The Adams Papers

L. H. BUTTERFIELD, EDITOR IN CHIEF

SERIES IV
PORTRAITS

John and Abigail Adams

Portraits of
John and Abigail Adams

by

ANDREW OLIVER

───────── ☆ ─────────

THE BELKNAP PRESS
OF HARVARD UNIVERSITY PRESS
CAMBRIDGE, MASSACHUSETTS
1967

Distributed in Great Britain by Oxford University Press · London

Funds for editing *The Adams Papers* were originally furnished by Time, Inc., on behalf of *Life,* to the Massachusetts Historical Society, under whose supervision the editorial work is being done. Further funds have been provided by a grant from the Ford Foundation to the National Archives Trust Fund Board in support of this and four other major documentary publications. In common with these and many other enterprises like them, *The Adams Papers* benefits from the continuing and indispensable cooperation and aid of the National Historical Publications Commission, whose chairman is the Archivist of the United States.

Library of Congress Catalog Card Number 67–11863 · Printed in the United States of America

This edition of *The Adams Papers*

is sponsored by the MASSACHUSETTS HISTORICAL SOCIETY

to which the ADAMS MANUSCRIPT TRUST

by a deed of gift dated 4 April 1956

gave ultimate custody of the personal and public papers

written, accumulated, and preserved over a span of three centuries

by the Adams family of Massachusetts

The Adams Papers

The acorn and oakleaf device on the preceding page is redrawn from a seal cut for John Quincy Adams after 1830. The motto is from Cæcilius Statius as quoted by Cicero in the First Tusculan Disputation: *Serit arbores quæ alteri seculo prosint* ("He plants trees for the benefit of later generations").

Foreword

The purpose of the Adams Papers editorial enterprise is to re-create the lives and minds of a remarkably articulate, influential, and durable American family. The editors have assumed that this could best be done by presenting a full and faithful record of what the Adamses wrote, in combination with what others wrote to them. But if the mass of their surviving papers constitutes by far the most valuable source for telling the story of the family, other important kinds of evidence also survive and sometimes furnish evidence at the very points where the documents falter or are entirely wanting. Successive Adamses wrote a great deal, for example, about their Quincy homestead—John Adams' "Peacefield," later simply "the Old House." They wrote, naturally, in fragmentary and allusive terms, telling of homecomings from diplomatic missions, the visits of Lafayette and other celebrities, the building of a new ell, marriages, deaths, and seasonal gardening and farming operations. Fortunately, however, the Old House, having been given by the family to the nation in 1946, still stands intact as the Adams National Historic Site. Surrounded by its 18th-century grounds and 19th-century outbuildings, filled with a fine clutter of four generations of Adams books, furniture, and other possessions gathered from many parts of the world, this great physical survival can be inspected and studied like a stratified archeological dig. It has been so studied, and will continue to be, in order to confirm, correct, and extend the written records.

Among the furnishings at the Old House are, of course, portraits. They are only a fraction of those known to have been taken of members of the family from the later 18th to the early 20th century. But life portraits and even their progeny in the form of replicas, hand copies, engravings, lithographs, and cartoons constitute a class of evidence peculiarly valuable to those concerned with penetrating the past. So obvious a truth hardly needs explanation. It has been a commonplace since one of the earliest and most influential European treatises on the painter's art. "Painting," said Jonathan Richardson in the introduction to his *Essay on the Theory of Painting* (1715), "gives us not only the persons, but the characters of great men. The air of the head and the mien in general give strong indications of the mind and illustrate what the historian says more expressly and particularly." In short, Richardson urged, if you read Clarendon, go on and improve upon him by studying the portraits of Van Dyck.

In accordance with this unexceptionable precept, historians and biographers have commonly, even routinely, embellished their books with portraits chosen with more or less care and reproduced with more or less fidelity. Lately something more has been attempted, no doubt because the study of iconography has become rapidly and markedly professional on both sides of the Atlantic. In the earliest of the truly comprehensive editorial enterprises organized in the United States, the Yale edition of *The Correspondence of Horace Walpole,* Mr. Wilmarth Lewis has been furnishing, with great labor and care, a full iconographic as well as documentary record. The files of original pictorial materials that he has gathered at Farmington, together with the analytical indexes to them, comprise a major new resource for the study of English life and taste in the 18th century. Similarly impelled to bring *all* relevant evidence to bear on the versatile career of Jefferson, Mr. Julian P. Boyd has from the outset of *The Papers of Thomas Jefferson* proceeded on the principle that illustrations should illustrate rather than merely embellish. He and his associates have followed Jefferson on his travels here and abroad, gathered old and new materials illustrating his encounters with men, regions, and works of art and mechanical genius, and, in the pictures they have reproduced and the detailed descriptions that accompany them, have vastly enlarged our knowledge of Jefferson and his time. Perhaps no better example of the blending of textual and iconographic evidence to achieve important new results could be cited than Mr. Boyd's presentation of Jefferson's Notes on American Medals Struck in France, in volume 16 of the *Papers*. Here diligent search and perceptive interpretation have combined to untangle a subject much written about but much misinterpreted by less persistent and discerning inquirers. At the same time the episode, which occupied Jefferson at intervals over several years, illustrates his character as a man of taste and his scrupulous methods in conducting public business.

With these and other examples before them, the editors of *The Adams Papers* have from the beginning seized hold of all iconographic evidence they have encountered that is pertinent to the four generations of the family with which they are concerned. They could be sure, for example, that everything gathered relating to Adams residences here and abroad and all likenesses of Adamses, major and minor, early and late, would ultimately prove useful, and in some cases vital, to their purpose. So too, very likely, would information about and pictures of surviving costumes, furniture (for example, the desk at which John Quincy Adams toppled over when he rose to speak in the House of Representatives in February 1848), and other relics and memorabilia.

The materials thus accumulated in reproduced form were put in rough order. (Human ingenuity has not yet devised a system, both simple and adequate, to catalogue a miscellaneous picture file.) They have answered reference questions and served as a reservoir from which to draw illustrations. But as the variety and quality of extant Adams portraits became apparent, the conviction grew that a separate work devoted to likenesses of the family must sooner or later be undertaken. The appearance in 1962 of both Mr. Alfred L. Bush's admirable *Life Portraits of Thomas Jefferson* and Mr. Charles Coleman Sellers' monumental and captivating *Benjamin Franklin in Portraiture* offered inspiring models and strengthened the editors' conviction. But even if they had possessed the scholarly competence to carry out such a project, the editors' own time and resources were wholly committed to the family papers. Funds and an expert hand to prepare a study of Adams portraiture would have to be sought outside the main enterprise.

As things turned out, these presented themselves promptly. Early in 1963 the editor in chief determined to ask Mr. Andrew Oliver, a New York lawyer who has long and constructively concerned himself with the work of historical societies and is a collector of and writer on American portraits, if he would serve as special editor of an Adams Papers portrait project. The meeting which followed was at dinner, with no announced agenda. After the editor had made his proposal, Mr. Oliver disclosed that he had come with the intention of volunteering his help in any way it might be useful to so important and attractive an undertaking. A grant for out-of-pocket expenses was obtained from the Charlotte Palmer Phillips Foundation, Inc., of New York City, and operations began. The first published results appear in this volume.

Although this study and catalogue of *Portraits of John and Abigail Adams* is intended to stand on its own feet as an independent work, and should be cited by its individual volume title in scholarly references, it stands in relation to *The Adams Papers* as a whole as the first volume in Series IV: Adams Family Portraits. A second volume, in preparation, will deal with the known likenesses of John Quincy and Louisa Catherine Adams. A third, treating the portraits of Charles Francis and Abigail Brooks Adams and of their children, will or at least may follow if the materials warrant it, but of this, for reasons suggested below, we cannot yet be sure.

Mr. Oliver took over the materials that had been gathered with more zeal than system in the Adams Papers office, and began filling out the record of Adams iconography by systematic inquiry in the innumerable places where one must inquire in this kind of undertaking. For John Adams he had recorded, by the time this volume went to press, nearly three dozen likenesses taken from life by more than twenty artists and sculptors between 1766 and 1825. Of these, about two dozen survive as originals; a few more are known in engraved or other derivative form; and the rest appear to be irrecoverably lost. His wife Abigail was much less frequently painted, but this is usual for Presidents' wives: whatever their natural claims may be to artists' attention, their likenesses do not have the talismanic value for the public that their husbands' do. As far as is now known, Abigail Adams was portrayed from life only eight times, and all of these likenesses, executed by seven artists between 1766 and 1812, are preserved.

While the very respectable run of portraits left by John Adams gives us a good idea of what he looked like at well-spaced intervals from age thirty to age ninety, the known portraits of John Quincy Adams substantially exceed those of his father in quantity and variety. Parental pride and financial resources had something to do with this; so did opportunity, combined with the simple fact of J. Q. Adams' being separated from members of his family for long periods. Other reasons, including a conscious urge on his part to patronize the arts, could also be offered, but this is not the place to develop them. In 1839, in the compulsive way he had of listing phenomena of all sorts, Adams set down on a paper later bound up in one of the "Rubbish" volumes of his Diary, a record of all the portraits for which he had sat that he could remember, beginning with the very Dutch-looking little boy done in crayons by Schmidt in the Netherlands in 1783, when Adams was sixteen. There are thirty-four entries for painted, sculptured, and medallic likenesses made at The Hague, London, Ghent, Boston, New York, Washington, and Quincy. But the list is not complete even for the period it covers, and still more portraits were to be painted of Adams in the last decade of his life. What is more, in the very year this list was compiled Louis Daguerre's extraordinary invention was announced to the world, and the daguerreotypes of "the old man eloquent" produced in the Washington studio of Brady and the Boston studio of Southworth & Hawes during the 1840's are among the masterpieces of early photographic art.

Thus the story of J. Q. Adams in portraiture spans sixty-five years, two continents, and all the older media plus the newest one. When completed it should take on value as a record of taste independent of its revelation of the person and character of the extraordinary man whose career forms such a long chapter of American history. No such claims can be made for the portraits of the next two generations of the family. The artist Delaroche is reported to have exclaimed upon seeing Daguerre's process demonstrated, "Painting is dead from this day!" He was far from right, but photography did have a depressing effect on portrait painting as a social phenomenon in the middle and later decades of the 19th century. In any case, the interest of Mr. and Mrs. Charles Francis Adams in the painter's art was mild, and they had few portraits painted. This was true also of most of their six children. Henry Adams, as commonly, was an exception. For him there is a distinguished though comparatively sparse sequence of likenesses from youth to old age; and quite as valuable in their way are the superb photographs that Marian Hooper Adams made of her husband, as well as of some members of his family, during the 1870's and 1880's. There is no portrait of either Charles Francis or Abigail Brooks Adams quite so evocative of character as Marian Adams' photograph of them together on the porch of the Old House in the summer of 1883.

Among the accumulations that by 1850 made the Old House in Quincy a combined museum, archives, and library, the family papers held first place in the Adams hierarchy of values, and that has remained true ever since. The safekeeping of the papers, meaning not simply their physical preservation but their preservation intact and undivided, has always been of the highest concern. Books came next in the family's esteem, but partly through choice and partly through necessity, the Adamses' immense accumulations of books have not enjoyed the same good fortune as their papers. Although the Old House and the Stone Library adjoining it are still crammed with books, whole libraries were given away in the 19th and early 20th century, sometimes in a manner that makes it possible for the scholar to reconstruct their contents, sometimes not. A few portraits take up the space of a great many books. During the lives of the first Charles Francis and his wife, room was found for nearly all the great portraits owned by the family between the Quincy homestead and the Adamses' town house on Mount Vernon Street in Boston. C. F. Adams died in 1886; after his widow's death in June 1889 the family no longer had a central headquarters, and there was doubt whether the Old House would be occupied thereafter at any season. It seemed best to divide the portraits, along with other heirlooms of exceptional monetary or sentimental value, among the five living children of C. F. Adams. This was done in the fall of 1889, and since then the natural course of things has led to their still wider dispersion. As Mr. Oliver's Catalogue shows, some have come back to Quincy while others have come to rest in great museums from Boston to Washington, where they can be enjoyed by the widest possible public. Happily several of the best are under the same roof as the family's papers in the Massachusetts Historical Society.

In spite of Mr. Oliver's diligence, other Adams likenesses no doubt continue to linger in obscurity. They may be important, or they may be merely interesting because they could add a little to the sum of our knowledge of a remarkable family. Since studies like the present one, by bringing out what *is* known, furnish leads to what is *not* known, the Adams editors confidently hope for and would be most grateful to receive further information on any aspect of Adams portraiture.

John Adams' views on art, like his views on science, have been only partially and tentatively studied and assessed. For him these two great fields of human endeavor were closely linked. Both had a strong appeal to the side of his mind which found the ideas of the Enlightenment congenial and inspiring, and he said trenchant things about both when that side of his mind dominated his mood and pen. But he had a whole other side, inherited from his Puritan forebears and reinforced by his rural New England upbringing. It often predominated and prompted him to warn his countrymen in strong terms against merely "ornamental" and "philosophical" accomplishments, since the real business of life in a young republic lies elsewhere. His letters and more formal writings contain many brief and some lengthy sermons on this theme, all the more emphatic in their tone, one cannot doubt, because he felt within himself the power of these allurements.

Adams' first encounter with a major artist shows the tension between his natural response to the world of art and his doubts about its entire wholesomeness. In a letter to his wife in the summer of 1776 he described a visit to "Mr. Peele's Painters Room" in Philadelphia. Adams was fascinated by this, to him, almost entirely new world, and wished, he said, that he "had Leisure and Tranquility of Mind to amuse myself with these Elegant, and ingenious Arts of Painting, Sculpture, Statuary, Architecture, and Musick. But," he concluded firmly, "I have not." Apparently it did not even occur to him to have his likeness painted at this great moment in history and in his own career by the leading artist of Philadelphia. Like the man in the joke who already had a book and therefore did not want another, Adams *had* a portrait—the agreeable but rather characterless pastel done by Blyth in Salem in 1766 (Fig. 1 in this book), typical of the paintings commissioned, produced, and hung as status symbols in colonial homes.

Less than two years after his visit to Peale's studio, this Yankee farmer and lawyer found himself in Paris at the center of the stage of European politics, surrounded by a "Richness, . . . Magnificence, and Splendor" of taste and habits of living that he told his wife were "beyond all Description." Nevertheless, he described them often and vividly, for at times he was nearly carried away with them. Such things, he supposed, were well enough in their place, but that place ought not to be America. His best comments are his humorous rather than his homiletic ones. In the great ornamental gardens at M. Bertin's country seat near Paris, Adams' host showed him "his Luxury, as he called it, which was a collection of misshapen Rocks . . . drawn together, from great distances, at the Expence of several Thousands of Guineas. I told him," said Adams, thinking of the granite outcrops on his Braintree farm, "that I would sell him a thousand times as many for half a Guinea." Adams saw, or thought he saw, how all this folderol of French *haut goût,* accompanied by dabblings in science as well as the arts, directly interfered with the business of the American mission to France, which was to win a war and a peace. Around his colleague Franklin there constantly hovered a crowd of fashionable ladies, admiring scientists who drew off Franklin's attention from diplomatic business to philosophical experiments, and artists eager to take more likenesses of the great man that they could peddle. To Adams, who received little such attention, they were all equally frivolous and diversionary if not downright wicked. On his second mission, having surfeited himself with tours of royal collections of art and natural history, while what he really wanted to do was to get on working terms with the French Foreign Office, Adams told his wife in a letter of May 1780: "I could fill Volumes with Descriptions of Temples and Palaces, Paintings, Sculptures, Tapestry, Porcelaine, &c. &c. &c.—if I could have time. But I could not do this without neglecting my duty." He added a passage that includes his most quoted observation (although it is still absent from the pages of Bartlett):

The Science of Government it is my Duty to study, more than all other Sciences. The Art of Legislation and Administration and Negotiation, ought to take Place [of], indeed to exclude in a Manner all other Arts. I must study Politicks and War that my Sons may have liberty to study Mathematicks and Philosophy. My Sons ought to study Mathematicks and Philosophy, Geography, natural History, Naval Architcture, navigation, Commerce and Agriculture, in order to give their Children a right to study Painting, Poetry, Musick, Architecture, Statuary, Tapestry and Porcelaine.

Such was Adams' curriculum for Americans of his own and ensuing generations. On the assumption that sons and grandsons will or should follow intellectual blueprints drawn by their fathers and grandfathers, it was not a bad one, and in his own family it actually worked out more or less in the way he planned. Meanwhile, in the flush of American success in the peace negotiations at Paris, Adams indulged his own craving for a little "Magnificence" now and then by going to London and sitting for two splendid portraits. The artists, of course, were American-born: West, who enjoyed immense prestige as historical painter to the King; and Copley, Adams' former fellow townsman, who was rapidly making his way into the best British society and art circles. The results may be seen in this volume (Figs. 18 and 9). West gave the most prominent place in his (unfinished) group portrait of the Peace Commissioners to Adams, probably because the first actual sketch was of Adams. The Copley portrait is a thing of magnificence indeed. Adams was painted full-length and heroic in size and stance—so far as his short round figure could be made to appear heroic—and furnished with all the worldly and mythological emblems of grandeur that could well be painted in without crowding. The portrait cost Adams a hundred guineas, which he paid on the spot.

As Mr. Oliver notes, Adams very soon developed a certain self-consciousness about "this Piece of Vanity." Evidently he was more relieved than troubled by its remaining in England, even though fully paid for, until after Copley died and Adams was an old man. It is not certain that Adams saw it after it finally reached America in 1817; at any rate it was never to hang in the Old House and remind him of the extravagant way in which he had memorialized a diplomatic career that he often complained had impoverished him.

All the portraits that followed were on a more modest scale, and nearly all of them were executed at the desire of someone other than the sitter. The sequence of Stuart portraits, for example, which has given us our most enduring conception of John Adams' features, began with a vote in the Massachusetts legislature in 1798. The artist was so dilatory that the vote was forgotten by the time the painting was completed and in fact—as Mr. Oliver has ingeniously shown—had become two different paintings (Figs. 64 and 67). But this is to anticipate the extraordinary story told in Chapter XVII, which is a

xiv

brilliant contribution not only to the history of American art on its upper and lower levels, but to the understanding of John Adams' historical reputation. If the second President was not taken to the great heart of the American people in the 19th century, the iconographic evidence assembled here helps to show why. In his monograph on *The Likenesses of Thomas More* (London, 1963), Mr. Stanley Morison demonstrates how fortunate and yet how accidental it was that "the real, historical reporting of Holbein's image" of More persisted through whole centuries during which the superb originals were lost from sight. The exact opposite occurred with John Adams, the successive debasements of the Stuart image transforming him by the 1840's "into a sort of toothless likeness of Washington." (For an example see Fig. 73.)

All this has now been traced in nice and copious detail by Mr. Oliver, and the correctives have been mercifully supplied. As if to compensate John Adams, and us, for the lost opportunities of his early life and the failure of Stuart's great portrait of 1798–1815 to become publicly known, three remarkable likenesses of Adams were taken in the last decade of his life. These were the Binon marble bust of 1818, which was executed for the town of Boston and captured the old philosopher as Josiah Quincy, Ticknor, and Emerson described him, with lightning flashes in his mind and thunder in his words (Fig. 91); the Stuart painting of 1823, at once the greatest and the most benign of all the portraits of John Adams (Fig. 93); and Browere's life mask of 1825, which Mr. Oliver pronounces "more than a likeness; . . . a facsimile" (Fig. 101), and hence a most valuable confirmation of how well the sculptor and painter had done.

It was in connection with Binon's bust that Adams said his final word on the plastic arts, and it was his strongest. Binon was pleased with his success and proposed to reproduce the bust in plaster for various people who had said they would like copies. Sternly, but with a kind intent, Adams warned the sculptor that he was "engaged in speculations that will never be profitable." The age of painting and sculpture had "not yet arrived in this country," he continued, "and I hope it will not arrive very soon. . . . I would not give sixpence for a picture of Raphael or a statue of Phidias." Adams did not elaborate here this extraordinary statement, but it is, of course, a hyperbolical phrasing of his old distrust of the arts as accompaniments, even instruments, of authoritarian government and religion, of the very sort vigorously reasserting themselves in the legitimist reaction current in Europe. "Every one of the fine Arts," he had argued in a letter to Jefferson not long before, "from the earliest Times has been inlisted in the Service of Superstition and Despotism. The Whole World at this day Gazes with Astonishment at the grossest Fictions because they have been immortalized by the most exquisite Artists, Homer and Milton, Phidias and Raphael. The Rabble of the Classic Skies and the Hosts of Roman Catholic Saints and Angells are still adored in Paint and Marble and Verse."

And yet, returning to Binon's request, Adams would not, and did not, deny it: "Artists have done what they would with my face and eyes, head and shoulders, stature and figure and they have made them monsters as fit for exhibition as Harlequin or Punch. They may continue to do so as long as they please." Surely a fortunate acquiescence, since it provided evidence refuting all of Adams' harsher judgments on the painter's art and enabling Mr. Oliver to spread before us this vivid and discriminating record of what a founder of the nation and its most illustrious family really looked like.

L. H. BUTTERFIELD
Editor in Chief

Contents

List of Illustrations

The formal statement of ownership of recorded portraits of John Adams is given in the entries in the Catalogue. The courtesy lines in the List of Illustrations commonly indicate ownership but in some instances indicate only the sources of photographs used for reproduction and permission to reproduce them. Dates given in the List may be approximate or conjectural; fuller information is given in the text.

Illustrations

Acknowledgments

For much of the purely factual, statistical details, names, dates, &c., of artists, recourse has been taken to that incomparable aid, Groce and Wallace, *Dictionary of Artists in America,* issued by The New-York Historical Society in 1957, my indebtedness to which cannot be adequately acknowledged. And this book could hardly have been possible without the aid of the helpful staff and excellent resources of the library of The New-York Historical Society.

Since this gathering of illustrations, collected as it was from all parts of this country, as well as from England and France, could not have been assembled without the generosity of the many individuals and institutions that own the portraits and engravings here reproduced, it is a duty to be gratefully undertaken to thank the following persons and institutions for their kindness in consenting to the reproduction of the portraits and engravings owned by them as indicated in the Catalogue: Adams National Historic Site, Quincy, Massachusetts; Charles Francis Adams, Dover, Massachusetts; Thomas Boylston Adams, South Lincoln, Massachusetts; American Scenic and Historic Preservation Society, Yonkers, New York; Boston Athenæum; Brooklyn Museum; Architect of the Capitol, Washington; Chicago Historical Society; City Art Gallery, Bristol, England; City of Boston; City of Quincy, Massachusetts; Mrs. T. Jefferson Coolidge, Boston; David M. Freudenthal, New York City; Frick Art Reference Library; Harvard University; Historical Society of Pennsylvania; Miss Ima Hogg, Houston; Independence National Historical Park, Philadelphia; Iselin Estate, Katonah, New York; Library of Congress; Massachusetts Historical Society; Metropolitan Museum of Art; Musée de Blérancourt; Museum of Fine Arts, Boston; National Gallery of Art; New England Historic Genealogical Society; New-York Historical Society; New York Public Library; New York State Historical Association; Pennsylvania Academy of the Fine Arts; Princeton University Library; Quincy Historical Society; Redwood Library and Athenaeum, Newport; Franklin D. Roosevelt Memorial Library, Hyde Park; John F. Seymour, Topanga, California; Smithsonian Institution; Society for the Preservation of New England Antiquities; Tulane University; Wadsworth Atheneum, Hartford; Mrs. Graham L. Russell, Upper Montclair, New Jersey; White House Historical Association; Henry Francis du Pont Winterthur Museum; Yale University Art Gallery; George Gray Zabriskie, New York City.

So, too, the extent to which the search and research have met with success and been most rewarding is in large measure due to the kindness and unselfishness of the many scholars engaged in historical pursuits who have been asked for information or help of one kind or another, or often simply to point the way out of the woods. At no point have I been faced with the dilemma of *meum* or *tuum*—all have given freely of their time, of their knowledge, and of their own personal discoveries. Lyman Butterfield, editor in chief of the Adams Papers, and his former associate editor Wendell D. Garrett, now of *Antiques* magazine, not only allowed me to dip freely and often into the bottomless well of their own inexhaustible knowledge of the Adamses but have been tireless in their assistance in reading every draft of this volume from manuscript to page proof and in making valuable corrections and additions. Latterly, Marc Friedlaender, another associate editor, and editorial associates and assistants Susan F. Riggs, Lynne Crane, and Glynn Marini have joined in these operations as well as in searching the farthest corners of the Adams archives for elusive facts that had escaped me. To list all of the others to whom I am indebted or to describe the particular aid of each would be difficult, but each of the following will know that his contribution has not been overlooked: Whitfield J. Bell Jr.; Julian P. Boyd; Samuel H. Bryant; Alfred L. Bush; Arthur B. Carlson; Josephine Cobb; Ulysse Desportes; Donald T. Gibbs; Mrs. Wilhelmina S. Harris; James J. Heslin; Cuthbert Lee; Bertram K. Little; A. Hyatt Mayor; Thomas Maytham; Marcus A. McCorison; David McKibbin; Ann Louise Coffin McLaughlin; Milo M. Naeve; Barbara Neville Parker; Mrs. Carl A. Pitha; Jules David Prown; Stephen T. Riley; Carolyn Scoon; Charles Coleman Sellers; Clifford K. Shipton; Theodore Sizer; David H. Wallace; Louise Wallman; Walter Muir Whitehill; Nathalie Wright; and Joseph B. Zywicki.

Editorial Method and Apparatus

Although it stands on its own feet as an independent work, this volume is planned as one in a series of volumes treating Adams family portraits, and the Portrait series is, in turn, a part of the over-all Belknap Press edition of *The Adams Papers*. Accordingly, while the contents and structure of the present volume markedly vary from those of other volumes so far published, and while this volume should be cited by its own individual title, it incorporates all the features of *Adams Papers* editorial practice, as well as format, that it feasibly can.

Thus it follows *Adams Papers* style in the presentation of texts; see the table of Textual Devices which follows. In the footnotes, and also in the Catalogue when necessary to distinguish between members of the Adams family bearing the same name, it employs the Adams Family Code Names (see below) adopted for use throughout the entire edition. The descriptions of MSS quoted and referred to are given in the shortened forms listed in the table of Descriptive Symbols below (though MS letters cited *without* accompanying symbols are assumed to be "RC's"—i.e. recipients' copies), and their institutional ownership is indicated in the forms shown in the table of Location Symbols below (with the exception that all MS Diaries of the Adamses are assumed to be in the Adams Papers, Massachusetts Historical Society).

With respect to the last two tables below, it should be pointed out that the appearance therein of any particular abbreviation or "short title" does not necessarily mean that the work in question is cited frequently *in this volume,* but that it has been used here in its shortened form either because it already has been or will be so frequently cited elsewhere (e.g. in the next volume of the Portraits series) that a short form for it has been devised for use wherever it may appear in *The Adams Papers.*

1. TEXTUAL DEVICES

[. . .], [. . . .]	One or two words missing and not conjecturable.
[. . .] ¹, [. . . .] ¹	More than two words missing and not conjecturable; subjoined footnote estimates amount of missing matter.
[ ]	Number or part of a number missing or illegible. Amount of blank space inside brackets approximates the number of missing or illegible digits.

[roman]	Conjectural reading for missing or illegible matter. A question mark is inserted before the closing bracket if the conjectural reading is seriously doubtful.
⟨*italic*⟩	Matter canceled in the manuscript but restored in our text.
[*italic*]	Editorial insertion in the text.

2. ADAMS FAMILY CODE NAMES

First Generation

JA	John Adams (1735–1826)
AA	Abigail Smith (1744–1818), *m.* JA 1764

Second Generation

JQA	John Quincy Adams (1767–1848), son of JA and AA
LCA	Louisa Catherine Johnson (1775–1852), *m.* JQA 1797
CA	Charles Adams (1770–1800), son of JA and AA
Mrs. CA	Sarah Smith (1769–1828), sister of WSS, *m.* CA 1795
TBA	Thomas Boylston Adams (1772–1832), son of JA and AA
Mrs. TBA	Ann Harrod (1774–1846), *m.* TBA 1805
AA2	Abigail Adams (1765–1813), daughter of JA and AA, *m.* WSS 1786
WSS	William Stephens Smith (1755–1816), brother of Mrs. CA

Third Generation

GWA	George Washington Adams (1801–1829), son of JQA and LCA
JA2	John Adams (1803–1834), son of JQA and LCA
Mrs. JA2	Mary Catherine Hellen (1807–1870), *m.* JA2 1828
CFA	Charles Francis Adams (1807–1886), son of JQA and LCA
ABA	Abigail Brown Brooks (1808–1889), *m.* CFA 1829
ECA	Elizabeth Coombs Adams (1808–1903), daughter of TBA and Mrs. TBA

Fourth Generation

JQA2	John Quincy Adams (1833–1894), son of CFA and ABA
CFA2	Charles Francis Adams (1835–1915), son of CFA and ABA
HA	Henry Adams (1838–1918), son of CFA and ABA
MHA	Marian Hooper (1842–1885), *m.* HA 1872
BA	Brooks Adams (1848–1927), son of CFA and ABA
LCA2	Louisa Catherine Adams (1831–1870), daughter of CFA and ABA, *m.* Charles Kuhn 1854
MA	Mary Adams (1845–1928), daughter of CFA and ABA, *m.* Henry Parker Quincy 1877

Fifth Generation

CFA3	Charles Francis Adams (1866–1954), son of JQA2
HA2	Henry Adams (1875–1951), son of CFA2

3. DESCRIPTIVE SYMBOLS

Dft	draft
FC	file copy
LbC	letterbook copy
MS, MSS	manuscript, manuscripts
RC	recipient's copy

4. LOCATION SYMBOLS

CtY	Yale University Library
DLC	Library of Congress
MBAt	Boston Athenæum
MBBS	Bostonian Society
MH	Harvard College Library
MH-Ar	Harvard Archives
MHi	Massachusetts Historical Society
MWA	American Antiquarian Society
NHi	New-York Historical Society
NNP	Pierpont Morgan Library
PHi	Historical Society of Pennsylvania
PPAmP	American Philosophical Society

5. OTHER ABBREVIATIONS AND CONVENTIONAL TERMS

Adams Papers

Manuscripts and other materials, 1639–1889, in the Adams Manuscript Trust collection given to the Massachusetts Historical Society in 1956 and enlarged by a few additions of family papers since then. Citations in the present edition are simply by date of the original document if the original is in the main chronological series of the Papers and therefore readily found in the microfilm edition of the Adams Papers (see below). The location of materials in the Letterbooks and the Miscellany is given more fully, and often, if the original would be hard to locate, by the microfilm reel number.

Adams Papers Editorial Files

Other materials in the Adams Papers editorial office, Massachusetts Historical Society. These include photoduplicated documents (normally cited by the location of the originals), photographs, correspondence, and bibliographical and other aids compiled and accumulated by the editorial staff.

Adams Papers, Fourth Generation

Adams manuscripts dating 1890 or later, now separated from the Trust collection and administered by the Massachusetts Historical Society on the same footing with its other manuscript collections.

The Adams Papers

The present edition in letterpress, published by The Belknap Press of Harvard University Press.

6. SHORT TITLES OF WORKS
FREQUENTLY CITED

AA, *Letters*, ed. CFA, 1840

    Letters of Mrs. Adams, the Wife of John Adams. With an Introductory Memoir by Her Grandson, Charles Francis Adams, Boston, 1840.

AA, *Letters,* ed. CFA, 1848

    Letters of Mrs. Adams, the Wife of John Adams. With an Introductory Memoir by Her Grandson, Charles Francis Adams, 4th edn., Boston, 1848.

AA2, *Jour. and Corr.*

    Journal and Correspondence of Miss Adams, Daughter of John Adams, . . . edited by Her Daughter [Caroline Amelia (Smith) de Windt], New York and London, 1841–1842; 2 vols.

Adams Family Correspondence

    Adams Family Correspondence, ed. L. H. Butterfield and others, Cambridge, 1963– .

Bemis, *JQA*

    Samuel Flagg Bemis, *John Quincy Adams*, New York, 1949–1956; 2 vols. [Vol. 1:] *John Quincy Adams and the Foundations of American Foreign Policy;* [vol. 2:] *John Quincy Adams and the Union.*

Bentley, *Diary*

    The Diary of William Bentley, D.D., Pastor of the East Church, Salem, Massachusetts, Salem, 1905–1914; 4 vols.

Biddle, *Old Family Letters*

    Old Family Letters: Copied from the Originals for Alexander Biddle, Series A, Philadelphia, 1892.

Bowen, *Centennial of Washington's Inauguration*

    The History of the Centennial Celebration of the Inauguration of George Washington as First President of the United States, ed. Clarence Winthrop Bowen, New York, 1892; commonly bound in 2 vols.

Bush, *Life Portraits of Jefferson*

    Alfred L. Bush, *The Life Portraits of Thomas Jefferson: Catalogue of an Exhibition at the University of Virginia Museum of Fine Arts*, Charlottesville, 1962.

Cappon, ed., *Adams-Jefferson Letters*

    Lester J. Cappon, ed., *The Adams-Jefferson Letters: The Complete Correspondence between Thomas Jefferson and Abigail and John Adams*, Chapel Hill, 1959; 2 vols.

CFA, *Diary*

> *Diary of Charles Francis Adams,* ed. Aïda DiPace Donald and David Donald, Cambridge, 1964– .

DAB

> Allen Johnson and Dumas Malone, eds., *Dictionary of American Biography,* New York, 1928–1936; 20 vols. plus index and supplements.

Dict. Amer. Fighting Ships

> U.S. Navy Department, Office of the Chief of Naval Operations, Naval History Division, *Dictionary of American Naval Fighting Ships,* Washington, 1959– .

Dunlap, *Arts of Design,* ed. Bayley and Goodspeed

> William Dunlap, *A History of the Rise and Progress of the Arts of Design in the United States,* ed. Frank W. Bayley and Charles E. Goodspeed, Boston, 1918; 3 vols.

Groce and Wallace, *Dict. Amer. Artists*

> George C. Groce and David H. Wallace, *The New-York Historical Society's Dictionary of Artists in America, 1564–1860,* New Haven and London, 1957.

JA, *Diary and Autobiography*

> *Diary and Autobiography of John Adams,* ed. L. H. Butterfield and others, Cambridge, 1961; 4 vols.

JA, *Legal Papers*

> *Legal Papers of John Adams,* ed. L. Kinvin Wroth and Hiller B. Zobel, Cambridge, 1965; 3 vols.

JA, *Letters,* ed. CFA

> *Letters of John Adams, Addressed to His Wife,* ed. Charles Francis Adams, Boston, 1841; 2 vols.

JA, *Works*

> *The Works of John Adams, Second President of the United States: with a Life of the Author,* ed. Charles Francis Adams, Boston, 1850–1856; 10 vols.

JCC

> Worthington C. Ford and others, eds., *Journals of the Continental Congress, 1774–1789,* Washington, 1904–1937; 34 vols.

Jefferson, *Papers,* ed. Boyd

> *The Papers of Thomas Jefferson,* ed. Julian P. Boyd and others, Princeton, 1950– .

Jefferson, *Writings,* ed. Lipscomb and Bergh
> Andrew A. Lipscomb and Albert Ellery Bergh, eds., *The Writings of Thomas Jefferson,* Washington, 1903–1904; 20 vols.

JQA, *Memoirs*
> *Memoirs of John Quincy Adams, Comprising Portions of His Diary from 1795–1848,* ed. Charles Francis Adams, Philadelphia, 1874–1877; 12 vols.

JQA, *Writings*
> *The Writings of John Quincy Adams,* ed. Worthington C. Ford, New York, 1913–1917; 7 vols.

MHS, *Procs.*
> Massachusetts Historical Society, *Proceedings.*

Niles' Register
> *Niles' Weekly Register,* Baltimore, 1811–1849.

NYHS, *Colls., Pubn. Fund Ser.*
> New-York Historical Society, *Collections, Publication Fund Series,* New York, 1868–

NYHS, *Quart.*
> New-York Historical Society, *Quarterly.*

Park, *Gilbert Stuart*
> Lawrence Park, comp., *Gilbert Stuart: An Illustrated Descriptive List of His Works,* New York, 1926; 4 vols.

PMHB
> *Pennsylvania Magazine of History and Biography.*

Prown, *Copley*
> Jules David Prown, *John Singleton Copley,* Cambridge, 1966; 2 vols.

Edmund Quincy, *Josiah Quincy*
> Edmund Quincy, *Life of Josiah Quincy of Massachusetts,* Boston, 1868.

Quincy, *Figures of the Past*
> Josiah Quincy [1802–1882], *Figures of the Past, from the Leaves of Old Journals,* ed. M. A. DeWolfe Howe, Boston, 1926.

Winsor, *Narr. and Crit. History*
> Justin Winsor, *Narrative and Critical History of America,* Boston and New York, 1889; 8 vols.

WMQ
> *William and Mary Quarterly.*

Portraits of
John and Abigail Adams

Introduction

"Every student and reader of History," Carlyle wrote in 1854, "who strives earnestly to conceive for himself what manner of Fact and *Man* this or the other vague Historical *Name* can have been, will, as the first and directest indication of all, search eagerly for a Portrait, for all the reasonable Portraits there are; and never rest till he have made out, if possible, what the man's natural face was like. Often I have found a Portrait superior in real instruction to half-a-dozen written 'Biographies,' as Biographies are written;—or rather, let me say, I have found that the Portrait was as a small lighted *candle* by which the Biographies could for the first time be *read,* and some human interpretation be made of them." [1]

Happily, portraits of John Adams are so numerous as almost to furnish for us a candelabrum, and that of high candle power! Each portrait is in fact a historical document, a primary source of importance to the student of history, of importance to any who seek to learn what manner of man Adams was. He has been described by his editor as "self-important, impetuous, pugnacious, tormented by self-doubts and yet stubborn to the point of mulishness, vain, jealous, and suspicious almost to the point of paranoia; and yet at the same time deeply affectionate and warm-hearted, 'as sociable as any Marblehead man,' irrepressibly humorous, passionately devoted all his life to the welfare of his country, and as courageous a statesman and diplomat as his country has ever had." [2] Yet what did he look like?

Adams had his own opinion of art and artists with respect to paintings of himself: "I have no Miniature," he wrote in response to a question in 1809, "and have been too much abused by Painters ever to sit to any one again." "My head has been so long the sport of painters, as my heart has been of libellers," he said in 1813. Even more bitterly in 1819 he complained: "The age of sculpture and painting have not yet arrived in this country and I hope it will not arrive very soon. Artists have done what they pleased with my face and eyes, head and shoulders, stature and figure and they have made of them monsters as fit for exhibition as Harlequin or Punch." [3] We seem to catch echoes here of

---

[1] Thomas Carlyle to David Laing, 3 May 1854, on the "Project of a National Exhibition of Scottish Portraits," in Thomas Carlyle, *Critical and Miscellaneous Essays: Collected and Republished,* Boston, 1860, 4:449.

[2] JA, *Diary and Autobiography,* 1:lxiv.

[3] JA to Skelton Jones, 11 March 1809 (LbC, Adams Papers, printed in JA

I

Dibdin's comment in his 1808 edition of More's *Utopia;* "Never perhaps," he wrote, "has it fallen to the lot of a human being to have his features so tortured and perverted as More's have been." [4]

Of course the other side of the coin reveals the most extraordinary interest in the finished portrait. Here are a few phrases culled at random from the family correspondence and diaries: "Let me know what you think of the bust"; "it will be an admirable likeness"; "get a frame for my picture"; "engage an engraver"; "have it taken from the engraver"; "have the portraits ready to be shipped"; "the portrait goes to you at once"; "try to get the portrait he has of my mother"; "buy of him that of my father"; "which of the pictures are mine"; "take care and obtain the original"; "never let it out from under his roof"; "hung up the portraits"; "a goodly collection." With a display of such concern, it is not surprising that the Adamses, father and son, never failed to sit to an artist when asked to.

In searching for a likeness of Adams we are more fortunate today than were our predecessors. Until the Centennial in 1876, most of the life portraits of John Adams were either lost or still in private hands, not open to view by the public; his face, if known at all, was known only through the medium of engravings—in most instances engravings made not from original life portraits but from copies of them.

Consider, for example, Stuart's portrait of Adams (Fig. 64), now the most familiar of all, commenced in 1798 but not finished until 1815. Over the next forty years, several dozen engravings of Adams appeared, in periodicals, histories, biographical dictionaries, and broadsides, described as having been engraved after this portrait by Stuart. Yet apparently not a single engraver had ever seen the original portrait; the engravings were derived from Bass Otis' copy, of a very poor copy, of Stuart's original, painted by his nephew Gilbert Stuart Newton when only nineteen years old. Each of these engravings was therefore at least thrice removed from the original source, and none bears more than a superficial resemblance to the original. Our forebears did not know what Adams looked like! It was not until 1856 that an engraver had access to Stuart's original portrait; then, for the first time, the public could see a fair reproduction of Stuart's version of Adams. Only two engravings, made prior to the 20th century directly from the original portrait have come to light. Such has been the experience with

Works, 9:613); JA to Joseph Delaplaine, 8 June 1813 (LbC, Adams Papers); JA to J. B. Binon, 7 Feb. 1819 (MBBS:Colburn Coll.).
    [4] Thomas More, *Utopia,* ed. T. F. Dibdin, London, 1808, p. cxv.

most of the other life portraits that were reproduced in engravings. It means that if we are to find the true likeness of the second President and not merely a superficial resemblance we must turn to the portraits themselves.

John Adams' name no doubt conjures up in everyone's mind's eye some likeness of him, though probably few are familiar with all the life portraits. For threescore years, from the age of thirty to the middle of his ninety-first year, Adams sat for his portrait, thirty or more times in all; sat to the greatest American artists of the day, whose very names alone stir the imagination of the student of American history and art—Copley, Mather Brown, West, Trumbull, C. W. Peale, and Stuart, to name some.

The resulting sequence of likenesses makes us wonder at the historical coincidences that could bring such artists and such a man together at such significant times and places. We might have had to know Adams only from the small pastel done by Blyth in 1766, or from the ungainly portrait by Winstanley that hangs on the balcony of the Stone Library adjoining the old Adams House in Quincy. But not so! History has raised up, time and again, artistic genius meet for the man and the moment; and so in our day we can see Adams the Aristocrat, by Copley; Adams the Patriot, by Trumbull; Adams the Peace Commissioner and Ambassador, by West and by Brown; Adams the President, by Stuart. We see a new dimension added by Saint-Mémin and the other silhouettists; Binon's marble of the octogenary carries the unmistakable conviction of truth; Stuart's last great masterpiece gives a priceless glimpse of the aged Argonaut, and lastly (and it was at the very last), rescued by chance from a century's oblivion, we can see Browere's magnificent, classical facsimile, the life mask of 1825. What an extraordinary progression! Each artist by some coincidence seems to have been best endowed in his own medium and style to catch and preserve the face and character, the very lifelikeness of the man at the moment—and each moment a mark on the measure of the history of the young republic. We can cry out with young Tarquin:

> *Hos habuit voltus, haec illi verba fuerunt,*
> *Hic color, haec facies, his decor oris erat.*[5]

If we look long at some of these portraits, we can almost hear the voice of that aged monk in Spain as he whispered to Sir David Wilkie, standing before a portrait from the brush of Velasquez, "That picture is a

[5] Ovid, *The Fasti*, bk. 2, lines 773–774.

3

reality, while all the generations that have gazed on it are but shadows." [6]

In the following pages there are reproduced all known life portraits, busts, and silhouettes of John Adams, as well as some of the more outstanding replicas, copies, and engravings.[7] These in the composite may show us, who are but the shadows, the reality that was Adams.

ANDREW OLIVER

[6] Quoted in Hampton L. Carson, *A History of the Historical Society of Pennsylvania,* Phila., 1940, 1:30–31.

[7] The terms "original," "replica," and "copy" should not be used interchangeably. An original is of course the artist's initial painting of the subject, a replica is the artist's own reproduction of this original, and a copy is the reproduction of the artist's work by another.

Benjamin Blyth

"Those Ladies and Gentlemen who please to favour him
with their employ, may depend on having good likenesses."
Advertisement, 1786.

On 25 October 1764, five days before his twenty-ninth birthday,
John Adams, the son of Deacon John Adams of Braintree, married
Abigail, daughter of the Reverend William Smith of Weymouth, nine
years his junior. Not long after this, the earliest known portraits of the
young pair were painted, in Salem, by the self-styled limner in crayons,
Benjamin Blyth.

The exact date of the painting of these pictures is not known. Internal evidence, in the form of inscriptions on the back of the pictures, is
misleading and incorrect in some respects. Two paper labels are pasted
on the back of each, obviously of different age, the upper and probably later one on white paper, the lower and earlier one on brown paper. The upper label on the portrait of John Adams (Fig. 1) reads:

> John Adams
> 2nd President of the United States
> Picture drawn by Blythe
> English Artist
> In America in 1763
> (Colored Crayon)

the lower one:

> John Adams
> Drawn by Blythe 1763
> (Coloured Crayon)
> Presented to Thomas B. Adams
> By his Mother.

On that of Abigail Adams (Fig. 2) the upper reads:

> Abigail Adams
> Wife of John Adams
> Picture drawn by Blythe
> English Artist
> In America in 1763
> (Colored Crayon)

1. JOHN ADAMS. PASTEL BY BENJAMIN BLYTH, 1766

2. ABIGAIL ADAMS. PASTEL BY BENJAMIN BLYTH, 1766

and the lower:

> Abigail Adams
> Drawn by Blythe, 1763
> (English Artist)
> Presented to her son Thomas B. Adams.

The handwriting of all the labels is so far unidentified.

John Adams records in his diary [1] for August 1766 a visit he and Abigail made to Salem to stay with her sister Mary, who had married John's long-time friend Richard Cranch. This visit, or a subsequent one in November of the same year, undoubtedly furnished the occasion for Blyth to paint the couple. The suggestion in the labels of a 1763 date is no more surprising than, and just as likely due to faulty memory years later as, the misspelling of Blyth's name by adding a final "e" and calling him an "English Artist." An excellent account of Blyth, including a checklist of some forty portraits, many of well-known Salem residents painted by him between 1766 and 1782, appears in an article by Henry Wilder Foote.[2] Blyth was born about 1746 and lived in Salem until about 1782, when he moved to Richmond, Virginia, where he continued his profession as limner in oil, crayons, and miniatures. The medium he used principally in Salem was pastel, although he did a few paintings in oil, not so successfully. The Reverend William Bentley, the Salem diarist, considered him a dauber but admitted that he had sometimes "taken likenesses." [3]

Although this representation of Adams gives little promise of the man he was to become, it does, perhaps, justify Abigail's comment at the time to her sister, "My Good Man is so very fat." [4] Half a hundred years later, writing to his friend and early law clerk, William Tudor, Adams recalled to mind his own appearance in his first days as a young lawyer:

> Whenever you shall find a Painter, Male or Female, I pray you to suggest a Scene and a Subject for the pencil.
> The Scene is the Counsel Chamber in the old Townhouse in Boston . . . February, 1761. . . . Samuel Quincy and John Adams had been admitted Barristers at that term. John was the youngest. He should be painted looking like a short, thick, fat Archbishop of Canterbury, seated at the Table, with a pen in his hand, lost in Admiration, now and then minut-

---

[1] JA, *Diary and Autobiography,* 1:318.
[2] "Benjamin Blyth, of Salem: Eighteenth-Century Artist," MHS, *Procs.,* 71 (1953–1957):64–107.
[3] Bentley, *Diary,* 3:470.
[4] To Mary Smith Cranch, 6 Oct. 1766, *Adams Family Correspondence,* 1:56.

ing those despicable Notes which you know that Jonathan Williams Austin, your fellow student in my office, stole from my desk and printed in the Massachusetts Spy, with two or three bombastic expressions interpolated by himself; and which your Pupil, Judge Minot, has printed in his history.[5]

The occasion he so understandably recalled was the great argument on the validity of Writs of Assistance, and it marked a turning point in his own political career.[6]

The marked contrast between the two portraits of John and Abigail has been pointed out by Bernard Bailyn. Of that of John Adams he wrote, "It is a likable but unimpressive face: round, rather soft-looking, bland, and withdrawn. It is an unfinished, uncertain, face, with no decisive lines or distinguishing feature. The composure seems artificial and posed." On the other hand, "Abigail's face is extraordinary, not so much for its beauty, which, in a masculine way, is clearly enough there, as for the maturity and the power of personality it expresses. . . . It is about as confident, controlled, and commanding a face as a woman can have and still remain feminine." [7] The point is well taken: Abigail's character is already formed; John's will develop, and the change will be revealed in later portraits.

From the labels, the earlier of which probably dates from the beginning of the 19th century, we can accept the fact that the pictures were given by Abigail, prior to her death in 1818, to her son Thomas Boylston Adams, her fifth and youngest child, born in 1772. T. B. Adams died in 1832, leaving a widow, who followed him thirteen years later, and a daughter, Elizabeth Coombs Adams, who died in 1903 at the age of ninety-five.

J. Q. Adams mentions seeing the portraits in 1835: "In the Evening visited Mr. and Mrs. John Greenleaf. . . . They have Portraits of my father and mother, in crayons, painted about the time of their Marriage in 1764, or as Mrs. Greenleaf says between the birth of my Sister Smith in 1765 and mine in 1767." [8] Mrs. John Greenleaf was the former Lucy Cranch, daughter of Richard and Mary Cranch, and was in a position, if anyone then was, to know something of the origin of the portraits.

Again, in 1839, J. Q. Adams records: "Mrs. Greenleaf has two Portraits, in Crayons, of my father and mother, which belong to me. They were taken in the year 1765, just after the birth of my Sister Abigail.

[5] 29 March 1817 (LbC, Adams Papers; printed in JA, *Works*, 10:244–246).
[6] See JA, *Legal Papers*, 2:106–147.
[7] Bernard Bailyn, "Butterfield's Adams: Notes for a Sketch," *WMQ*, 19:249–250 (April 1962).
[8] Diary, 21 June 1835.

3. JOHN ADAMS. ENGRAVING BY G. F. STORM, 1840

And Mrs. T. B. Adams claims them, as having been given to her by my mother. They were taken by my Aunt Cranch from the House at the foot of Penn's hill, when my mother was in England, to save them from the dampness of an empty house, and they have remained there about 55 years."[9] If the diarist had taken the date from the labels (1763, even though incorrect), he would probably also have accepted the ownership of Mrs. T. B. Adams from the same source. We hear rumblings, however faint, of controversy such as has raged in countless families over the ownership of family portraits. Only a month later

[9] Same, 7 Aug. 1839.

4. ABIGAIL ADAMS. ENGRAVING BY OLIVER PELTON, 1840

J. Q. Adams capitulated on the point of ownership, noting in his diary in reference to the picture of his father, "Mrs. T. B. Adams claims it as having been given to her, by my mother with her own of the same date. I admit the claim." [10]

The claim having been admitted, the portraits passed on the death of Mrs. T. B. Adams to her daughter, Elizabeth Coombs Adams. Dr. Foote states that Elizabeth left them to her cousin's son, the second C. F. Adams,[11] yet in Bowen's *Centennial*[12] they are recorded as be-

[10] Same, 5 Sept. 1839.
[11] Foote, "Benjamin Blyth, of Salem," p. 81.
[12] Bowen, *Centennial of Washington's Inauguration*, 2:425.

11

longing to C. F. Adams in 1892, years before Miss Adams died. Apparently she had given or sold them to him long before, as he wrote in his diary of November 1879, "Hung up the E. C. Adams portraits of John and Abigail Adams." [13] From C. F. Adams, they passed to his son, the second Henry Adams, on whose death they passed to his brother, the late John Adams of South Lincoln, who presented them to the Massachusetts Historical Society in 1956 and 1957.

Pastel copies of each (Cat. Nos. 7, 10), identical in size and deceptively like, done in 1904 by May Hallowell Loud, now belong to the Quincy Historical Society and hang in the John Quincy Adams Birthplace in Quincy.

Each of the portraits has been several times engraved, although without marked success. In another diary entry, referring to the pastel of his father, J. Q. Adams wrote, "Mr. George Bancroft wishes to have this portrait of my father engraved, to introduce it into his history of the United States; and I told Mrs. Greenleaf I would send for it." [14] A month later he records delivering it to Mr. Bancroft, adding, "He has engaged an engraver by the name of Storm to engrave it." [15] G. F. Storm was a stipple engraver who had come to Philadelphia from England in about 1834 and in his brief stay in the United States engraved a number of portraits. His engraving of Adams (Fig. 3), also in stipple, appeared first in Charles Francis Adams' edition of *Letters of John Adams, Addressed to His Wife,* and later in Volume 4 of Bancroft's *History,* [16] but it fails as a good reproduction or in catching the pastel effect of the original.

Engravers of Abigail's picture were even less successful. The first Charles Francis Adams, engaged in publishing a collection of letters of his grandmother, relates the difficulties encountered in having her portrait engraved by Oliver Pelton, the banknote engraver. "I went to town taking in with me the picture of my grandmother for the Engraver. I got it in safely and now feel as if I was really launched upon the sea of Authorship." [17] Again a few months later, "The Engraving however, a revised and finished copy of which was furnished to me today is a very poor performance and mortifies me much. I took it out with me to Quincy for the purpose of taking the decision of the mem-

[13] CFA2, Diary, 9 Nov. 1879 (Adams Papers, Fourth Generation).
[14] Entry of 7 Aug. 1839.
[15] Entry of 10 Sept. 1839.
[16] *Letters of John Adams, Addressed to His Wife,* ed. Charles Francis Adams, Boston, 1841, vol. 1, frontispiece; George Bancroft, *History of the United States,* Boston, 1839–1874, vol. 4 (published in 1852), frontispiece.
[17] CFA, Diary, 9 June 1840.

bers of the family upon it." [18] His father thought the engraving "wretchedly executed." Charles' remonstrances to the engraver produced some effect, and he set about to improve his plate, but the family were never entirely satisfied. Mrs. de Windt inquired of J. Q. Adams why his son didn't substitute the portrait of his grandmother engraved from Stuart's portrait, instead of the other which gave such great dissatisfaction. But, in the end, Pelton's engraving (Fig. 4) was used, not only in this edition of letters, but many years later by C. F. Adams in his edition of his grandparents' *Familiar Letters*—the book that beyond all others made John and Abigail Adams known to American readers.[19]

Despite the unsatisfactory result of attempts to engrave Blyth's pastels, they have long remained favorites of the family, and are a provocative pair of likenesses with which to begin our quest.

[18] Same, 21 Sept. 1840.
[19] *Familiar Letters of John Adams and His Wife Abigail Adams, during the Revolution*, N.Y., 1876.

II

Reinier Vinkeles

Early in the last quarter of the 18th century, the Dutch artist Reinier Vinkeles accomplished the unusual feat of engraving his own portrait on the same plate with those of two brother artists, Isaak Schmidt and Juriaan Andriessen.[1] Schmidt, born in Amsterdam in 1740, was one of the founders of the Amsterdam Drawing Academy; Vinkeles, also born in Amsterdam, a year his junior, became secretary of the Academy; hence their friendship. It is not surprising, therefore, to discover that in 1782, when John Adams, as the newly recognized Minister Plenipotentiary from the United States to the Dutch Republic, was living in Holland with his young son, the sixteen-year-old John Quincy Adams, their portraits should be taken by these two, the son, appropriately in pastel, by Schmidt, the father in a more formal engraving by Vinkeles.

Vinkeles had been a pupil of Jan Punt and of Le Bas at Paris, and had been later summoned to St. Petersburg by the Empress Catherine. He returned to Amsterdam in 1772, and there continued his extraordinarily productive career, producing by the time of his death in 1816 upwards of 2,500 engraved plates, the majority of which were of his own design.[2]

Two engravings of Adams were made by Vinkeles. One (Fig. 5) was issued by the Amsterdam publisher William Holtrop as a frontispiece to the Dutch translation of Adams' "Novanglus" essays, which had originally been printed in the *Boston Gazette* in 1775 in reply to the articles signed "Massachusettensis," written by the loyalist lawyer Daniel Leonard who later became Chief Justice of Bermuda. This, the first collected edition of these essays, was circulated at Adams' instance to inform the Dutch of the events leading up to the American War of Independence, as well as to inspire confidence in himself as his country's negotiator. It would have been thought helpful, therefore, if the essays could be accompanied by a striking likeness of their author.

The Dutch publication was evidence of but another facet of Ad-

---

[1] Michael Bryan, *Bryan's Dictionary of Painters and Engravers,* ed. George C. Williamson, London, 1903–1905, 5:308.

[2] Emmanuel Bénézit, ed., *Dictionnaire critique et documentaire des peintres, sculpteurs, dessinateurs et graveurs,* new edn., Paris, 1948–1955, 8:585.

JOHN ADAMS, Schildknaap, Minister Plenipotentiaris der XIII Vereenigde Staaten van Noord-Amerika, bij de Republijk der VII Vereenigde Nederlanden.

5. JOHN ADAMS. ENGRAVING BY REINIER VINKELES, 1782

15

ams' diplomatic method. From his earliest days in Holland he had made friends with the Dutch journalists and taken advantage of every opportunity to develop favorable public opinion by publication in the press of articles on America, its intellectual activities, the justice of its cause, and the likelihood of its success. In April 1782 he succeeded in accomplishing what was considered impossible, having himself formally recognized as the Ambassador of the United States of North America to their High Mightinesses the States General of the United Netherlands. If a proud, firm, self-confident expression can be detected in Vinkeles' engravings it can well be explained by Adams' recent and quite remarkable diplomatic triumph.[3] Inscribed below the engraving appears the legend, "Reinr. Vinkeles, ad viv. del. & sculp. 1782," which can be fairly expanded and translated, "Drawn and engraved 1782 from life by Reinier Vinkeles." On a double page at the end of the volume there was advertised a folio engraving of Adams by Vinkeles, as well as the projected publication of a similar one of Washington. The engraving of Adams and the titlepage of the book have both been reproduced in John Adams' *Diary and Autobiography.*[4] No copy of the folio engraving has come to light.

The second engraving of Adams by Vinkeles (Fig. 6) is closely similar to the first, although undoubtedly separately engraved. It, too, is inscribed as being "ad viv." and was reproduced in 1888 in Winsor's *Narrative and Critical History.*[5] In 1791, Vinkeles had also engraved a portrait of the Comte de Vergennes, four years after his death, after a portrait by Antoine Callet. The engraving is a faithful copy, in much detail, and has also been reproduced in Adams' *Diary and Autobiography.*[6] The significance of this engraving is not only the curious fact that Vergennes looks out from within the identical frame which surrounds Adams in Fig. 6, but also that the engraving of Vergennes is not inscribed as "ad viv." It was not a life portrait but a copy of one. We can then safely consider Vinkeles' engraving of Adams as a life portrait.

As for the value of these engravings as likenesses of Adams, we must consider not only Vinkeles' enormous productivity as an index of his popularity which must to a degree presuppose the ability to get a likeness but also, for example, his detailed and accurate copy of Callet's portrait of Vergennes. Any strangeness in Adams' features might be accounted for by the fact that Adams is seen through the eyes of a

[3] See JA, *Diary and Autobiography,* 2:442–458; 3:1–29.
[4] Same, vol. 3, facing p. 32.
[5] Vol. 6:36.
[6] Vol. 4, facing p. 162.

6. JOHN ADAMS. ENGRAVING BY REINIER VINKELES, 1782

Dutchman and has been graven on the plate with a correspondingly Dutch cast to his features. This was the only image of Adams available to many Europeans at this time. But it was apparently satisfactory to Adams, whose esteem for the Dutch people was so high in 1782 that he thought of himself as almost half a Dutchman.

III

Unknown Artist, 1783

In the August 1783 issue of the *European Magazine,* published in London, there appeared an unsigned engraving of Adams bearing the inscription "From the Original Portrait in the Possession of Edmund Jennings, Esq." The engraving (Fig. 7) serves as an illustration to an article titled "Anecdotes of His Excellency John Adams, Minister Plenipotentiary of the States of North America to their High Mightinesses the States General of the United Provinces." A headnote to the article characterizes the illustration as "a striking likeness from an original Portrait."

A brief, though informative and interesting, account of Edmund Jenings (as he himself spelled his name) appears in John Adams' *Diary.*[1] Born in Annapolis, Maryland, in 1731, Jenings lived most of his life in London in "cultivated leisure," making frequent visits to Brussels, Paris, and elsewhere on the Continent, where he weathered the later years of the Revolution. In this way he came into close contact with Adams, and proved helpful to him in keeping channels open to the London press. Adams thought so well of him that he proposed him as secretary to the American Peace Commissioners in Europe, though, to Adams' intense annoyance, Franklin, very adept at nepotism, got ahead of him with Jay's approval of his grandson, William Temple Franklin, for the post. Although some thought his conduct devious during the war, Jenings was a loyal supporter of American sentiments and an admirer of John Adams, and it was quite in keeping with his association with Adams for him to have procured his portrait to be painted. Assuming that the engraving after Jenings' portrait of Adams fairly reproduces the original, we can surmise that the painter was French or Dutch, the cast of Adams features having a decidedly foreign tinge; yet the likeness compares favorably with Copley's portrait of a few months later (Fig. 9). There is, however, no basis from which to hazard a guess as to who the artist was.[2] The engraving bears no signature, though the work resembles a similar engraving of Silas Deane made in October 1783, signed "W. Angus." The engraving of

[1] Vol. 2:355–356.
[2] There is the possibility that the Jenings portrait was one of the "lost miniatures" mentioned in Chapter XXI.

His Excellency JOHN ADAMS.

7. JOHN ADAMS. ENGRAVING BY AN UNKNOWN ARTIST, 1783

His Excy. *JOHN ADAMS Esqr.*

J. Norman Sc.

8. JOHN ADAMS. ENGRAVING BY JOHN NORMAN, 1784

Adams could have been the work of William Angus (1752–1821), who, in England, would have had ready access to Jenings' portrait of Adams. It was reproduced twice in the late 19th century: first in the *Magazine of American History* in 1884, and then by Winsor in his *Narrative and Critical History* in 1888.[3] In the former case the engraving is inscribed: "From a portrait executed in London in 1783." This of course was not so, as Adams only arrived in London in October 1783, whereas this engraving had first appeared in August 1783. The inscription does suggest that the publisher in 1884 may have thought the engraving derived from Copley's portrait, which was executed in London in November or December 1783. Like the engraving, the article on Adams in the *European Magazine* is unsigned. It contains, however, so many details coinciding with entries in Adams' own diary and in his correspondence, that it is almost certain that Jenings, who commonly contributed to English newspapers and periodicals, was its author.

JOHN NORMAN

The *Boston Magazine,* in its February 1784 issue, published a short biographical sketch entitled "Character of his Excellency John Adams Esq.," accompanied by a striking, though crudely drawn, line engraving of Adams (Fig. 8) by the English-born engraver John Norman. By about 1774, Norman had come to Philadelphia from London, and six or seven years later moved to Boston. He became one of the publishers of the *Boston Magazine,* and later produced the first work on architecture published in America. The only likenesses of Adams now known to have been in existence in February 1784 are the Blyth portrait of Adams as a young man in 1766 (Fig. 1), the Vinkeles engraving of 1782 (Fig. 5), Jenings' portrait and its engraving (Fig. 7), and Copley's most recently finished work (Fig. 9). There is no evidence or likelihood that Norman could have yet seen Copley's painting, and we may conclude that his engraving must have been a free adaptation of the *European Magazine*'s reproduction of Jenings' portrait, tempered possibly by Norman's personal recollections of Adams before he went to Europe.

[3] George C. Eggleston, "Our Twenty-one Presidents, Part I: The First Ten— Washington to Tyler," *Magazine of Amer. History,* 11:93 (Feb. 1884); Winsor, *Narr. and Crit. History,* 7:90.

IV

John Singleton Copley

"Copeley is the greatest Master, that ever was in America."
John Adams to Abigail Adams, August 1776.

On 3 September 1783, the definitive Treaty of Peace with Great Britain was signed in Paris. A month later Adams, just risen from a sickbed, set out for London from his residence at Auteuil accompanied by his son John Quincy. There he soon fell in with John Singleton Copley, whom he had long known and admired in America. Copley had left America in 1774, and by 1783, now aged forty-six, had made his mark in London with such pictures as *The Death of Major Pierson* and *The Death of the Earl of Chatham*. It was only natural that he should have sought to paint Adams' portrait, not only as that of an old acquaintance, but as one who was now in the ascendancy, who had helped lead his country not only into the Revolution but out of it into an independence now firmly recognized.

Before the end of the year the great portrait was completed (Fig. 9), and Copley was paid the handsome sum of one hundred guineas for it.[1] A striking picture, 7 feet 9¾ inches x 4 feet 10 inches in size, it shows Adams, the size of life, sword at his side, in a brown velvet court dress, striking a dramatic and aristocratic pose. He holds in his hand a scroll, perhaps a counterpart of the Treaty of Paris; before him on the table lies a map of America, and at his feet the world, in the form of a globe. Though Copley was never at a loss in selecting a fitting pose for his sitters, it is not hard to detect in the setting of this painting, the hand of the master statesman and diplomat, the successful negotiator, and his Country's plenipotentiary. Despite his recent illness, Adams appears in the fullness of health and vigor. The frustrations to which he had been subjected over the years and the enforced separation from Abigail had not overcome him. Only a few years before he had written to Abigail from Passy, "I never had so much Trouble in my Life, as here, yet I grow fat. The Climate and soil agree with me—so do the

---

[1] "London Decr. 10 1783 Recd. of John Adams Esquire, one hundred Guineas in full for his portrait. J. S. Copley" (Adams Papers).

9. JOHN ADAMS. OIL BY JOHN SINGLETON COPLEY, 1783

Cookery and even the Manners of the People, of those of them at least that I converse with, Churlish Republican, as some of you, on your side the Water call me." [2]

The detail of Adams' head, shown in Fig. 10, is revealing and should be compared with West's portrait of the same period (Fig. 19) and Trumbull's of a few years later (Fig. 23). The similarity is striking; each clearly caught a likeness.

Almost immediately after the portrait was finished, Adams departed for Amsterdam to secure a loan from the Dutch to restore and bolster the credit of the United States. There he remained until August 1784. Meanwhile, after months of planning, canceling of plans, delays, and frustrations, Abigail with her daughter set sail with a "fine wind" for England in the ship *Active*. On 21 July, after a voyage of thirty days, they were "set down at Lows Hotel in Covent Gardens." [3] One of the first things Abigail did was to visit Copley's studio. "I have been to see a very Elegant picture of Mr. Adams," she wrote to her sister, "which belongs to Mr. Copely, and was taken by him. It is a larg full length picture. He is drawn with a Globe before him; the Map of Europe in his hand and at a distance a female figure representing Innocence, and Peace. It is said to be an admirable likeness." [4] This was a poignant comment; Abigail had not seen her husband for more than four and a half years!

Adams himself was self-conscious about the portrait, perhaps because of its aristocratic appearance. During the summer of 1784 he sought to have it framed, writing to his son, "Desire Mr. Copeley to get a Frame made for my Picture and do you give him the Money. He will tell you how much and give you a Receipt. The Frame should be made, to take to Pieces, so that it may be removed to the Hague or to Boston, in time. Thus this Piece of Vanity will be finished. May it be the last." [5] Some years later, in 1793, when John Stockdale, the London bookseller, proposed to have the Copley portrait engraved for use as the frontispiece to his new edition of Adams' *Defence of the Constitutions of Government of the United States,* Adams confessed, "I should be much mortified to see such a Bijou affixed to those Republican Volumes." [6]

Since this is the only known life-sized portrait of Adams, it is of in-

[2] 13 Feb. 1779 (Adams Papers, printed in JA, *Letters,* ed. CFA, 2:45).
[3] AA to Mary Smith Cranch, 6–30 July 1784 (MWA, printed in AA, *Letters,* ed. CFA, 1848, p. 172).
[4] To Elizabeth Smith Shaw, 28–30 July 1784 (DLC:Shaw Family Papers).
[5] To JQA, [post 1 June 1784] (Adams Papers).
[6] JA to John Stockdale, 12 May 1793 (British Museum: Add, MSS,. 24329:2–3).

10. JOHN ADAMS. DETAIL OF FIGURE 9

terest to discover whether it be a correct representation. Fortunately we are supplied with excellent evidence of the process used in its painting, in the person of John Quincy Adams, who was present at the time. Many years later, in 1845, John Quincy was sitting to the artist George P. A. Healy at the command of the French King, Louis Philippe, who was forming a collection of portraits of the principal characters of the American Revolution and the early days of the Republic. With compass in hand Healy asked permission to measure Adams' head, at which Adams observed that "of all the artists to whom I have sat, you are the first since Copley to use the compass." He went on to add that he had seen Copley, when painting his father's full-length portrait, measure not only his father's face but also his arms and legs.[7] This account of Copley's careful technique, developed after his arrival in England, is borne out by the preliminary sketch he made for Adams' portrait, which has been preserved and is now owned by the Metropolitan Museum of Art (Fig. 11). With many others it remained in the possession of Copley's family following his death, first as the property of his wife, then of his son, Lord Lyndhurst, and was even preserved in the same house at 25 George Street, Hanover Square, until sold at auction at Christie's in February 1864 at the sale of Lord Lyndhurst's library. At that sale this drawing was part of lot 170, which consisted of drawings for portraits; it was bought by Edward Basil Jupp, from whom it passed, with others, to Martha Babcock Amory, a granddaughter of Copley. The drawings ultimately descended to Linzee Amory of Boston, who gave them to a servant, whence in May 1946 they came into the hands of the art dealers Charles D. Childs of Boston and Harry Shaw Newman of New York, who jointly acquired the entire collection. This drawing was sold but later came back into Newman's hands and was again sold, with many others, to the Metropolitan Museum of Art in 1960.

Copley's exactitude is apparent from the way in which the figure of Adams is sketched onto the paper, divided as it is by vertical and horizontal lines, with the head and center of gravity perpendicularly above his right leg, which bears his weight. Although in the finished portrait the position and gesture of the left hand are varied, yet the head and right arm, the turn of Adams' body, and the stance agree closely with the preliminary drawing and maintain the same measured proportions.

[7] Marie de Mare, G. P. A. Healy, American Artist, An Intimate Chronicle of the Nineteenth Century, N.Y., 1954, p. 144–145; George P. A. Healy, Reminiscences of a Portrait Painter, Chicago, 1894, p. 157.

11. JOHN ADAMS. PRELIMINARY DRAWING FOR FIGURE 9, 1783

28

The Hon.ble JOHN ADAMS

12. JOHN ADAMS. ENGRAVING BY NOBLE, 1786

Copley had no lack of faith in his own ability or in the merit of his work. He knew his likeness of Adams would not only appeal to the family but would also be in demand as a source for engravings. Consequently he retained possession of the painting for that purpose. It was not until thirty-four years later that the picture finally came into possession of the Adamses.

It was first reproduced early in 1786 by the English engraver Noble, the upper part only, the engraving (Fig. 12) appearing in the February issue of *The New London Magazine,* prefacing a two-page memoir of "The Life of his Excellency John Adams, Minister Plenipotentiary from the United States of North America, to the Court of London." [8] It is there quite unjustifiably described as "a striking Likeness elegantly engraved by Noble," and the reader is advised, lest he fail to

[8] Facing p. 70.

13. JOHN ADAMS. ENGRAVING BY HALL, 1794

notice it from the engraving, that those "who have an opportunity of knowing his Excellency Mr. Adams trace in his features the most unequivocal marks of probity and candour." On the opposite page is a companion engraving by the same artist of an excellent likeness of Franklin. It is hard to see how Noble did so well in one instance and yet fell so wide of the mark in the other! (The taste of *The New London Magazine* was catholic; the following articles in that issue are entitled: "Account of the Organ of Hearing in Fish," and "A Caution against Drunkenness.")

Noble presumably had access to the painting while it was in Copley's possession. So also did the English artist Hall, who in 1794 engraved the bust only for the frontispiece to Stockdale's edition of the *Defence*. This engraving (Fig. 13), the bijou of Adams' mortification, is the source of many that followed and is a well-executed and faithful likeness.

The portrait next appeared on exhibition at the Royal Academy in 1796. The first American to reproduce it was James Smither, the engraver and seal cutter of Philadelphia who, accused of treason, had left for New York in 1778 and returned only after the peace in 1786. Smither died in September 1797, and his engraving (Cat. No. 22), published in Philadelphia by William Cobbett in February of that year, must have been one of his last efforts. Smither had no access to the original portrait and closely followed Hall's work.

One of the earliest American engravers on copper, Amos Doolittle of Connecticut, produced and published, using either Hall's or Smither's work as his model, a striking broadside (Fig. 14), dated 14 August 1799, entitled "A New Display of the United States." Adams is depicted as President, surrounded by the great seals of the sixteen states and surmounted by an eagle, displayed, holding in its talons a branch and spear, and a ribbon on which is inscribed C. C. Pinckney's purported defiance, "MILLIONS FOR OUR DEFENCE—NOT A CENT FOR TRIBUTE." Doolittle, who was born in Cheshire, Connecticut, in 1754, early trained as a jeweler and silversmith, and taught himself the art of engraving. He is perhaps best known as a historical artist for his series of four views of the battles of Lexington and Concord, engraved and printed by him in 1775, though drawn by Ralph Earl. A second engraving by Doolittle appeared as a frontispiece to the May 1801 issue of the *Connecticut Magazine,* a modification of the earlier example reversing the pose (Cat. No. 25).

Although several other engravings of the Copley portrait will be found listed in the Catalogue, the anachronism published by Thomas Gimbrede (Fig. 15), the French-born miniaturist and engraver, is worth mentioning here. Gimbrede, who had come to America in 1802 and settled in New York, published in 1812 an engraving showing the first four Presidents within separate ovals, before folds of drapery and crossed flags. The source of the four engravings is of interest. Washington, Jefferson, and Madison are taken from Stuart's portraits of 1795, 1805, and 1804 respectively. Adams had also sat to Stuart, in 1798, but by 1812 Stuart had not yet finished his portrait. Gimbrede must have cast about for a satisfactory likeness of Adams and finally settled on Copley's 1783 painting—probably through the medium of Hall's or Smither's engraving, with the result that Adams, who was scarcely three years younger than Washington, and eight and sixteen

14. JOHN ADAMS. ENGRAVING BY AMOS DOOLITTLE, 1799

32

years older than Jefferson and Madison, appears by far the youngest of the group.

All this time the original portrait, though paid for, remained out of the possession of the family. In 1800 Copley wrote to Adams:

I have been for a long time, waiting for an opportunity of making an Engraving from the portrait, I painted for you when you were in this country; and I think the times and cast of politicks are now such as to insure it an honourable reception *in this Country,* as well as in America; on this conviction Mr. Heath, an Engraver of the first abilities in this country, is engaged to do it as a companion to one of General Washington engraved by the same Artist, from a picture painted by Stuart. . . . I wish the hair as you now wear it may be added instead of the wig, for this purpose I have committed to the care of Mr. Berry who will have the honour to deliver this letter to you a Sketch or outline of the head, and request you will have the goodness to sit to Mr. Stuart while he puts the hair to it, and Mr. Berry will send it back to me.[9]

Not a word was said about sending the original which belonged to Adams.

There is no record that Adams ever sat to Stuart for the purpose requested, nor of Heath's ever finishing his engraving. In 1811 John Quincy Adams wrote from St. Petersburg to his brother to say that he had requested Copley to deliver the portrait to Mr. Boylston but supposed it would be some time before it would be done.[10] Four years later John Quincy recorded in his diary: "I spoke to Mr. Copley about the full length Portrait of my father, painted by him in the year 1783. He said it had long been in the hands of an engraver, who was making an engraving from it. But he would speak to him and have it returned. Mr. Trumbull told me the engraver was Heath." [11]

Early in the next year, following Copley's death in September 1815, John Quincy Adams again noted in his diary: "We paid a visit however to Mrs. and Miss Copley, whom we found at home. I enquired for the picture of my father which is still at the engraver's. . . . I told her I should be glad to send my fathers Picture to America next Summer, and would have it taken either from the engraver's where it now is, or from her house, as would be most agreeable to her. She proposed sending for it, and said it would probably want new varnishing. She complained of the engraver who had undertaken to engrave it, but had never finished the work, although Mr. Copley had paid one third

[9] 4 March 1800 (Adams Papers).
[10] To TBA, 13 May 1811 (Adams Papers, printed in JQA, *Writings,* 4:70).
[11] Entry of 15 June 1815.

15. WASHINGTON, JEFFERSON, MADISON, AND ADAMS.
ENGRAVING BY THOMAS GIMBREDE, 1812

part of the expence of it." [12] A not unnatural complaint after sixteen years!

Finally, the same diary reports in June 1817, "I wrote a Note to Mrs. Copley requesting her to have the Portraits of my Father and Sister ready to be shipped for Boston whenever Coll. Aspinwall sends for them." [13] They went at last by the ship *Galen* and arrived safely, but the portrait of Adams had not yet found a permanent home. A few months later Abigail Adams, writing from Quincy to her daughter-in-law, confessed: "Mr. Boylstone has solicited so warmly to have the portrait of your Father to place in his House, that we have finally agreed that he should take it, with a promise from under his Hand that he will deliver it to my son when ever he shall call for it, which promise I have in writing. He will take good care of it. Here it was in danger of getting injured." [14] This last fear is understandable considering that the rooms of the Old House in Quincy were low studded and the portrait almost eight feet tall, without its frame.

Ward Nicholas Boylston, Adams' second cousin, in acknowledging receipt of the painting shows how greatly he valued it. He wrote to John Adams from his house, the Hermitage, in Jamaica Plain, Massachusetts:

My dear Cousin:
That I may prove to you and my Dear Mrs. Adams, the high estimation of the value I attach to the picture you have confided to my care—I sent immediately for a blacksmith, and had an Iron fender made to go round the lower part, as a protection from the careless brush of the Housemaid, or the incautious Foot of those who might otherwise wish to come too near it. The room is every day aird, and the door kept lock'd, and the key in Mrs. Boylstons pocket, and no one sufferd to see it, without either she or myself are with them. As soon as it's known that I am the possessor of it, I shall expect to be visited by all the Amatuers of the fine arts in Boston and its vicinity, and assume the office of Sir Clement Cotterell (who I conclude was the Master of Ceremonies at St. James in your day), to introduce all the strangers of distinction who may visit Boston, to an acquaintance with the portrait, when they are not so fortunate as to be known to the original.[15]

The portrait remained in Boylston's possession. Charles Francis Adams saw it there in the early 1820's.[16] Since John Adams himself made

---

[12] Entry of 31 Jan. 1816.
[13] Entry of 6 June 1817.
[14] To LCA, 17 March 1818 (Adams Papers).
[15] 24 March 1818 (Adams Papers).
[16] Martha Babcock Amory, *The Domestic and Artistic Life of John Singleton Copley, R.A.*, Boston, 1882, p. 87.

16. JOHN ADAMS. ENGRAVING BY AN UNKNOWN ARTIST, CA. 1850

17. JOHN ADAMS. OIL BY AN UNKNOWN ARTIST

no disposition of it at his death, Boylston, with the tacit consent of the family, left the portrait by will to Harvard College where it was noticed with approbation in 1837 by President Jackson on the occasion of his receiving an LL.D. at the hands of Harvard's President Josiah Quincy.[17] There it remains to this day, in the Fogg Art Museum.

There is only one known engraving of the entire portrait (Fig. 16). It appears in Charles Francis Adams' edition of *The Works of John Adams*,[18] and is unsatisfactory, lacking in grace and falling quite short of a likeness. It ill compares with Hall's work for Stockdale, despite Charles Francis Adams' comment in 1872, referring to Hall's engraving: "But a much better engraving of the entire picture was made by my direction, which will be found prefixed to the title-page of the fifth volume of my edition of his life and works, published more than twenty years ago."[19]

Although Copley's portrait was many times engraved, very few copies in oil have been found. One (Fig. 17), is owned by the Museum of Fine Arts, Boston. It is only 20 x 13½ inches in size, and may have been painted in Copley's studio before the original came to the United States. It has had a checkered career. It appeared in the Martin Colnaghi sale of October 1908 described as a portrait of Admiral Lord George Anson. This was but a wild guess, as at that time there was hanging in the National Portrait Gallery (transferred there from the British Museum in 1879) a fine portrait of Admiral Anson, after Reynolds, and the resemblance between the two is remote. In 1920 the picture was illustrated in a life of the artist John Zoffany where it was again described as of Admiral Anson painted by Zoffany.[20] A short time later it was sold at Christie's described as "a merchant," by Copley,[21] and so passed into American hands. On reaching Boston, the subject was readily identified and the picture purchased by the Museum of Fine Arts.

Another copy in oil (Cat. No. 34), a little smaller than Copley's original, was painted in 1946 by John M. Carpenter and hangs among the collections of the Bostonian Society in the Old State House, Boston.

[17] "Extracts from the Journal of Benjamin Waterhouse," ed. William R. Thayer, Cambridge Hist. Soc., *Procs.*, 3 (1909):30–31.
[18] Frontispiece to vol. 5, published in 1851.
[19] Quoted in Martha Babcock Amory, *The Domestic and Artistic Life of John Singleton Copley, R.A.*, Boston, 1882, p. 87–88.
[20] Lady Victoria Manners and G. C. Williams, *John Zoffany, R.A., His Life and Works, 1735–1810*, London, 1920.
[21] Unidentified newspaper clipping in MBAt:Portrait Collection.

V

Benjamin West

"Our immortal countryman."
John Adams to the *Boston Patriot*, May 1812.

On 30 November 1782 the Preliminary Treaty, concluding the war with Great Britain, was signed in Paris. Representing the States as Peace Commissioners were Franklin, Adams, Jay, and Laurens, with William Temple Franklin as secretary. The British were represented by their plenipotentiary, Richard Oswald, and his secretary, Caleb Whitefoord. Not long after the conclusion of the peace negotiations, Benjamin West, since 1772 historical painter to George III, commenced his sketch (Fig. 18) for a large painting to commemorate the signing of the Treaty.

This was West's first step in carrying out the bold plan he had confided to his former pupil Charles Willson Peale on 4 August 1783:

I wrote you by Mr. Vaughan my intention of composing a set of pictures containing the great events which have affected the revolution of America; for the better enabling me to do this, I desired you to send what ever you thought would give me the most exact knowledge of the costume of the American armys, portraits in small, either painting or drawing, of the conspicuous characters necessary to be introduced into such a work. I now embrace my friend Capt. Falconer the opertunity to make the same request and that you would on his return to this country send me (on consulting some able friend) what you might have in readyness with his plan for such an undertaking. I mean the arrangement of the subject most expressive and most painted as for instance—The cause of the quarel; the commencement of it; the carying it on; the Battles; alliances &c. to form one work to be given in eligant engravings call'd The American Revolution. This work I mean to do, at my own expense and to employ the first engravers in Europe to carry them into execution not having the least dout as the subject has engaged all the powers of Europe, all will be interested in seeing the event so portraid. I have made Capt. Falconer a confident in such things who will have a pleasure in conphering with you.[1]

This ambitious scheme never materialized. West undoubtedly dropped the project as one which he felt would have given great offense at

[1] Quoted in Charles Henry Hart, *Benjamin West's Family*, Phila., 1908, p. 11–12.

18. AMERICAN COMMISSIONERS AT THE PRELIMINARY PEACE NEGOTIATIONS WITH GREAT BRITAIN. OIL BY BENJAMIN WEST, CA. 1783

Court. The single sketch of the Preliminary Treaty and a painting of the *Reception of the American Loyalists by Great Britain in 1783* were all that West produced in this field.[2]

Born in Springfield, Pennsylvania, in 1738, West had commenced his career as an artist in and about Philadelphia, but in 1759 went abroad, first to Italy and finally in 1763 to London. This was at a time when a general enthusiasm for the arts was sweeping over England, and West's pictures quickly made a favorable impression. Before long he attracted the attention of the King and soon began to fill the royal halls and residences with what Stuart facetiously called his "ten-acre pictures." Many of the larger ones are still on display at Kensington Palace, others at Buckingham and Windsor, though no longer so prominently displayed.

West's career as Court painter continued for years, ending only when his patron became insane. During the war, his position as a royal favorite understandably aroused hard feelings on the part of many Americans, yet he nevertheless generously went out of his way to aid his countrymen. It was Americans in particular who came to study under him—Peale, Brown, Trumbull, Stuart, Morse, and Allston, to name a few. Until close to the end of his life West considered himself an American. Exactly when Adams sat to West for his likeness in the sketch of the *Preliminary Treaty* we cannot be sure, but it must have been late in 1783. In his last autobiographical communication to the *Boston Patriot,* dated 17 February 1812, Adams compared his reception by ministers of state on the one hand, and by Mr. West on the other. "I did not ask favours," he wrote, "or receive anything but cold formalities from ministers of state or ambassadors. I found that our American painters had more influence at court to procure all the favors I wanted, than all of them. Mr. West asked of their majesties permission to shew me and Mr. Jay, the originals of the great productions of his pencil such as Wolfe, Bayard, Epaminondas, Regulus, &c. &c. &c. which were all displayed in the Queen's Palace, called Buckingham House. The gracious answer of the king and queen was, that he might shew us 'the whole house.' . . . We gazed at the great original paintings of our immortal countryman, West, with more delight than on the very celebrated pieces of Vandyke and Reubens; and with admiration not less than that inspired by the cartoons of Raphael." [3]

[2] *The Reception of the American Loyalists* was engraved by Henry Moses and is mentioned in Lorenzo Sabine's *American Loyalists,* Boston, 1847, p. 527, and reproduced in James Grant Wilson's *Memorial History of New York,* N.Y., 1892–1893, 2:574.
[3] JA, *Diary and Autobiography,* 3:150.

John's admiration for West was shared by Abigail, who wrote in her journal in July 1784 that "The 2 most celebrated painters now in Britain are Americans Mr. Copeley and Mr. West."[4]

The guided tour Adams described took place in November 1783; in January of the following year he crossed the North Sea with his son John Quincy in order to bolster his country's credit in Amsterdam. The close association with West was undoubtedly the result of, or had provided the opportunity for, Adams' sitting to the artist for the sketch prior to his journey to Holland. Franklin's likeness was modeled after a miniature taken from the portrait by the French artist Joseph Siffred Duplessis, lent to West in 1784 for the purpose.[5] The British representatives to the peace negotiations died before the sketch was completed. In its unfinished state the sketch includes, from left to right, Jay in olive tan, Adams in light tan, Franklin in dark dress, Laurens in red, and the head only of William Temple Franklin. The merest shapes in the unfinished portion of the canvas point to where Oswald and Whitefoord were to have appeared, and the spaces even in their pregnant emptiness lend a balance and proportion to the whole. Despite its incomplete condition the painting is a masterly and imposing representation of the American Commissioners. Measuring 28½ x 36½ inches, it now hangs over the mantel in one of Winterthur's most characteristic dining rooms contemporary with the Peace of 1782. Not least significant is the fact that Adams is the most prominent, central figure of the group. He was clearly making the most of his recent victory in Paris. It was no coincidence that in the short two months he was in London, before he crossed over to Holland, his portrait was taken by both West and Copley, two of the most eminent artists of the day, and that each portrait was done in a manner best suited to display the world statesman to advantage.

Many years after the sketch was painted John Quincy Adams recorded his conversation with West in London in 1817, a day or so before Adams was to set sail on his return to America. From Newman Street, London, West wrote to J. Q. Adams: "Should you be at home at any hour this evening, I will have the honour to wait on you and Mrs. Adams with the sketch I made of your Father and the American Commissioners of Peace in 1783—and at the same time to wish yourself, and Family a pleasant passage to your native Land."[6] Adams responded the same day from Craven Street: "We shall be at home in

[4] Same, p. 165.
[5] Charles Coleman Sellers, *Benjamin Franklin in Portraiture*, New Haven and London, 1962, p. 399.
[6] 6 June 1817 (Adams Papers).

the evening and very happy to see you." [7] In a brief entry in his diary the next day, he reports: "Mr. West sent me the sketch which he made for a picture of the Peace of 1782. He promised me last Evening that he would finish it. He has all the American negotiators, but not Oswald, nor Whitefoord." [8] A few weeks later, when at sea and with time on his hands, J. Q. Adams caught up on his diary by expanding his account of events before leaving London:

I mentioned that Mr. West, with Zerah Colburn [an American mathematical prodigy then on tour] and his father spent the Evening of 6 June with us. Mr. West then told me that he had in the year 1783 made a Sketch for a Picture of the Peace which terminated the War of the American Revolution, which he would send me to look at the next Morning, as he accordingly did. I then recollected having seen it before, at the time when my father was sitting to him for his likeness in it. The most striking likeness in the picture, is that of Mr. Jay. Those of Dr. Franklin and his Grandson W. T. who was Secretary to the American Commission, are also excellent. Mr. Laurens and my father though less perfect resemblances are yet very good. Mr. Oswald, the British Plenipotentiary, was an ugly looking man, blind of one eye, and he died without leaving any picture of him extant. This Mr. West alledged as the cause which prevented him from finishing the picture many years ago. Caleb Whitefoord the Secretary of the British Commission is also dead; but his Portrait exists from which a likeness may be taken. As I very strongly expressed my regret that this Picture should be left unfinished Mr. West said he thought he could finish it, and I must not be surprised if some day or other it should be received at Washington. I understand his intention to be to make a present of it to Congress. . . . We sent back his sketch of the Picture of the Peace of 1782. [9]

West did not make good his promise, and the sketch, never completed, remained in his possession until his death in 1820. It was then sold, at the sale of his paintings at Christie's, to Joseph Strutt, from whom it descended to his nephew Edward Strutt, the first Baron Belper of Belper, who died in 1880. From his successor, the second Lord Belper of Kingston, Derby, it was purchased in 1916 by the elder J. Pierpont Morgan and passed to Winterthur in 1943. Its first public appearance in the United States was at its exhibition at the Brooklyn Museum in 1917. [10] A copy in oil by an unknown artist was made for

---

[7] 6 June 1817 (LbC,, same).

[8] Entry of 7 June 1817.

[9] Entry of 21 July 1817. West erred in thinking Oswald had left no portrait of himself; his portrait had been painted in 1747 by De Nune and is reproduced in color as the frontispiece to *Richard Oswald's Memorandum,* ed. W. Stitt Robinson, Charlottesville, Va., 1953.

[10] *Brooklyn Museum Quarterly,* 4 (1917):81; illustrated at p. 78.

19. JOHN ADAMS. DETAIL OF FIGURE 18

44

George Grote, the historian of Greece, and given a century ago by Grote and his wife to John Jay, the grandson of one of the American Commissioners. Another copy, in oil, was given to the State Department by Cass Canfield of New York and his son, having originally belonged to Lewis Cass, American Minister to France from 1836 to 1844.

West's grasp of the historical significance of the moment, so apparent in this fragment, can only occasion regret that he went no further with the project he had revealed to Peale. In his grand plan, however, he was happily succeeded by John Trumbull, who had an equal if not greater talent for recognizing and preserving the outstanding events in the life of the new Republic. Trumbull's *Declaration of Independence* (Fig. 22), the first of his series, of lasting and national significance, is in every way a realization of West's dream. The detail of Adams in this sketch (Fig. 19), reproduced in the same size as the original, gives us within a small compass a remarkable likeness, one that is not only entirely consistent with other contemporary paintings but is itself one of the great portraits of Adams.[11]

[11] Mr. Sellers gives many more details on West's rendering of Franklin in this group portrait and also different dates for the production of the painting, namely, "1784–85," with John Adams added "ca. 1785–88." However, if J. Q. Adams actually saw his father sitting for West, it must have been late in 1783, the only period when father and son were in London together. The result of that sitting may of course have been only a preliminary sketch, and the final figure of Adams could have been painted in afterward from further sittings during Adams' ministry in London, 1785–1788. See Charles Coleman Sellers, *Benjamin Franklin in Portraiture,* New Haven, 1962, p. 398–401.

VI

Mather Brown

"Painter to the American Ambassador's family."
Abigail Adams 2d to John Quincy Adams, July 1785.

Adams had no sooner joined his wife and daughter in London on 7 August 1784, after a separation of four years and a half, than they all set out together, the next day, for Paris. Here they joined Jefferson and for nine months lived in close, friendly intercourse with him, strengthening the bond that had been forged between the two men eight years before at Philadelphia. Abigail herself developed a strong attachment to Jefferson and felt the pangs of her loss of his association when she and Adams returned to London the following May. To Jefferson she wrote on 6 June 1785 of her departure from Paris:

I own I was loth to leave my garden because I did not expect to find its place supplied. I was still more loth on account of the increasing pleasure, and intimacy which a longer acquaintance with a respected Friend promised, to leave behind me the only person with whom my Companion could associate with perfect freedom, and unreserve: and whose place he had no reason to expect supplied in the Land to which he is destinied.[1]

A month earlier, writing to her sister, she had characterized that "respected Friend" as "one of the choice ones of the earth."[2] With such a bond of friendship between these two men, it was but natural in that age that they should desire to exchange portraits.

The young American artist Mather Brown was active in London for some years after 1781. Born in Massachusetts in 1761, he had been a pupil of Gilbert Stuart, and like so many other young artists had come to London to study under Benjamin West. By 1784 he had rented a house in Cavendish Square and become a popular portraitist. A glowing account of Brown was given by young Abigail to her brother John Quincy Adams:

By the way, I must not omit to tell you, that a rage for Painting has taken Possession of the Whole family, one of our rooms has been occu-

[1] 6 June 1785 (DLC: Jefferson Papers, printed in Cappon, ed., *Adams-Jefferson Letters,* 1:28).
[2] To Mary Smith Cranch, 8–10 May 1785 (MWA, printed in AA, *Letters,* ed. CFA, 1848, p. 248).

46

pied by a Gentleman of this profession, for near a fortnight, and we have the extreme felicity of looking at ourselves upon Canvass. The Paper yesterday had this paragraph . . . "Copely and Brown are exerting their skill upon their illustrious Country Man Mr. Adams the American Ambassador." *I expect it will be next that Mr. Brown is painter to the American Ambassador's family.* He was very sollicitous to have a likeness of Pappa, thinking it would be an advantage to him, and Pappa Consented. He has taken the best likeness I have yet seen of him, and you may suppose is very Proud, when so many have failed before him. Mamma has set for hers, and I followed the example. It is said he has taken an admirable likeness of my Ladyship, the Honble. Miss Adams you know. It is a very tasty picture I can assure you, whether a likeness or not. Pappa is much pleased with it, and says he has got my character, a Mixture of Drolery and Modesty. I wish we could have the other three yourself and Charles and Thomas. I think we should make a *respectable Group*. He has a good likeness of Mamma, too.[3]

Despite the obvious satisfaction of the family with the three portraits mentioned, only one—that of "my Ladyship"—has remained in the family. It hangs in the Long Room of the Old House in Quincy. That of Adams himself has disappeared; the "good likeness of Mamma" survives (Fig. 21).

In the spring of 1786, during a visit to England, Jefferson sat to Brown, probably at the instance of Adams (though on 25 April 1786 Jefferson paid Brown £10 for the picture), and the portrait has remained in the Adams family ever since. Abigail first mentioned it in a letter to Jefferson the following July when she took the "opportunity of paying my respects to a Gentleman for whom I entertain the highest esteem, and whose portrait dignifies a part of our room, tho it is but a poor substitute for those pleasures we enjoy'd some months past."[4]

It wasn't long before Jefferson reciprocated his desire to obtain a portrait of Adams. "Will you," he wrote to Adams' son-in-law, William Stephens Smith, in October, "undertake to prevail on Mr. Adams to set for his picture and on Mr. Brown to draw it for me? I wish to add it to those of other principal American characters which I have or shall have: and I had rather it should be original than a copy."[5] Jefferson had surely seen Adams' 1785 likeness by Brown and apparently wanted a new likeness. No progress was made, however, and Jefferson must have pursued Adams himself on the subject, or at least Abigail.

[3] 4 July–11 Aug. 1785 (Adams Papers).
[4] 23 July 1786 (DLC:Jefferson Papers, printed in Cappon, ed., *Adams-Jefferson Letters*, 1:145).
[5] 22 Oct. 1786 (Jefferson, *Papers*, ed. Boyd, 10:479).

We find her writing to Jefferson in the summer of 1787: "Mr. Adams will write you. He has not a portrait that he likes to send you. Mr. Trumble talks of taking one. If he succeeds better than his Brethren, Mr. Adams will ask your acceptance of it."[6] On the last day of 1787 Jefferson again wrote to Smith, "I must remind you also of Mr. Adams's picture, as I should be much mortified should I not get it done before he leaves Europe."[7] No doubt he had learned that on 5 October Congress had voted that "The honble. John Adams . . . be permitted agreeably to his request, to return to America at any time after the 24th. day of February . . . 1788,"[8] and realized, in view of Adams' strong desire to return home, how little time was left.

Smith replied in January, "I have again attacked Mr. Adams on the subject of the picture and he has promised if Mr. Trumbull on his return will take it, he will send it to you and I will take charge of it when finished if necessary."[9] Jefferson must have misunderstood this note as implying that Trumbull himself was to paint the picture, for he promptly replied to Smith, "With respect to Mr. Adams's picture, I must again press it to be done by Brown, because Trumbul does not paint of the size of the life, and could not be asked to hazard himself on it. . . . I must not be disappointed of Mr. Adams's."[10]

So the correspondence continued, with urging and impatience on Jefferson's part, and patience and cooperation on the part of Smith, as well as Trumbull, who was then a frequent correspondent with Jefferson. In February word arrived from Trumbull, "Have spoken to Brown who promises; but I am afraid will not perform as Mr. Adams has little time to spare. (Of that little however He will give me a part.) Brown says you paid him ten pounds for your picture. Do you mean I should pay the same for the other???"[11] Again, on 6 March, "Brown is busy about the pictures. Mr. Adams's is like. Your's I do not think so well of."[12] The "Your's" referred to was apparently a replica in process of the 1786 portrait of Jefferson.

The sittings were concluded by the end of March, and on the 30th of the month Adams left London with Abigail, bound for Falmouth whence not long afterwards they embarked for home on the ship *Lucretia,* of Boston. In May, Jefferson wrote again to Trumbull, "I omit-

[6] 10 July 1787 (DLC:Jefferson Papers, printed in Cappon, ed., *Adams-Jefferson Letters,* 1:186).
[7] 31 Dec. 1787 (Jefferson, *Papers,* ed. Boyd, 12:484).
[8] *JCC,* 33:612.
[9] 16 Jan. 1788 (Jefferson, *Papers,* ed. Boyd, 12:517).
[10] 2 Feb. 1788 (same, p. 588).
[11] Trumbull to Jefferson, 22 Feb. 1788 (same, p. 622).
[12] Trumbull to Jefferson, 6 March 1788 (same, p. 647).

ted in mine of Mar. 27. from Amsterdam to tell you that I wished to pay Mr. Brown the same for Mr. Adams's picture as I had paid him for my own. You say mine does not resemble. Is it a copy? Because he agreed that the original should be mine, and it was that I paid him for." [13] To this the reply was, "I believe what He means to send you of yourself to be the copy, and that Mr. Adams thus [will receive?] the original. They shall now be sent to you with the Polyplasiasmos"; [14] followed a month later with advice that, "The Polyplasiasmos picture will come with those from Brown, which are not quite ready." [15]

Patience was rewarded; at last the picture was finished and Brown was paid the £10 agreed upon, the receipt, "by the Hands of Mr. Trumbull," being dated 2 July 1788.[16] Two final letters close the exchange. From Trumbull in August, Jefferson received the welcome tidings, "The Diligence which leaves this tomorrow will bring you Brown's two pictures [i.e. the replicas of Adams and Jefferson], your polyplasiasmos, and a picture of Genl. Washington which belongs to Mr. De La Fayette, and which you will be so good to send him. They are all in one case." [17] To this he responded, "The pictures are received in good condition." [18]

On his return to America by the end of 1789 Jefferson brought with him Adams' portrait (Fig. 20), which remained in his possession at Monticello until his death in 1826. In 1828 it was exhibited at the

[13] 18 May 1788 (same, 13:178). Alfred L. Bush in his *Life Portraits of Jefferson* concluded that Jefferson ultimately received the original of himself by Brown, and JA the copy (p. 15). The difficulty with this conclusion is twofold. In the first place, the portrait that Adams received is signed "M. Brown P. 1786." It is hard to believe that a replica painted in 1788 would have been signed "P. 1786." In the second place, the 1786 portrait was in fact delivered to JA and is mentioned by AA in July 1786 as dignifying a part of her room. If Bush were correct in his conclusion, it would presuppose that in 1788 JA gave up the 1786 original and took back the replica. This we doubt, and no mention of such an exchange has been found.

[14] Trumbull to Jefferson, 23 May 1788 (Jefferson, *Papers*, ed. Boyd, 13:199). Jefferson had written to Trumbull 13 Nov. 1787, "If you could do me the favor also to bring me one of the copies taken without the pencil (I forget the hard name by which they call it; it is greek however) I should be glad of it." The "hard name" has been interpreted: "The multiplying or copying pictures in oil colours by a mechanical or chymical process, as invented by Mr. [Joseph] Brook, was at first stiled POLYPLASIOSMOS, a Greek word, signifying multiplication" (same, 12:358).

[15] Trumbull to Jefferson, 20 June 1788 (same, 13:280).

[16] "His Excellency Thos. Jefferson Dr. to Mr. Brown.

	£
To A Portrait of Mr. Adams	10.0.0
paid by the Hands of Mr. Trumbull	10.0.0
July. 2d. 1788. MB.	10.0.0"

(MHS, *Procs.*, 47 [1913–1914]:33.)

[17] 15 Aug. 1788 (Jefferson, *Papers*, ed. Boyd, 13:519).

[18] 10 Sept. 1788 (same, p. 597).

20. JOHN ADAMS. OIL BY MATHER BROWN, 1788

21. ABIGAIL ADAMS. OIL BY MATHER BROWN, 1785

Boston Athenæum; and it was sold at auction at Chester Harding's Gallery on School Street, Boston, on 19 July 1833. It was bequeathed to the Athenæum in 1908, on the death of George Francis Parkman, who presumably had inherited it from the purchaser at the 1833 sale; today it hangs in the Trustees' room.

Although the painting is a well-drawn, colorful representation, it presents Adams with a cold, formal, matter-of-fact expression, lacking the vigor and animation of Copley's or Trumbull's pictures. But we have the judgment of Trumbull, the master painter, borne out by comparison with West's or Copley's, or his own, that it is "like."

Clearly visible on the table before Adams can be seen a large volume labeled "Jefferson Hist. of Virginia." In May 1785, just before the Adamses left Paris for England, Jefferson had sent Adams a copy of his *Notes on the State of Virginia,* two hundred copies of which had been printed in Paris that month for distribution to Jefferson's friends. Adams was enthusiastic in his praise of the volume. "I thank you kindly for your Book," he wrote. "It is our Meditation all the Day long. I cannot now say much about it, but I think it will do its Author and his Country great Honour. The Passages upon slavery, are worth Diamonds. They will have more effect than Volumes written by mere Philosophers. The Ladies say you should have mentioned West and Copeley at least among your American Genius's, because they think them the greatest Painters of the Age." [19] Though the artist used some artistic license in the size of the volume and its title, there can be little doubt that, by conspiring to have the volume so prominent in the portrait, as a sort of visible evidence of the bond between them, Adams was returning to Jefferson a compliment that must have been warmly received. Brown's portrait of Adams has been many times reproduced, photographically, in published works, but no engraving of it has come to light.

In the Colonnade of the Hall of Fame for Great Americans, at New York University, there is a bust of Adams in bronze (Cat. No. 43), the work of the Massachusetts sculptor John Francis Paramino. The sculptor allegedly worked from Copley's and Brown's portraits of Adams, though the bust more resembles the latter. Presented by the Massachusetts Society of the Sons of the Revolution, the bust was unveiled on 13 May 1924 by the late John Adams of South Lincoln, a great-great-grandson of the second President.

This famous exchange of portraits between Adams and Jefferson leaves us with a mystery so far unsolved. Brown painted two portraits

[19] 22 May 1785 (NNP, printed in Cappon, ed., *Adams-Jefferson Letters,* 1:21).

each of Jefferson and Adams; and both received one of each. At one time, therefore, Jefferson possessed both a portrait of himself and one of Adams, and Adams similarly had one of Jefferson and one of himself. The mystery is that by strange coincidence the portrait each man had of himself is lost, that of Adams done in 1785 and that of Jefferson in 1788. No trace or mention of either after 1788 has come to light. It is possible that the two portraits are still in existence but no longer identified. Brown's 1785 portrait of Abigail Adams for a time met a similar fate, and disappeared from sight until recent times.

In October 1948 there appeared a notice in *Panorama*,[20] beneath a likeness of Abigail Adams (Fig. 21):

> Portrait of Abigail Adams, 1744–1818. By Ralph Earl, 1751–1801. Signed. Published for the first time. Painted probably in England in 1785 and shows marked English influence. An important addition to the recorded works of Earl. Oil on canvas 30¼ x 21½ inches. 18th Century carved gold leaf frame. $2,500.

This appears to have been all that was known of the portrait at that time. What has since been discovered of its provenance is only its recent history. It had been owned in 1928 by H. A. Hammond Smith, exhibited at the Inaugural Exhibition of The Museum of the City of New York in 1932, listed as item No. 768 at the Erskine Hewitt sale of 22 August 1938, where it was described as "Portrait of a Lady," painted "about 1800," and brought $310 at auction. In the 1930's it was examined and recorded by the late William Sawitzky in preparation for his book on Ralph Earl, and later sold to Miss Frances Eggleston of Oswego, New York, passing subsequently from her to the New York State Historical Association at Cooperstown, New York, its present owner. Recently it was lent to the White House and hung prominently in the China Room on the ground floor. As early as 1932 it was described as being signed "R. Earl, Pinxt.," but it was not until 1948 that the sitter was recognized as Abigail Adams. A comparison with the Blyth pastel (Fig. 2), or the Stuart of 1800 (Fig. 66), leaves no room for doubt in this respect. This is undoubtedly Abigail as she appeared in 1785, aged forty, painted some time after her arrival in London from Paris in May of that year.

Ralph Earl, who had resided in England since 1778, left that country in 1785 and is recorded as being in Rhode Island in October of that year. If he were the painter of this portrait, it would have had to

[20] Published by the Harry Shaw Newman Gallery, later the Old Print Shop, in New York City.

have been painted at some time between Abigail's arrival in England late in May and Earl's departure in September or even earlier. That Adams family portraits were being painted during that period we know from young Abigail's letter to her brother quoted above. Brown was there called "painter to the American Ambassador's family"; he had painted John Adams, "Mamma has set for hers, and I followed the example." Even the newspaper commented that "Copeley and Brown are exerting their skill upon their illustrious Countryman Mr. Adams." But not a word of Earl! And yet this portrait of Abigail is a striking portrayal of the handsome, resolute, and able wife and partner of the Ambassador. Surely it merited a word of approval!

The fact is that Abigail's portrait (Fig. 21) is actually the "good likeness of Mamma" done by Brown in 1785. The stumbling block has been that the painting appears to be signed "R. Earl." But even this disability has given way to close scrutiny. On careful examination it now appears that the Earl signature is on top of the varnish and therefore at once suspect! From this discovery it can be conjectured that some enterprising owner of the handsome portrait of an unknown lady chose at random from the possible artists who might have painted it and selected Earl, adding his name—on top of the varnish. Then, the subsequent discovery that the subject was Abigail required dating the painting to the very short period between May 1785 and Earl's departure from England, the exact date of which is not yet known, and leaves us wholly without any explanation of why this much-painted and articulate family never so much as mentioned Earl.

How much of this speculation might have been eliminated if the artist had only signed his name and added the name of the subject! We are reminded of the remark of the philosopher John Locke when Kneller was painting his portrait for Anthony Collins: "Pray get Sir Godfrey to write on the back of my Lady Masham's picture, 'Lady Masham,' and on the back of mine, 'John Locke.' This he did to Mr. Molyneux's: it is necessary to be done, or else the pictures of private persons are lost in two or three generations." [21]

[21] Quoted in Walter F. Tiff, *Gossip about Portraits*, London, 1867, p. 138.

VII

John Trumbull

"To his country he gave his SWORD and his PENCIL."
Memorial tablet erected at Yale in 1843.

Just as the signing in 1776 of the "Declaration" of the independence of their country was remembered by Adams and Jefferson as the greatest achievement of their careers, so also has Trumbull's small canvas of that *Declaration of Independence* (Fig. 22) been held to be his greatest work and the one which alone would assure him an illustrious place in the annals of American history and art.

In 1780, shortly after concluding a brief, though not undistinguished, military career, Trumbull sailed for Europe with a view to furthering his profession by studying under Benjamin West. After a short stay in Paris, where he procured from Franklin a letter of introduction to West, he went to London. Scarcely had he commenced his studies under West when he was arrested in retaliation for the execution of Major André. He spent seven months in prison, being released only on condition that he leave the country, not to return until peace was declared. This he did, with Copley and West his sureties, and it was four years before he returned, again placing himself under the hand of West.

At the age of twenty-eight Trumbull took the torch from West and, as he later wrote, "began to meditate seriously the subjects of national history, of events of the Revolution." [1] Now it was that he embarked on that grand, patriotic scheme which, flowering into a series of epic paintings, formed the unique pictorial record of historic moments in the early hours of the new republic.

By the spring of 1786 he had completed his *Battle of Bunker's Hill* and *Death of Montgomery*, which he carried with him later that year when he journeyed to Paris to visit Jefferson. During this visit he conceived the plan of the *Declaration*, drawing with profit on Jefferson's memory and enthusiasm. In the collections of Yale University there are preserved a sketch made by Jefferson outlining his recollection of the interior of Independence Hall and Trumbull's preliminary drawing

[1] *The Autobiography of Colonel John Trumbull, Patriot-Artist, 1756–1843,* ed. Theodore Sizer, New Haven, 1953, p. 88.

22. DECLARATION OF INDEPENDENCE. OIL BY JOHN TRUMBULL, 1787–1796

for the picture, bearing Trumbull's endorsement: "The first idea of the Declaration of Independence, Paris, Sept. 1786." He returned to London in November of that year, and, as he said, "went on with my studies of other subjects of the history of the Revolution, arranged carefully the composition for the Declaration of Independence, and prepared it for receiving the portraits, as I might meet with the distinguished men, who were present at that illustrious scene." [2] For this purpose he painted from life no less than thirty-six of his characters, on little 3- or 4-inch oval mahogany panels, later copying many of them into the painting. He also had a receptacle made for holding the canvas, so that he could carry it about with him in his carriage while in search of the original signers.

In this way he took Adams. "In the course of the summer of 1787, Mr. Adams took leave of the court of St. James, and preparatory to the voyage to America, had the powder combed out of his hair. Its color and natural curl were beautiful, and I took that opportunity to paint his portrait in the small Declaration of Independence." [3] We can, perhaps, afford a smile at Trumbull's recollection, after the lapse of thirty-seven years, of the beauty of the "color and natural curl" of the hair of the fifty-two-year-old ambassador. It certainly is not borne out by the small *Declaration,* although there is some evidence of a reddish tinge to Adams' hair in the later and larger adaptations of the picture.

The *Declaration* was completed about 1796, and remained in Trumbull's possession until 1832, when with many others of his paintings it was transferred to Yale College under the terms of an indenture dated 19 December 1831 prepared by Yale's President Jeremiah Day which provided in turn for Trumbull an annuity of one thousand dollars, which he continued to receive until his death in 1843 at the age of eighty-eight.

In 1848, the sculptor Horatio Greenough expressed admiration for the way Trumbull had dealt with a weighty and difficult subject. "I admire in this composition the skill with which Trumbull has collected so many portraits in formal session, without theatrical effort in order to enliven it, and without falling into bald insipidity by adhering to trivial fact. These men are earnest, yet full of dignity; they are firm yet cheerful; they are gentlemen; and you see at a glance that they meant something very serious in pledging their lives; their fortunes, and their sacred honor." [4]

[2] Same, p. 146–147.
[3] Same, p. 147.
[4] Quoted in John F. Weir, *John Trumbull,* N.Y., 1901, p. 55–56.

The likeness of Adams, as Trumbull caught it, is at once penetrating and convincing, surpassed if at all only by Stuart's last portrait of the aged former President. Chubby and rotund, serious in expression but not worried, the delegate from Massachusetts is seen with hand on hip, confidently occupying a prominent position in the front ranks of that band of patriots. Though in the garb of 1776, this is the Adams of 1787. A glance at Trumbull's portraits of Adams done after 1791 will show how closely they resemble it. The entire canvas measures only 21 x 31 inches and each head is less than 2 inches in size, yet within that tiny area Trumbull has painted a head of Adams (Fig. 23) which for likeness and detail of expression compares favorably with his own later life-sized head or with Brown's or Copley's.

In February 1816 Congress commissioned Trumbull to execute four large paintings, to be drawn from his smaller canvases of a quarter century earlier, to be placed in the rotunda of the Capitol, for which he was ultimately to receive $32,000. On learning of the project, Adams wrote, "Your Country ought to acknowledge itself more indebted to you than to any other Artist who ever existed; and I therefore heartily wish you success."[5] J. Q. Adams saw the "first chalking out" of the great picture in September 1817,[6] but it was not entirely finished until 1819; the other three not until several years later. It was to be late in 1826 before they would finally take their places in the rotunda of the Capitol.

The *Declaration,* before being taken to Washington, was exhibited, to the displeasure of some members of Congress, in New York, Philadelphia, Boston, and Baltimore. In Boston the public was invited to view the picture in Faneuil Hall, and, with an admission fee of twenty-five cents a person, $1,701 was collected. At the request of Trumbull, Adams went to the exhibition in Boston, making one of his last public appearances. Of it he reported to Jefferson, "Trumbull with a band of Associates drew me by the Cords of old Frien[d]ships to see his Picture on Saturday where I got a great Cold. The Air of Ph[an]euil Hall is changed. I have not been Used to catch Cold there."[7] Years later, the author and abolitionist Edmund Quincy described the occasion:

I well remember being one of the party which accompanied Mr. Adams to see Trumbull's picture. Faneuil Hall was full of spectators when we arrived, and what impressed the scene upon my boyish memory was the re-

[5] To John Trumbull, 1 Jan. 1817 (CtY:Mason-Franklin Coll., printed in Trumbull's *Autobiography,* ed. Sizer, p. 311).

[6] JQA, Diary, 13 Sept. 1817.

[7] 8 Dec. 1818 (DLC:Jefferson Papers; printed in Cappon, ed., *Adams-Jefferson Letters,* 2:530).

23. JOHN ADAMS. DETAIL OF FIGURE 22

spectful manner in which all the men took off their hats when Mr. Adams entered leaning on my Mother's arm, and remained uncovered while he stayed. Room was made for him by common consent, so that he could see the picture to the best advantage. He seemed carried back to his prime of manhood, and to the most famous scene of his life, and he gave his warm approval to the picture as a correct representation of the Convention.[8]

J. Q. Adams records his opinion of the painting as he saw it shortly before its completion: "I cannot say I was disappointed in the Execution of it, because my expectations were very low, but the picture is immeasurably below the dignity of the subject. It may be said of Trumbull's talent, as the Spaniards say of heroes who were brave on a certain day—He has painted good pictures. I think the old small picture far superior to this large new one. He himself thinks otherwise."[9] Let it be added to Trumbull's credit that Adams modified his opinion when he saw the picture in place at last in 1826: "His four pictures are placed, and in such a favourable light, that they appear far better than they had ever done before."[10]

Sometime after 1831 and before 1840, Trumbull again reproduced in oil the *Declaration* (Fig. 24), this time with four companion pieces, one-half life-sized—6 x 9 feet—replicas of the originals, though with modifications. The five paintings were purchased from Trumbull's executors in 1844 by a group of public-spirited gentlemen of Hartford and, being presented to the Wadsworth Atheneum, were considered the most important acquisition of the newly formed art gallery. But age had taken its toll. By comparison with the original, conceived half a century earlier, this last version of the *Declaration* is a disappointment. Curiously enough, apart from a general lowering of quality and loss of touch, the striking difference is that, without exception, each of the persons represented is made to appear in the later version markedly younger than in the original. Perhaps this is merely a subjective reaction to be expected of the aged artist. Another noticeable variation is in the architecture of the room, the Wadsworth Atheneum version showing but one door behind the gathering, rather than two, as in the original. This change reflects the differences of opinion that early existed as to just how the room actually appeared in 1776. Edward Savage's rendering (Fig. 51) is now thought to be closest to the fact.

From the very earliest moment, Trumbull had had in mind the advantages to be derived from having his proposed series of small his-

[8] Edmund Quincy, *Josiah Quincy*, p. 371.
[9] Diary, 1 Sept. 1818.
[10] Same, 28 Nov. 1826.

24. DECLARATION OF INDEPENDENCE. OIL BY JOHN TRUMBULL

torical canvases engraved for widespread distribution. West had pointed this out to him and had also explained the detailed steps necessary for it. Nevertheless it was to be thirty years before the engraving of the *Declaration* was actually put in process.

J. Q. Adams' diary reflects his conversations in London in June 1815 with Trumbull on this subject: "He had now engaged his passage to return to America, and expected to sail in about a Month. That he intended to open a subscription for engraving his Pictures of the Declaration of Independence, and of the Battle of Princeton. . . . I told him I thought those engravings would succeed in America, but he could not expect many of them to be sold here. He said if the Print was well executed he could reckon upon about two hundred that would be taken by Collectors of Prints, as specimens of Art. They were always indifferent about the subject." [11]

Niles' Weekly Register, published in Baltimore, in February 1818 carried the advertisement for subscriptions for the proposed engraving: "*Mr. Trumbull,* has issued proposals for the publication of his picture of THE DECLARATION OF INDEPENDENCE, of which he is engaged in painting an enlarged copy for the decoration of the Capitol. Every American of feeling, who can spare the necessary money, will rejoice in being able to decorate his house with a picture at once commemorative of the most striking event of our history, and itself a proof of its perfection in that branch of the Fine Arts." [12]

The man selected to make the engraving was Asher B. Durand, a young artist born in Jefferson Village (later Maplewood), New Jersey, in 1796, who had received his apprenticeship with the New York engraver and lithographer Peter Maverick and later become his partner. On learning of his capabilities, Trumbull employed Durand and wrote a glowing letter about the young artist to Francis C. Gray, the prominent Boston lawyer: "With regard to the engravings of Mr. Durand. . . . It gives me much pleasure to state that there is but one opinion of the remarkable merit of this engraver; & that the ablest judges are most liberal of their praise. . . . Mr. Allston thinks them proofs of singular talent. Mr. Stuart says that they are specimens of the highest art, & that he should not hesitate to have any of his works engraved under his own eye & in conformity with his directions, by this artist." [13]

Durand received $3000 for making the plate for the engraving

[11] Same, 15 June 1815.
[12] *Niles' Register,* 14:15 (28 Feb. 1818).
[13] 22 March 1820 (quoted in Trumbull's *Autobiography,* ed. Sizer, p. 321).

25. DECLARATION OF INDEPENDENCE. ENGRAVING BY ASHER B. DURAND, 1823

63

(Fig. 25), yet the venture was but another printmaking failure. Although dated 1820, the plate was not completed, nor engravings available, until 1823, some thirty-two years after the painting had been finished. But despite Trumbull's financial disappointment, Durand's work is entitled to high praise and in this undertaking went far toward establishing his reputation. His lines are strong and sure, the figures stand out in clarity of detail, and the import of the moment so well portrayed by Trumbull is fairly caught and preserved. Trumbull was enthusiastic. He sent a print to Jefferson with a letter full of pride and nostalgia:

I have the pleasure of saying that not only has the engraving been finished with great beauty but the printing has been executed with uncommon success. It is delightful to me, that after the lapse of so many years, this work which I meditated, and you assisted me to arrange, at Chaillot, in the year 1786, is at last completed. Rarely does it occur that two individuals, advanced as we then were on the road of life, remain to see the completion of a favorite project at the end of thirty-seven years. The event was great beyond all others in the history of man; the actors in it were men who not only by that act, but by the consistent and undeviating patriotism of their subsequent conduct deserve to live in the memory of mankind to the end of time; and I thank God that I have possessed (to use the beautiful language of Dr. Johnson) "Calmness of mind, and steadiness of purpose" to complete this memorial of such men and such an act. May I not, my dear sir, without excessive vanity, say with Horace, "Monumentum exegi aere perennius," will not my name live, under the shadow of their glory.[14]

Later in the same month he wrote Lafayette a similar letter: "I have sent to you a small case containing a proof impression of a print which has been engraved here from my painting of the 'Declaration of Independence' by a young engraver, born in the vicinity, and now only twenty-six years old. This work is wholly American, even to the paper and printing, a circumstance which renders it popular here and will make it a curiosity to you, who knew America when she had neither painters nor engravers nor arts of any kind, except those of 'stern utility.'"[15] In 1826 Trumbull presented J. Q. Adams, then President, with a large portfolio containing the *Declaration* and three others of the series "inscribed on the outside of the Port-Folio, as presented by

[14] 1 Oct. 1823 (quoted in Weir's *Trumbull*, p. 39–40); *Exegi monumentum aere perennius* ("I have finished a monument more lasting than bronze"), from Horace, Ode XXX, bk. iii, line 1.
[15] 20 Oct. 1823 (quoted in John Durand, *Life and Times of Asher B. Durand*, N.Y., 1894, p. 26).

26. JOHN ADAMS. OIL ON MAHOGANY PANEL
BY JOHN TRUMBULL, 1792

him to the President of the United States, 1826." [16] The engravings
are still preserved in the Stone Library adjoining the Old House in
Quincy. Over the years the *Declaration* has had an enormous popularity and has been engraved many times, in the United States and
abroad, in many sizes, alone and surrounded by or enclosed within fac-
similes of the Declaration itself with the signatures appended to it.
But none has equaled Durand's youthful masterpiece.

Although the Adams of the *Declaration* was unquestionably Trumbull's best likeness of Adams, it was not his only one. The catalogue
of the 1802 exhibition of the Columbian Gallery listed as No. 16,
"A portrait of J. Adams, late President. / Original Painter's name /

[16] JQA, Diary, 30 Nov. 1826.

J. Trumbull." [17] A review of the exhibition appeared in several editions of the *Morning Chronicle* for November and December 1802 and January 1803, signed "An Admirer of the Polite Arts." [18] The Trumbull full-length is described as "executed in a good style, and a faithful likeness," and was said to have been owned by Edward Savage. This painting is now unlocated. It may have been taken to Boston when Savage's collection was reassembled there as the Columbian Museum, and have been destroyed in 1803 when a large part of the collection was burned. Perhaps it and a companion, unfinished, portrait of Samuel Adams (No. 14 in the exhibition), had been painted as studies in preparation for the *Declaration*.

Among the large collection of miniatures in the Trumbull Gallery at Yale is a small oval, 4 x 3 inches, painted on a mahogany panel (Fig. 26) showing Adams when Vice President, inscribed: "John Adams / first Vice President of / the United States of America / & one of her ministers at / the conclusion of peace / with G. Britain in 1783 / Painted by J. Trumbull / at Philadelphia 1792." This miniature was acquired by Yale in 1832 as part of the collection transferred under the 1831 indenture. The style of wig is unfamiliar on Adams, but the likeness in other respects is faithful and compares well not only with the Adams of the *Declaration* but also with the next two to be considered.

Trumbull painted his last portrait of Adams in 1793 or 1794. Two of this period are known, one undoubtedly a replica of the other. One (Fig. 27) early belonged to John Jay, perhaps was commissioned by him, and passed from his descendants to "Bedford House," the historic Jay mansion at Katonah, New York. The earliest notice of the other (Fig. 28), probably the replica, was on the occasion of its gift to Harvard College in 1794 by Andrew Craigie, the land speculator and later the builder of the Craigie Bridge from East Cambridge to the North End of Boston. In the minutes of the meeting of the President and Fellows of Harvard College, held 26 August 1794, there is recorded: "Voted, that the thanks of this Corporation be given to Andrew Craigie, Esquire, for his generous and very acceptable present to this University of two elegant Portraits, the one of the President of the United States, the other of the Vice President." [19] The portrait of the

---

[17] The Columbian Gallery was then at the Pantheon, No. 80 Greenwich Street, New York City, near the Battery.

[18] Rita Susswein Gottesman, "New York's First Major Art Show, as Reviewed by Its First Newspaper Critic in 1802 and 1803," NYHS, *Quart.*, 43:295 (July 1959).

[19] MH–Ar.

27. JOHN ADAMS. OIL BY JOHN TRUMBULL, 1793

President was Trumbull's replica of his likeness of Washington painted in Philadelphia in May 1793, which was purchased by Yale in 1832.[20] We can only speculate that Craigie, seeing the originals of both Washington and Adams in Trumbull's possession in 1793 or 1794, commissioned him to paint replicas of both for Harvard. Dunlap records seeing both at Harvard in 1797:

Mr. Adams the present president of ye U S has lately presented a very valuable collection of French books from his private library. They have a museum here. In a very handsome room opposite the library is the celebrated orrery made by Mr Pope of Boston, in this room are pictures of the benefactors of the Colledge, & of Messrs Washington & Adams, 2 of the first, one by Trumbull & an execrable thing by Savage. Mr. Adams's is by Trumbull & at first did not appear to me like him, but on examination I found it accurate, except the tasty air which the painter has diffused over it.[21]

Both pictures of Adams (Figs. 27, 28) are remarkably like the Adams of the *Declaration,* the only significant difference being in the style of Adams' hair and his clothes. The firm yet chubby face, the seriousness of Adams' expression are quite like. This is Adams the Vice President; this is a step beyond the progression from Blyth (Fig. 1) to Copley (Fig. 9) to West (Fig. 16) and to the Trumbull of the *Declaration* (Fig. 22). Reversing Trumbull's oval miniature (Fig. 26) with the aid of a mirror, will show that it, too, is strikingly similar. It is this very consistency that renders Trumbull's representations so authoritative, so worthy of reliance in our search for the likeness of Adams.

[20] John H. Morgan and Mantle Fielding, *The Life Portraits of Washington and Their Replicas,* Phila., 1931, p. 170.
[21] Entry of 12 Dec. 1797, *Diary of William Dunlap (1766–1839),* NYHS, Colls., Pubn. Fund Ser., vols. 62–64, N.Y., 1929–1930, 1:188.

28. JOHN ADAMS. OIL BY JOHN TRUMBULL, 1793

VIII

Charles Willson Peale

"The industrious and ingenious Mr. Peale
of the Museum at Philadelphia."
John Adams to François Adriaan Van der Kemp, November 1804.

Adams' first recorded meeting with Peale is entertainingly described in his letter to Abigail of 21 August 1776: "Yesterday Morning," he wrote, "I took a Walk, into Arch Street, to see Mr. Peele's Painters Room. Peele is from Maryland, a tender, soft, affectionate Creature. . . . He has a Variety of Portraits—very well done. But not so well as Copeleys Portraits. Copeley is the greatest Master, that ever was in America. His Portraits far exceed Wests. . . . He [Peale] is ingenious. He has Vanity—loves Finery—Wears a sword—gold Lace —speaks French—is capable of Friendship, and strong Family Attachments and natural Affections." [1] He was quite obviously taken by Peale's charm and his collection of books on art, his portraits, miniatures, and models. "I wish I had Leisure," he added wistfully, "and Tranquility of Mind to amuse myself with these Elegant, and ingenious Arts of Painting, Sculpture, Statuary, Architecture, and Musick. But I have not. A Taste in all of them, is an agreable Accomplishment." [2]

Thus far, no records have come to light revealing a further association between Peale and Adams. The painter was a mild Antifederalist, though he heartily welcomed the adoption of the Constitution in 1788. When Peale was forming his gallery of distinguished persons, however, he and Adams must have met again. It was while Adams was Vice President, probably in 1794, that Peale painted his portrait (Fig. 29), measuring about 23 x 19 inches, the same size as so many of the collection in his Museum. Adams would have recalled their meeting fifteen years before and undoubtedly enjoyed Peale's enthusiasm for painting and science. The painting when completed must have joined that of Jefferson and others which hung in Peale's Museum. Although we cannot tell precisely when it was painted, it was first listed in Peale's *Historical Catalogue* of 1795. It remained in the Museum col-

[1] *Adams Family Correspondence,* 2:103–104.
[2] Same, p. 104.

70

29. JOHN ADAMS. OIL BY CHARLES WILLSON PEALE, CA. 1794

71

lection until the auction sale on 6 October 1854 in Philadelphia, where it was listed as No. 48 in the Catalogue. The New York dealer, P. E. Erben, purchased it for sixty dollars [3] for the City of Philadelphia, and it is now on permanent loan to Independence National Historical Park. For years it hung in Independence Hall, where Adams had been so active at the time it was painted, only being removed to storage during the recent restoration of the Hall.

The picture has the warm colors so characteristic of Peale; Adams appears of florid complexion, with a light gray coat and waistcoat, and gray-green harmonizing background. It was reproduced in Clarence Bowen's *History of the Centennial* (1892) and engraved for the 1898 edition of John Fiske's *Critical Period of American History,* but except for these occasions, it has not received much notice other than as originally a part of the Peale Museum collection and now at Independence Hall.

[3] *Peale's Museum Gallery of Oil Paintings . . . Catalogue of the National Portrait and Historical Gallery, Illustrative of American History . . . Formerly Belonging to Peale's Museum,* Phila., 1854 (NHi, photostat copy)

IX

James Peale

James, younger brother of Charles Willson Peale, after serving with the Continental Army during the Revolution, settled in Philadelphia, where, under his brother's instruction, he turned to painting, specializing in miniatures, until his sight began to fail in 1818. Sometime in the 1790's James painted a small portrait of Adams (Fig. 30), measuring only 10¾ x 8¾ inches. On the reverse of the painting appears the inscription "John Adams by James Peale, Pinx." This portrait appeared as No. 107 in the catalogue of the Peale exhibition at the Pennsylvania Academy of the Fine Arts in 1923, having belonged formerly to Mrs. A. L. Stevenson of Hempstead, Long Island.[1] It was mentioned later in an article by Frederic F. Sherman when it was in the possession of The Ehrich Galleries in New York.[2] It is presently unlocated and is illustrated here from a photograph in the possession of the Frick Art Reference Library. As a likeness it is not convincing. Adams is shown wearing a wig, but of a kind not usual for him during the last decade of the century. The face shows very little expression although that could be accounted for by the blurred reproduction. On the basis of appearances only, it would not have been accepted as a likeness of Adams, were it not for its inclusion in the Peale Exhibition of 1923, at a time when the canvas itself was available for inspection. It is entirely possible that the portrait was incorrectly attributed.

[1] *Catalogue of an Exhibition of Portraits of Charles Willson Peale and James Peale and Rembrandt Peale,* Phila., 1923.

[2] "Two Recently Discovered Portraits in Oils by James Peale," *Art in America,* 21:114 (Oct. 1933).

30. JOHN ADAMS. OIL BY JAMES PEALE, CA. 1795

X

The Sharples

"Sharples for the expression."
George Washington Parke Custis to
Thomas William Channing Moors, 1857.

Shortly before Adams was elected President, there came to America and settled in Philadelphia a talented family of artists and incipient artists, who in the course of a decade or so produced a multitude of little portraits of almost every prominent American of the day. James Sharples (or Sharpless, as his name was spelled, and apparently sometimes pronounced), the father and master artist of the family, emigrated from England with his third wife, Ellen, who had been his pupil, their two children, James Jr. and Rolinda, and a son Felix by his second wife.[1] For eight years, until the family returned to England for the first time, James painted, indeed proliferated, his charming little portraits, only 9 x 7 inches, likenesses of Washington, Adams, Jefferson, Hamilton, Rush, Burr, Monroe, and a host of others. The list is almost endless; each was a gem.

William Dunlap tells us that Sharples' "successful practice in this country was in crayons, or pastels, which he manufactured for himself; and suited, in size, to the diminutive dimensions of his portraits, which were generally *en profile,* and, when so, strikingly like." The profile was produced with the aid of the pantograph or physiognotrace, and the details of the features were added, not in pastel, as commonly believed, but in tempera, using colored crayons, which the artist kept finely powdered in small glass cups, applied with a camel's hair pencil to a thick, gray, soft-grained, woolly-textured paper. Most of his portraits he finished in one sitting and his price "for the profile was $15; and for the full-face (never so good) $20."[2]

John Adams' likeness must have been first taken by Sharples late in 1796 or early in 1797, shortly before he assumed office as President.

[1] Katharine McCook Knox, *The Sharples, Their Portraits of George Washington and His Contemporaries,* New Haven, 1930, contains a full account of James Sharples and his family, and excerpts from his wife Ellen's diary (now in the City Art Gallery of Bristol, England), on which, and on *Lippincott's Magazine* of March and Dec. 1871 and Feb. 1872, I have drawn for family history.

[2] *History of the Rise and Progress of the Arts of Design in the United States,* N.Y., 1834, 2:70–71.

Two Sharples portraits of Adams of this date have survived, one (Fig. 31) belonging to Miss Ima Hogg of Houston, Texas, and the other (Fig. 32) to the Royal West of England Academy and on permanent loan to the City Art Gallery of Bristol, England. These two almost mirror one another, yet close scrutiny reveals a few trifling though real differences: the depth of the crease by the top waistcoat button, the fold of the waistcoat collar, and the shadowing of the sitter's farther eye. They cannot be two independent original portraits. One must be a replica by Sharples himself or perhaps a copy by Ellen or one of their children. Any doubt of the identity of the sitter is dispelled by the appearance in *The American Universal Magazine* of 20 March 1797 of an engraving (Fig. 33), bearing the inscription "Houston Sculpt. John Adams. / President of the United States." The engraving, scarcely 3 inches in size, appears immediately preceding a report of the speeches of Adams and Jefferson "on entering on the Duties of President and Vice President of the American Republic," and serves to date the Sharples portrait to a time early in 1797 or late in 1796.

Houston, who used alternately a single or double "H.," or "H.I.," as his initials, had just come to Philadelphia from Ireland, where he had contributed to the *Hibernian Magazine,* among other things, a fine engraving of that noble Irish barrister John Philpot Curran, a man whose warmth of heart and ability and courage as a lawyer must have excited the admiration of Adams. For a few years Houston applied his art in Philadelphia, producing engravings of Washington, Rittenhouse, Kemble as Richard III, and others, including Adams taken after both Sharples and Williams. David McNeely Stauffer in his *American Engravers upon Copper and Steel* considered him one of the earliest good stipple engravers in this country.

As was not uncommon, Houston's engraving of Sharples' Adams reverses the image—Adams now facing to the right—but if the engraving can be seen in a mirror, the exactness of the engraved reproduction is striking. We cannot be sure which of the two Sharples portraits was followed by Houston, but it would seem likely that it was Fig. 31. The sweeping curve of the edge of Adams' coat in the engraving and the clearness of his farther eye, more clearly resemble those features of the Hogg example, and the crisp, finished appearance suggests that it is the original and the Bristol example but a replica or copy.

Most of the history of these two pastels must be conjectured from what is known of the peregrinations of the Sharples family and their

31. JOHN ADAMS. TEMPERA BY JAMES SHARPLES, 1796–1797

32. JOHN ADAMS. TEMPERA BY JAMES SHARPLES, 1796–1797

JOHN ADAMS.

President of the United States.

33. JOHN ADAMS. ENGRAVING BY H. HOUSTON, 1797

collection of little portraits. James and Ellen returned with their children to England in 1801 and came back to America again in 1809. During the eight years' sojourn in England, Ellen and the children devoted themselves to improving their skill in painting and in making duplicates of James' portraits. Ellen recorded in her diary for December 1804:

> During the year 1804 copied in miniature Mr. Adams, President of the United States, Mr. Jefferson, President, Gen. Hamilton, Commander in Chief of the Forces of the U. S., Chancellor Livingston, Mr. B. Livingston, Mr. Gallatin, Dr. Priestly, 2nd of Gen. Washington, executed in a very superior style to the one done of him last year, as are all the latest pictures. This manifest improvement as I persevere is very pleasing to me.

The family proficiency in copying James' works became so advanced that, lacking a signature, it is not always possible to be sure which are by Sharples himself and which are copies by Ellen or some one of the children. By the time of his death in New York in 1811, at the age of fifty-nine, there was in the family's possession an extraordinary collection of little portraits, several hundred, both originals and copies. Many of these Ellen took with her when she sailed back to Liverpool on May 25 of that year with young James and Rolinda. Others—"most of the portraits of distinguished Americans," as she wrote in her diary —she left with Felix as his patrimony.

Ellen survived all her children and died in 1849 at the age of eighty, bequeathing her estate, including three- or fourscore of portraits and numerous small pencil copies of others, to the Bristol Fine Arts Academy, later the Royal West of England Academy, founded by her, from which they were all placed on continuing loan in the City Art Gallery of Bristol.[3] Among these is Fig. 32, as well as many counterparts of others in this country.

Not long after Sharples' death, the New York *Public Advertiser* repeatedly carried an advertisement which announced that "The Collection of Original Portraits of Distinguished American Characters painted by the late James Sharples, Esqr. are for sale."[4] Felix had evidently set right to work. From New York the young itinerant artist traveled south, painting little portraits by the way and taking his precious collection with him. In the course of his travels and while visiting the Winder family at Yeardley, Northampton County, Virginia, in

---

[3] From John H. Morgan and Mantle Fielding, *The Life Portraits of Washington and Their Replicas,* Phila., 1931, p. 397, it appears that Ellen bequeathed 97 portraits to the Academy, of which 57 were painted by James Sharples.

[4] New York *Public Advertiser,* April–June 1811.

1813, he ran short of the funds required for a hasty journey he was compelled to make. He solved the emergency by borrowing $150 from a generous member of the Winder family, pledging the collection of portraits as security for the loan, to be repaid on his return. But he never returned; one report was that he was drowned fording a nearby river. The loan was never repaid nor the pledge redeemed. The collection remained for years in the possession of the Winders, hanging for a time in Peale's Museum in Philadelphia. Some of the portraits were destroyed by Union troops in 1861 after the Winders had moved to Accomac; perhaps 130 or so survived, their unique value finally recognized. When hidden away for safety, they were taken out of their frames, which in many instances bore the only record of the identity of the sitter. Subsequent identification after the War, and matching of frame to picture, all identical in size, was to say the least difficult and in many instances impossible. In *Lippincott's Magazine* for December 1871 there appeared an account of the then current whereabouts of the collection:

> At present the collection is temporarily in the possession of several gentlemen of Baltimore, who have undertaken to identify those pictures of which the names have been lost by the aid of the original Sharpless catalogue, contemporary likenesses and personal recognition; and especially by those duplicate portraits which Sharpless delivered to the families of his more distinguished sitters.

With the approach of the Centennial of the Declaration of Independence the group was sold at auction, a large number purchased by or for the City of Philadelphia being now on permanent loan to Independence National Historical Park. Others were widely dispersed, but they still come to light from time to time. All have attained a value in the marketplace that is the pride of the owner and the envy and despair of the collector.

Through Ginsburg and Levy, Inc., of New York, Miss Hogg acquired the original of Fig. 31 in 1957, but the seller had not been able to discover anything of its past history.[5] There is no record of its ever having been in the possession of any member of the Adams family, and it is more than likely that it was one of those sold at auction in 1874. It seems logical to presume that Houston's engraving (Fig. 33), made soon after the painting of the original, would have been taken from the original; this supports the conclusion that Miss Hogg's is that one. But an appealing argument can be made that the freshly widowed

[5] Letter to the author from Benjamin Ginsburg, 17 Dec. 1963.

Ellen would surely have taken with her on her sad journey home to England those portraits done by her husband's hand, rather than her own or her children's copies. That the Bristol example is the original finds support from Alfred Bush, who concluded that the Bristol example of Sharples' Jefferson is entitled to priority as an original over the counterpart at Independence Hall.[6]

In attempting to match portrait to frame, the Baltimore group designated as Adams a profile of a young man which was subsequently bought for the City of Philadelphia and even today hangs as a supposed likeness of Adams at Independence Hall (Fig. 34). It cannot, however, be accepted as Adams, although it has often been published as his likeness.[7] Charles Henry Hart questioned it in 1917,[8] and Katharine McCook Knox in 1930.[9] Not only does it not resemble any known likeness of Adams, it represents a man of not more than forty years of age at a time when Adams was over sixty.

Sharples, however, did draw a profile of Adams known from two copies in oil and from a pencil sketch by Ellen. The Adams profile, with a companion piece of Washington, and a pair representing Judge William Cushing and his wife, all by Sharples, hung (according to a note in the *Boston Transcript* of 25 January 1887) in the dining room of the Cushing home in Scituate until Mrs. Cushing's death in 1834. The Washington and Adams then descended to Mrs. Cushing's nephew Henry Bowers and in 1843 were lent by him to John Quincy Adams for copying. On 6 June 1844, Mrs. J. Q. Adams wrote to her son Charles Francis Adams that his father had had three or four portraits of himself taken (referring probably to those then recently done by Marchant, Bingham, and Lambdin) and that he had "given two crayon drawings to Mr. Marchant to be copied," [10] undoubtedly the two he had borrowed from Bowers. From 122 Bleecker Street, New

[6] *Life Portraits of Jefferson*, p. 37–38.

[7] In, for example, Bowen, *Centennial of Washington's Inauguration*, 1892; Dunlap, *Arts of Design*, ed. Bayley and Goodspeed, 1918, vol. 2; *McClure's Magazine*, vol. 17 (1901); Frederic Austin Ogg, *The Pageant of America*, New Haven, 1952, vol. 8; and elsewhere.

[8] C. H. Hart to Wilfred Jordan, Curator of Independence Hall, 14 May 1917: "Sharples was in Philadelphia in 1796 when John Adams was in his 60th year, portly and with very acquiline nose as shown in Stuart's portrait of the previous year when the dome of his head was perfectly bald. A comparison of the Sharples with the Stuart of about the same period will show both are not of the same person" (MS in Independence National Historical Park). Hart is, of course, referring to the Stuart now usually attributed to the year 1798, i.e. Fig. 64. A comparison with the other Sharples Adamses not then available to Hart is even more convincing.

[9] Knox, *The Sharples*, p. 63, 94.

[10] This and the two letters quoted immediately below are in the Adams Papers.

34. UNKNOWN SUBJECT. TEMPERA BY JAMES SHARPLES, CA. 1800

York City, on 18 May 1844, Marchant wrote to J. Q. Adams in Washington:

Your kind favor acquainting me with your reception of my copies of the Portraits of the two Presidents, together with your satisfaction in regard to them, came timely to hand. I might probably have achieved much greater artistical effect particularly in their draperies (of which I fear some may complain) but as I knew the greatest possible fidelity of likeness to the original your object, I thought it safer to make as literal a transcript as was in my power in every respect. . . .

My terms for the copies of which you were pleased to inquire are, one hundred each, which is the price that I have received for portraits of the Bust, for some years.

J. Q. Adams in turn wrote to Bowers on 27 July of that same year:

I send the two pictures which you had the goodness to leave here last September to be delivered to you or your order at my son's office, No. 23 Court Street, Boston, with many thanks for the use of them. I have been so much pleased with them that I have had exact copies of them made in oil by Mr. Marchant, a distinguished portrait painter in N.Y.

Marchant's copy (Fig. 35) of the Adams, together with his copy of Washington, passed from John Quincy Adams to his granddaughter Mary Louisa Adams (Mrs. William Clarkson Johnson), and finally to her granddaughter Mary Louisa Adams Clement, a descendant of John Adams through two of her grandparents and so entitled to a double portion of the Adams birthright. The little copy hung at Edge Hill in Warrenton, Virginia, until 1951, when, with many other Adams portraits, including Stuart's replica of the former President when aged eighty-nine (Fig. 94), it was presented by Miss Clement to the Smithsonian Institution, where it now hangs.

Edward Dalton Marchant was, of course, well known to J. Q. Adams at that time, having, by 1844, painted three portraits of him. Born in Edgartown, Massachusetts, in 1806, he exhibited his works on several occasions at the National Academy, of which he was an associate member, and painted many of the prominent men both of New York and Philadelphia. His copy of Sharples' Adams produces in oil a profile likeness of Adams, but his dark background reflects his own style rather than the soft tone of the typical Sharples. The fine sharp profile and the light powdered hair are a strong reminder of what the original must have been like.

As Katharine McCook Knox said in her remarks at the opening of the Adams-Clement Collection at the Smithsonian Institution in 1951,

35. JOHN ADAMS. OIL BY EDWARD D. MARCHANT, 1843

"fortunately for all of us these same Sharples portraits of George Washington and John Adams, which John Quincy Adams ordered Marchant to copy, were still in the possession of Henry Bowers at late as 1854."[11] On 6 March 1854 Bowers wrote to his cousin Samuel Wetmore:

Allow me to present to you, with my regards, two small pictures, copies in oil of the original likenesses of Washington and Adams taken by Sharpless in 1796. These copies were painted by an esteemed relative of mine, and I trust they will not be the less valued by you on that account. How well he has succeeded, you have just had an opportunity to judge. In a note which came with the pictures my friend writes: "I have tried my best to make my pictures like the originals and have gone over them several times. It is not so easy to copy from a crayon, as to copy from a picture in oil, when painting in oil; but I think they look as much like those of Sharpless as could be reasonably expected."[12]

How these two copies descended from Wetmore is not known, but they were purchased in 1930 by William H. Bliss of New York and given by him to his daughter Mrs. Charles Warren of Washington, D.C., who in 1964 bequeathed them to Mrs. Graham L. Russell of Upper Montclair, New Jersey, that of Adams being reproduced here as Fig. 36. It no doubt follows, as closely as oil can follow tempera, the soft, shaded background and deep blue tones that are such a familiar stamp of Sharples. This second copy of Adams has also been attributed to Marchant, but I have not been able to verify that Marchant was Bowers' "esteemed relative," and the style of the two copies is quite different.

The Bowers original of Adams by Sharples has so far eluded search (unless it is Fig. 39), but John Quincy Adams' favorable judgment of it is evidence that it was highly acceptable to him as a likeness of his father.

Among the many pencil copies of her husband's portraits that Ellen Sharples bequeathed to the Bristol Fine Arts Academy are two of Adams. These sketches are but 3 x 2½ inches in size and yet are remarkable in the manner in which they reproduce in miniscule James' larger tempera portraits. One of them is undoubtedly the "miniature" mentioned by Ellen in her diary in 1804. The three-quarter view of Adams facing left (Fig. 37) is obviously a copy of the Hogg or Bristol tempera (Fig. 31 or Fig. 32). The other (Fig. 38), in profile, could

[11] Typewritten copy of "An Extension of the Remarks made by Katharine Mc-Cook Knox on the occasion of the Opening of The Adams-Clement Collection at the Smithsonian Institution on April 18, 1951" (Adams Papers Editorial Files).
[12] Same.

36. JOHN ADAMS. OIL BY AN UNKNOWN ARTIST, 1854

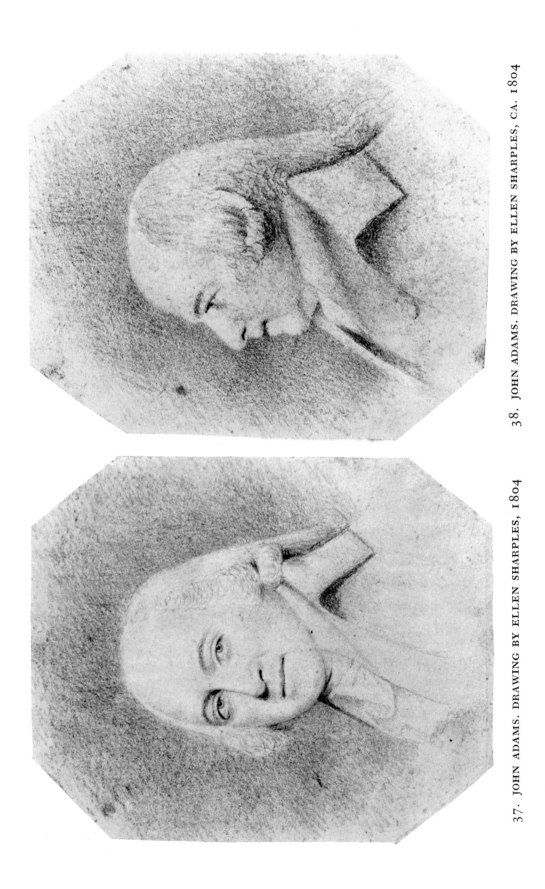

37. JOHN ADAMS. DRAWING BY ELLEN SHARPLES, 1804

38. JOHN ADAMS. DRAWING BY ELLEN SHARPLES, CA. 1804

39. JOHN ADAMS. TEMPERA PROBABLY BY JAMES SHARPLES, CA. 1797

well be a copy of the original owned years later by Bowers and followed by Marchant.

The last of this group to be considered is a faded and time-worn pastel or tempera of Adams (Fig. 39), now hanging in the John Quincy Adams Birthplace in Quincy, and belonging to the City of Quincy. This portrait, only 7 x 5½ inches (perhaps cut down from 9 x 7 inches—Sharples' usual size), has a tag attached to it evidencing its former ownership by Elizabeth Coombs Adams, John Quincy Adams' niece, who died in 1903 in her ninety-sixth year. A note on the back of the frame, written in her aged hand, reads: "Now October 1895—one hundred years ago 1795. Colored Pastel taken of John Adams at The Hague, Holland when he was Minister there by the same artist who painted the pastel of John Quincy Adams at 16." The pastel of John Quincy Adams referred to was by the Dutch artist Isaak Schmidt. It is now regrettably unlocated, but, fortunately, had at one time been not only copied but engraved and photographed, and the several reproductions are a delightful representation of the lad as he appeared at age sixteen, in his best blue coat and powdered hair. Miss Adams' note, however, is clearly in error. Adams was at The Hague in 1783 when John Quincy Adams was sixteen, not in 1795, and in 1783 Adams wore a heavy wig and was considerably younger looking than this profile. Copley's portrait of Adams (Fig. 9) and West's (Fig. 18), both painted in 1783, resemble neither in hair style nor in costume the pastel which, if by Schmidt, must also have been done in 1783. Tradition, though often unreliable, is dangerous to meddle with, but I incline to the view that this faded pastel profile is by Sharples, not Schmidt, and that it was painted not in 1783 but in 1796. It may be the original from which Ellen Sharples made one of the pencil miniatures (Fig. 38), perhaps even that from which Marchant and Bowers' esteemed relative made their copies, reversing the image for variety.[13] There is a strong resemblance, both in the profile and in the shape of the collar, between the Birthplace pastel, the two oil copies of the lost Sharples, and Ellen's pencil sketch, but the deteriorated condition of the surface of the pastel makes it difficult to compare the features closely. Something might be learned if the back of the little painting could be examined. What is left of the surface coloring, the soft gray and faded blue tones, is consistent with its having been painted by Sharples. Let the curious but compare closely, or

[13] Sharples profiles facing to the right are quite rare. Of the 32 profiles of Washington reproduced in Knox's *The Sharples,* only one faces right, and not even one of the 60 little pencil copies done by Ellen. From this it can fairly be conjectured that the Bowers original copied by Marchant faced to the left.

superimpose, one on the other, the three profiles: Marchant's copy of the Bowers original (Fig. 35), Ellen's sketch of the original profile (Fig. 38), and the Birthplace profile (Fig. 39).

Though there is no positive external evidence that any one of these Sharples examples is a life portrait, yet the profiles are certainly typical of Sharples' profiles and hence presumably produced by means of the pantograph or physiognotrace which presupposes an actual sitting by the subject. There is, moreover, a happy consistency in all of them that adds a measure of assurance to our acceptance of them, with John Quincy Adams' judgment, as, in the composite, a likeness of Adams at the time he became President. It is a strange quirk of fortune that, with the exception of the brief appearance of Houston's engraving (Fig. 33), the only one of the group that has been brought before the public and which has thereby had any effect in shaping the public image of Adams is Fig. 34, which is not a likeness of Adams after all!

XI

William Joseph Williams

The Presidential election of 1796 set off a rush to supply portraits and engravings of the second President, to satisfy the ever-increasing public curiosity and desire not only to be familiar with, but even to possess a copy of, the likeness of the new President.

It was at about this time that Adams' portrait was taken by the younger William Williams (later William Joseph Williams). As in the case of the early Sharples portraits, two likenesses of this date by Williams are extant. One (Fig. 40) is owned by The Pennsylvania Academy of the Fine Arts. The other (Fig. 41) belongs to the Adams National Historic Site in Quincy and hangs in the Old House dining room. Adams himself makes no direct mention of either of these portraits, but a letter to him from the artist throws some light on their origin. Williams wrote mentioning Adams' "obliging condescensions" to him when "I had the honor to draw your Picture, about three years ago" and applying for the post of professor of "Drawing and Designing" in one of the military schools recommended by Adams to Congress. "Since I had the honor of seeing your Excellency," he added, "I have been occupied in the College of George Town as Professor of Painting and Drawing." [1] The late Henry Adams (HA2) assigned this letter to August 1798, based in part on John Adams' interest at the time in the establishment of military schools. Georgetown University has found no records indicating Williams' connection with the College in the 1790's, and suggests that he may not have had the position of Professor but merely had been available to give private lessons to interested students.[2] Williams was born in New York in 1759, the son of the better-known William Williams who was the early instructor in painting of Benjamin West and who died in an almshouse in Bristol, England, about 1798. The elder Williams painted many well-known paintings, examples of which hang today in the Brooklyn Museum, Winterthur, and elsewhere. The younger Williams was introduced by Ferdinando Fairfax to General Otho H. Williams in 1793, as a deserving artist who had "received a good education, studied Divinity,

[1] Undated letter [Aug. 1798?] (Adams Papers).
[2] Letter to the author from the Librarian of Georgetown University, 21 Jan. 1964.

92

40. JOHN ADAMS. OIL ON WOOD PANEL
BY WILLIAM JOSEPH WILLIAMS, CA. 1795

93

41. JOHN ADAMS. OIL ON WOOD PANEL
BY WILLIAM JOSEPH WILLIAMS, CA. 1795

and actually officiated in one of the lower Parishes of this State; but not receiving a sufficient support (as is too commonly the case in Virginia) has determined to pursue the Bent of Genius, and to resume again the Pencil, from the exercise of which he had in early youth received some remarkable and very encouraging testimonies of approbation." [3] He was converted to Roman Catholicism in 1820, and then added a middle name, Joseph. Active in Philadelphia from 1793 to 1797, he painted a portrait of Washington in his Masonic regalia, and it was undoubtedly during this period that he took Adams. For a few weeks late in 1793 he advertised his services as portrait painter in Baltimore, "should any ladies or gentlemen be desirous of having their likenesses taken," the price to be "according to the style and manner of painting." [4] In 1798 he married the second of three wives and was at the time living near Washington.

The portrait hanging in the Old House (Fig. 41) is painted on a wood panel and measures 17 x 14 inches. It was given to the Old House by Henry Adams, whose acquisition of the picture is described in a letter written from Washington to his brother Brooks, 26 March 1909:

The portrait goes to you at once. I suppose Charles Henry Harte will tell you more about it. When he last wrote he was going to be appendicited, and I've not heard whether he came through. He said the portrait was by William Williams. I paid him $250 for it. As I start for Paris at once, by the Adriatic on Wednesday, I have to clear out all the goods now. [5]

The likeness belonging to the Pennsylvania Academy (Fig. 40) was a part of the John Frederick Lewis Memorial Collection acquired by the Academy in 1933 shortly after Mr. Lewis' death. He had apparently bought it at auction because with it came a page torn from an unidentified auction catalogue showing a reproduction of the painting and the legend "John Adams, attributed to James Sharples, Lot No. 11." It, too, is painted on a wood panel. Despite the suggested attribution to Sharples, the late William Sawitzky considered this attribution as without foundation. Not only are these two paintings too closely alike to be each an original, it would also have been difficult to recognize the sitter in either as Adams, were it not for the appearance in

[3] John F. Williams Jr., "William J. Williams, Portrait Painter, and His Descendants" (typescript, NHi), Supplement, 1948, p. 4.
[4] *Baltimore Daily Repository*, 14 Nov. 1793, quoted in Williams, "Williams," p. 3.
[5] MH:HA–BA Corr. (typescripts in Adams Papers, Fourth Generation).

His Excellency JOHN ADAMS President of the United States of America.

Respectfully Dedicated to the Lovers of their Country and Firm Supporters of its Constitution

Drawn & Engraved by H. Houston.

Published by D. Kennedy 22 S. Market St. Philad.ª

42. JOHN ADAMS. ENGRAVING BY H. HOUSTON, CA. 1797

His Excellency

JOHN ADAMS, Esqᴿ.

President of the United States of America

Published, September 1ˢᵗ ....

43. JOHN ADAMS. ENGRAVING BY H. HOUSTON, 1797

97

1797 of an engraving by Houston (Fig. 42) inscribed "Drawn and Engrav'd by H. Houston / His Excellency John Adams President / of the United States of America / Respectfully Dedicated to the Lovers of their Country / and Firm Supporters of its Constitution." This engraving shows which of the two Williams versions was followed by Houston. The clue is in the position of the index and middle fingers of Adams' right hand; in the Old House example they are close together—touching—whereas in the Academy version they are held apart exactly as in Houston's engraving. This suggests that the Academy's picture is the original by Williams, and the other a replica or a copy.

The identity of the artist is established by another engraving by Houston (Fig. 43), dated 1 September 1797 (though appearing in other states, undated), inscribed in part "W. Williams pinxt—R. B. Freeman Excudit—H. H. Houston Sculpt." The likeness is comparable, though Adams faces to the right, and the ruffles of his shirt now form a sort of rosette. Still a third engraving (Cat. No. 76) was made by Houston and appeared in the *Philadelphia Monthly Magazine* of July 1798, described as "a good likeness, engraved from an original painting, and finished in a superior manner." It was a frontispiece to a brief memoir of Adams which includes a characteristic and valuable anecdote of Adams taken from *A Tour in Holland* by "an American," namely Elkanah Watson, who had visited the American Minister at The Hague in 1784:

> I must not omit to tell you that if I had not exerted myself, I should probably have witnessed the unpleasant scene of one of the most brilliant characters of this age (Mr. A——), scrambling in a muddy canal, his wig afloat upon the surface, and all from a laudable zeal to save a child then drowning; the moment he saw the struggling infant bobbing on the top, I thought he would have darted headforemost into the canal, regardless of his personal safety: But I restrained his impetuosity for a moment, as a lusty fellow had that instant soused himself in.[6]

These several engravings by Houston, good representations of the original, were followed more or less closely by Cornelius Tiebout in 1800 (Cat. No. 79); by John Scoles, whose tiny engraving (Fig. 44) appeared in *The New Universal Biographical Dictionary* in 1805; and in a somewhat younger appearing likeness (Fig. 45) engraved by Benjamin Tanner for the *Literary Magazine and American Register* in

[6] *A Tour in Holland, in MDCCLXXXIV*, Worcester, Mass., 1790, p. 83–84. Watson continued: "In popularity and influence at this court, Mr. A—— undoubtedly bears the palm in the diplomatick body. He is universally esteemed, for his profound penetration and extensive political knowledge, the first character our western world has yet produced" (p. 84).

45. JOHN ADAMS. ENGRAVING BY BENJAMIN TANNER, 1804

44. JOHN ADAMS. ENGRAVING BY JOHN SCOLES, CA. 1800

46. JOHN ADAMS. DRAWING BY AN UNKNOWN ARTIST

1804.[7] I have in my possession a sanguine drawing of Adams (Fig. 46) on old worn paper, glued to a panel, in an 18th-century black pine frame. This drawing closely resembles Houston's engraving of 1 September 1797, even to the rosette of the shirt ruffle, and may well be contemporary with that engraving; it may even be the sketch from which the engraving was executed.

The Williams representation of Adams was a popular one and appeared in many versions over the first quarter of the 19th century. It compares favorably with the Sharples portraits, the principal and most noticeable difference being in Adams' nose, which in Williams' likeness is characteristically Roman, whereas in Sharples' it is less familiarly aquiline.

[7] James Hardie, *The New Universal Biographical Dictionary and American Remembrancer of Departed Merit,* N.Y., 1805, 1:68; *Literary Magazine and American Register,* Aug. 1804, frontispiece.

XII

William Winstanley

Our late-18th-century forefathers, searching the newspapers for sources of entertainment or enlightenment, were no doubt attracted by the notice that appeared in the New York *Daily Advertiser* of 21 August 1798:

John Adams Esq. President of the United States, to be seen at the Museum for one week only an original full length portrait painting, of an excellent likeness, of his Excellency John Adams, Esq. President of the U.S. This beautiful painting was lately taken from life by Mr. Wm. Winstanley, now of this city. This, with many late additions to the museum, renders it much more pleasing and respectable. Also two very vigorous and beautiful variegated living Rattle Snakes, will be seen at the Museum for one week only. N.B. The Museum has been much approved within the last six months.[1]

It is hard to say from this distance whether it was the Winstanley painting or the variegated reptiles that added to the respectability of the Museum. No doubt the "living Rattle Snakes" have long since returned to dust; the "beautiful painting" (Fig. 47), preserved in fine condition, now belongs to the Adams National Historic Site at Quincy and hangs in the Stone Library there.

William Winstanley came to America from England as a young man some time prior to April 1793; from 1795 to 1799 he practiced his art in New York City, returning to England not long after 1801. He is better known for his landscapes than for his portraits. A pair of his paintings of the Hudson River, now hanging at Mount Vernon, were sold by him to Washington in April 1793 for 93 guineas apiece. A year later, Washington bought two of his views of the Potomac for $93.33; they are now part of the Lewis-Custis Collection at the Smithsonian Institution. In 1801 there appeared in a Boston newspaper a prospectus for a series of eight American views to be engraved by Winstanley in aquatint.[2] Dunlap's account of Winstanley's copying Stuart's

---

[1] Quoted in Rita Susswein Gottesman, *The Arts and Crafts in New York, 1777–1799*, NYHS, *Colls., Pubn. Fund Ser.*, vol. 81, N.Y., 1954, p. 24.

[2] Boston *Mercury and New England Palladium*, 24 Nov. 1801 (quoted in J. Hall Pleasants, "Four Late Eighteenth Century Anglo-American Landscape Painters," *Amer. Antiq. Soc., Procs.*, 52 (1942):301–324, esp. p. 316).

47. JOHN ADAMS. OIL BY WILLIAM WINSTANLEY, CA. 1798

portrait of Washington, and attempting to palm off the copy as an original Stuart, is familiar even if not authenticated.[3] Only three original portraits by Winstanley are recorded, the two of Adams illustrated here (Figs. 47, 48) and one of Abraham Mortimer Walton owned by The New-York Historical Society. J. Hall Pleasants considered Winstanley's copies of Stuart's Washington better than any of his own original portraits, those of Adams and Walton being "but indifferent —perhaps third, rather than second, class work."[4]

Where the full-length portrait of Adams hung after parting company with the snakes is not known. It was first brought to the family attention by Clarence W. Bowen in 1891. At the same time Charles Francis Adams 2d, writing to Theodore F. Dwight, said he had never heard of it before and wondered if Dwight knew of it.[5] Bowen told Dwight that the portrait was at the Boston Museum.[6] It was illustrated in Bowen's *Centennial* and described as a likeness of Adams when minister at The Hague, the information purporting to be taken from an inscription on the back of the painting.[7]

Only two years later Charles Henry Hart offered the painting for sale to Henry Adams, on 28 March 1893, and on 18 April of the same year sent it on approval, restating the price as $1,000. Henry Adams wrote immediately from Washington to his brother Charles, giving an amusing description of the painting:

How are you off for great-grandfathers? . . . Now I receive from Philadelphia a full length portrait of John Adams painted during the Presidency by an Englishman named Winstanley, and I want to know what to do with it. Frame and all, it measures 52 x 44 inches. The figure stands 33 inches high, and the body is almost a third larger than it should be, compared with the legs. It is very well painted though ill drawn, and is in some respects a really fine portrait. . . . The fact is, I don't want it, and have no money. Do you care to take it? Nothing but weariness of accumulation, and poverty of bank-account checks my buying it now.[8]

Charles wrote promptly to his brother John that, if Henry thought the picture good, he, Charles, would put up the money to buy it, not

[3] Dunlap, *Arts of Design,* ed. Bayley and Goodspeed, 1:234–235.

[4] Pleasants, "Four Landscape Painters," p. 319.

[5] CFA2 to Theodore F. Dwight, 31 Aug. 1891 (Adams Papers, Fourth Generation).

[6] Clarence W. Bowen to Theodore F. Dwight, 17 Sept. 1891 (same).

[7] The inscription was said to read: "John Adams, when minister for the United States to Holland at the court of the Hague from 1782 to 1785, where this picture was painted by Winstanley" (Bowen, *Centennial of Washington's Inauguration,* 2:425–426; see also William Dunlap, *History of the Rise and Progress of the Arts of Design in the United States,* N.Y., 1834, 1:394–395).

[8] 22 April 1893 (Adams Papers, Fourth Generation).

48. JOHN ADAMS. OIL BY WILLIAM WINSTANLEY, CA. 1798

49. JOHN ADAMS. WOODCUT BY AN UNKNOWN ARTIST, 1845

knowing where to hang it but suggesting the "Art Museum." [9] In the end it was bought by Henry and added to the collection at the Old House.

Winstanley's second portrait of Adams is the half-length (Fig. 48), 26½ x 21½ inches in size, now belonging to the American Scenic and Historic Preservation Society and hanging in Philipse Manor Hall in Yonkers, New York. It was part of the collection left to that Society by Alexander Smith Cochrane at his death in 1929. In 1917 it had been exhibited in the Museum of the Brooklyn Institute of Arts and Sciences.[10] Its origin and former ownership are obscure. That it is an independent work is unlikely; in all probability it is but a modified replica of the full length. Whatever may be said of either from an artistic point of view—and it can't be very favorable—our interest in the two paintings is the marked similarity in the appearance of Adams, compared with the likeness by Williams (Fig. 40 or Fig. 41). We can be assured this is the same sitter and that somewhere between these pairs of portraits rests the then true likeness of the second President. Here we see the second President, threescore years of age, firm of face, vigorous and determined, bald-domed, but with his own hair, or possibly a wig, fluffed over his ears, and evidence of a pigtail and bow behind. In age he compares suitably with what is believed to be Stuart's first like-

[9] To JQA2, 24 April 1893 (same).
[10] Catalogue of an Exhibition Held in the Museum of the Brooklyn Institute of Arts and Sciences, Brooklyn, 1917, p. 127; illustrated at p. 134.

50. JOHN ADAMS. MEZZOTINT BY GEORGE GRAHAM, 1798

ness (Fig. 67), taken in 1798, though younger looking than in Stuart's later version (Fig. 64).

No engraving claiming on its face to be taken of either of these two portraits has been found. Two are known, however, that perhaps can be said to be taken from Winstanley's full-length. One is the 2½-inch woodcut caricature (Fig. 49) which appeared in 1847 and was described as "From an Anonymous American Portrait." [11] The other is the better-known, though scarce, engraving by George Graham (Fig. 50). Graham worked in stipple and mezzotint about 1800 and produced several other folio engravings, including portraits of Samuel Adams, Hamilton, and Commodore Hull, all of which are now scarce and have long been coveted by collectors.[12] Examples of Graham's engravings of John Adams are owned by the Metropolitan Museum of Art, the Adams National Historic Site, and one in color by the New England Historic Genealogical Society. At the Barrett sale at the Anderson Gallery, 3 January 1927, a copy sold for $300, the catalogue stating that there were then only three known impressions. It is not unlikely that Graham had seen Winstanley's full-length portrait of Adams—perhaps even with the "Rattle Snakes"! Adams' pose, hand outstretched holding the Constitution, became a popular one and was evidently followed in the 1865 lithograph of Washington and Lincoln by Charles Shober, which shows Washington in a stance like Adams', holding in one hand the Constitution, as did Graham's Adams, and with an inscription, reminiscent of Graham, "Behold Oh America, Your Sons. The Greatest Among Men."

[11] Robert Sears, *The Pictorial History of the American Revolution*, N.Y., 1847, p. 188.
[12] Dunlap, *Arts of Design*, ed. Bayley and Goodspeed, 3:304.

XIII

Edward Savage

Trumbull's *Declaration* must be compared with Edward Savage's *The Congress Voting Independence* to appreciate fully the two artists' different methods of composition and painting. Savage's picture (Fig. 51) was begun in Philadelphia about 1796, worked on for years, and added to until the artist's death in 1817. The figures are taken from various sources; some perhaps from life, others, such as Franklin, from likenesses by other artists. Adams might have been painted from life, although no mention of the subject has yet been found among his diaries or correspondence. If his is a life portrait, it must have been added to the painting some time before March 1801 when Adams returned to Quincy, leaving Washington the morning of Jefferson's inauguration. From internal evidence alone the likeness poses a question. It bears no more than a superficial resemblance to other contemporary likenesses (such as Fig. 31 or Fig. 40), yet it is closely like Savage's other portrait of Adams (Fig. 53), done at about the same time. One could well be taken from the other, and each could be drawn from memory or be a free rendering of some other artist's work.

Mention of Savage's group painting appears in the 1847 catalogue of the old Boston Museum on Tremont Street, where it is described as "Signers of the Declaration of Independence and view of the Hall where it was adopted. An original picture by E. Savage." [1] In 1892, Charles Henry Hart acquired the painting from Moses Kimball, the proprietor of the Boston Museum, and it was purchased from him in 1904 by the Historical Society of Pennsylvania. For many years it was thought to have been an unfinished work by Robert Edge Pine, completed by Savage. Hart was of this opinion, but in 1956 James M. Mulcahy concluded that the work was wholly that of Savage. [2] The interior

---

[1] No. 127 in *Catalogue of the Paintings, Portraits, Marble and Plaster Statuary . . . in the Collection of the Boston Museum*, Boston, 1847, p. 11.

[2] James M. Mulcahy, "Congress Voting Independence: The Trumbull and Pine-Savage Paintings," *PMHB*, 80:74–91 (Jan. 1956). Hart's thesis presupposed that the painting had survived the burning of the Columbian Museum in 1803. Mulcahy produces evidence not only that the entire contents of the Museum were destroyed but that all records indicate that Pine's paintings were life-sized rather than small (29⅞″ x 19½″) like this painting and would have been exceedingly difficult to rescue from a fire. In favor of Savage's authorship Mulcahy cites Savage's note to Jefferson in 1803 about "one of my Proposals for Publishing the Print of the Decla-

51. THE CONGRESS VOTING INDEPENDENCE. OIL BY EDWARD SAVAGE, CA. 1796–1801

52. THE CONGRESS VOTING INDEPENDENCE. ENGRAVING OF FIGURE 51
BY EDWARD SAVAGE

of the Hall appears quite different from its representation in any of Trumbull's three versions, and it is now generally agreed that Savage's rendering presents "as true a picture of the Assembly Room of Independence Hall as we are ever likely to find." [3]

The picture has been but once engraved (Fig. 52), at some time between 1801 and 1817, although the engraving was never completed. Less than a year after Savage's death, his son wrote Trumbull:

> Boston, April 11th, 1818
> Sir,—I take the liberty to write to you concerning the print of Congress '76 wich my Farther (late Edward Savag) had nerely conpleated. the same subject I understand you are about Publishing. as the one will hurt the other I do propose seling the Plate and Paper to you on liberal conditions, which I wish you to name in your letter if you see fit to write on the subgect. the Plate is now in a situation that it may be Finis'd in a few weeks. Yours &c &c   Edw Savage

Col. Trunbull
P.S. Direct yours E. S. Boston [4]

Trumbull apparently misunderstood the offer and, believing that it included the original painting, replied stiffly:

> Mr Ed Savage   New York 30th April 1818
> Sir,—Your fav, of the 11th offering to sell me the plate & painting prepared by your Father of the Congress of 1776, came duly to hand. My Painting of the subject was begun more than 30 years ago and all the heads were soon after secured. My composition is also nearly completed; so that the works of Mr. Savage cannot be of any possible use to me. My copper-plate cannot be finished in less than 2 or 3 years, so that, as yours is nearly ready I shall not interfere with your publication.
> I am your obt servt   JT

Trumbull quite evidently was not impressed with Savage's reputation as an engraver and was not the least concerned with the possibility of competition; at least he was not going to buy out his competitor. His letter, however, sheds some light on the date of the completion of his own painting of the Declaration.

---

ration of Independence which I intend to finish as Soone as Possible," as well as the exchange of letters between Savage's son and Trumbull in 1818 about the painting and its engraving. Mulcahy's argument is logical and persuasive.

[3] Same, p. 91.

[4] This letter and Trumbull's reply were bought by Charles Henry Hart at the sale of Trumbull's MSS and correspondence in Philadelphia and presented by Hart to the Massachusetts Historical Society. They are quoted in his paper, "Edward Savage, Painter and Engraver, and his Unfinished Copperplate of 'The Congress Voting Independence,' " MHS, *Procs.*, 2d ser., 19 (1905):1–19, see esp. p. 2–3.

The Savage plate next appears when presented to the Massachusetts Historical Society in 1859 by Samuel T. Snow of Boston. The gift was announced to the Society on 10 November 1859 by Leverett Saltonstall in the absence of Snow. He explained that many years before a party of play actors had left the plate with an innkeeper in payment of their board, and he, after keeping it for twenty years, brought it to Boston.[5] How it passed from Savage's son to the actors was not told.

Many engravings produced by Savage in the 18th century are now believed largely the work of his able and later famous apprentices, David Edwin and John Wesley Jarvis, both of whom left him in 1801. However, Savage's painting of the *Congress* was in no sense completed by 1801, so it is more than likely that the engraving is mostly if not entirely the work of Savage himself. Harold E. Dickson attributed it to him principally on the basis of its inexpert character.[6]

That Savage painted a portrait of Adams, other than the small one in his *Congress,* we know from an engraving that appeared at the end of the year 1800 or early in the following year. This engraving (Fig. 53) appeared in its first state inscribed "Published by E. Savage Oc. [or Dc.] 10, 1800." In a second version the plate was retouched and the inscription changed to "Painted by E. Savage in 1800." The painting from which the engraving was taken is unlocated. In 1801 Savage moved from Philadelphia to New York and there opened his Columbian Gallery with "original American Historical Paintings taken from the most interesting subjects." The collection probably included not only his own portraits of Adams but also Trumbull's full-length portrait of Adams (Cat. No. 49) as well as Savage's likeness of Jefferson. Some years later the collection was reassembled as the Columbian Museum in Boston and a large part of it destroyed by fire on 15 January 1803. Both Trumbull's and Savage's portraits of Adams, as well as Savage's Jefferson, have never since been seen and were presumably burned. Judging Savage's portrait of Adams only from the engraving, little can be said in its favor except that it is not inconsistent with the small likeness of Adams in Savage's *Congress.* Though it shows a man years older than the Williams or Sharples series, it bears more than a passing likeness to Winstanley's ungainly full-length (Fig. 47).

Whether this engraving is actually the work of Savage has been seriously questioned. It is inscribed only as being published by him. The fact that Savage ceased the publishing of engravings after Edwin and

---

[5] Same, p. 1–2.

[6] Harold E. Dickson, *John Wesley Jarvis, American Painter, 1780–1840, with a Checklist of His Works,* N.Y., 1949, p. 46–47.

53. JOHN ADAMS. ENGRAVING BY EDWARD SAVAGE, 1800

54. JOHN ADAMS. OIL BY WILLIAM M. S. DOYLE, CA. 1800

Jarvis left him suggests that they had taken more than a trifling part in his earlier work, and each of them is known to have been proficient in his own right. What we do know of Savage's own work is the unfinished engraving of the *Congress*. It is probable that the engraving of Adams (Fig. 53) is the work of David Edwin. Alfred L. Bush reached a like conclusion with respect to the so-called Savage engraving of Jefferson.[7]

One of the proprietors of the Columbian Museum was William M. S. Doyle (1769–1828), a portrait and miniature painter and sil-

[7] Bush, *Life Portraits of Jefferson*, p. 56–58.

55. JOHN ADAMS. ENGRAVING BY NATHANIEL DEARBORN

houettist.[8] Dunlap lists as among his works his portraits of Governor Caleb Strong, Isaiah Thomas, and John Adams. That of Adams (Fig. 54) is now unlocated and its reproduction here is taken from Bowen's *Centennial,* where it is described as being owned by the old Boston Museum.[9] Despite the poor quality of the reproduction, it is clear that Doyle's painting and Savage's engraving stemmed from the same

[8] "Correct Profiles. DOYLE—MINIATURE PAINTER, *Columbian Museum, bottom of Milk-street,* INFORMS his Friends and the Public, that he paints Miniatures, Profiles and Portraits, in a neat and correct stile, at various prices. His Physiognotrace is correct and expeditious, completing Profiles from 25 cents to 2 dollars.
"Profiles traced free of expence to the visitors of the Museum." (*Boston Gazette,* 2 Jan. 1804.)
[9] Bowen, *Centennial of Washington's Inauguration,* 1:18.

56. JOHN ADAMS AND GEORGE WASHINGTON. ENGRAVING
BY JOHN BOWER

source. A thought that readily occurs is that Doyle had seen Savage's painting before the fire of 1803 and had later simply copied it, by memory, aided by the 1800 engraving.

Another member of this group is the engraving of Adams by Nathaniel Dearborn (Fig. 55). Born in Massachusetts in 1786, Dearborn took up wood engraving and copperplate printing in Boston about 1811, and became one of the city's leading engravers. He would have had ready access to the Columbian Museum and to the old Boston Museum and would hence have been familiar with both Savage's 1800 engraving and Doyle's painting. His own engraving is a rather inept reproduction of one or the other, though it most resembles Savage's.

Last to be considered is the small vignette engraving by John Bower (Fig. 56). Though a poor work, it obviously is taken from the Savage or Doyle painting or from one of the engravings. It appears with a companion vignette of Washington which was engraved after the "execrable thing" by Savage that was seen by Dunlap in the possession of

117

Harvard College in 1797.[10] No other reproductions of Savage's Adams have come to light, which suggests that it was not a likeness that was warmly received.

Perhaps the most provocative and perplexing aspect of this Savage series is its relation to the problem of dating the Stuart likeness of 1798–1815 (Fig. 64). The series most resembles Winstanley's portrait (Fig. 47), but there is a sufficient correspondence to Morse's "unpleasing likeness" (Fig. 68) to cause us to wonder if Adams' general appearance changed much between 1800 and 1815, from age sixty-five to eighty.

[10] Entry of 12 Dec. 1797, *Diary of William Dunlap* (1766–1839), NYHS, *Colls., Pubn. Fund Ser.,* vols. 62–64, N.Y., 1929–1930, 1:188. Adams, not sharing Dunlap's opinion, bought from Savage a copy of the "execrable" portrait of Washington, paying "forty six and two thirds dollars" for it on 17 April 1790 (Louisa Dresser, "Edward Savage," *Art in America,* 40:195 [Autumn 1952]). The portrait of Washington now hangs in the dining room of the Adams National Historic Site in Quincy.

XIV

Charles Balthazar Julien Fevret
de Saint-Mémin

*"Those Ladies and Gentlemen who please to favour him
with their employ, may depend on having good likenesses."*
Advertisement, 1787.

Through the medium of Charles Balthazar Julien Fevret de Saint-
Mémin's physiognotrace portrait of Adams we are privileged to look on
Adams in profile, mechanically reproduced, as he must in fact have appeared at the opening of the 19th century. Two examples of Saint-
Mémin's Adams are preserved, one (Fig. 57) owned by the Metropolitan Museum of Art, and the other (Fig. 58) by George Gray Zabriskie
of New York City and the Museum of Fine Arts in Boston.

Saint-Mémin, born in Dijon, France, in 1770, emigrated to America
and settled in Philadelphia in 1797, where he remained for several
years. He took profiles apace and scarcely an American of any note escaped sitting to his mechanical contrivance. The newspapers of the day
carried advertisements headed "Physiognotrace Likenesses Engraved,"
providing the information that:

The subscriber begs leave to inform the public that he takes and en-
graves portraits on an improved plan of the celebrated *physiognotrace* of
Paris, and in a style never introduced before in this country. A great number of portraits of distinguished persons who honored the artist with their
patronage at New York may be seen at S. Chandron's, No. 12 south Third
street or at the subscribers, No. 32 South Third street. He delivers with
the original portrait, the plate engraved and twelve copies of the same.

St. Mémin [1]

The process, graphically described and illustrated with Edme Quene-
dey's sketch of the physiognotrace in Howard C. Rice Jr.'s "Saint-
Mémin's Portrait of Jefferson," [2] was painless and quick, the results accurate, intimate, and pleasing. We are brought much closer to our
subject, he appears more lifelike, more so perhaps than in a photograph. The portrait was finished, life-sized, in black crayon on pink-

---

[1] Quoted in *Catalogue of Engraved Portraits by Fevret de Saint-Mémin, 1770–
1852,* Washington, n.d., p. 6.
[2] *Princeton Univ. Libr. Chronicle,* 20:182–192 (Summer 1959).

tinted paper. The process was invented by Gilles-Louis Chrétien in 1786 and immediately achieved popularity abroad, Saint-Mémin being the first to introduce it in America.

Although the exact date of the taking of Adams' profile is not known, there was ample opportunity during most of his administration for Adams to have sat to the physiognotrace machine; or, if not while living in Philadelphia, he could have found time to stop in Saint-Mémin's studio on his way north to Quincy at the close of his administration. Adams' diary and correspondence are silent on the subject. Although it is entirely possible that Adams' profile was engraved in small size, like Jefferson's and so many others, no trace of any engraving has been found.

Saint-Mémin remained in the United States, moving from city to city, setting up his shop, and taking profiles until his return to France in 1814. During this time he produced many hundreds of separate portraits, most of which were reduced to small engravings. Collections of his prints, numbering over eight hundred in one case, can now be found in the Princeton Library, the Pierpont Morgan Library, and The Corcoran Gallery of Art,[3] but none of these includes a likeness of Adams. The two illustrated here are all that are known to survive. Upon Saint-Mémin's return to France, Louis XVIII appointed him curator of the Museum of Dijon, a post which he filled until 1852, when he died "in the bosom of the Catholic Church, in the faith of which he had lived faithful, in the midst of the infidelity of the end of the eighteenth century and during a long sojourn upon a Protestant soil."[4]

The source of these two drawings is similar. Framed with the Zabriskie example is a fragment of old paper inscribed, "John Adams—Original Crayon Portrait physiom-traced by St. Manmin of Paris. Presented by Wm. H. Huntington to Hon. John Bigelow." It was in Paris in 1861 that Bigelow, the journalist and diplomat, first met Huntington, who for almost a generation was Paris correspondent for the *New York Tribune*. The gift must have been some years after that, perhaps at the time Bigelow became Minister to France, a post once filled by Adams himself—a coincidence providing an occasion for the gift. Bigelow in time gave the drawing to his friend John A. C. Gray, the great-grandfather of its present owner.

[3] Fillmore Norfleet, *Saint-Mémin in Virginia: Portraits and Biographies*, Richmond, 1942, p. 23, 27.
[4] Elias Dexter, *The St.-Mémin Collection of Portraits; Consisting of Seven Hundred and Sixty Medallion Portraits, Principally of Distinguished Americans*, N.Y., 1862, p. 8.

57. JOHN ADAMS. PHYSIOGNOTRACE
BY C. B. J. FEVRET DE SAINT-MÉMIN, CA. 1800

121

On the back of the Metropolitan's drawing is inscribed in an old hand, "John Adams—Président des Etats Unis d'après nature au physiognotrace 1800 à 1801"; and in a later hand, "St. Mémin." It was received by the Metropolitan Museum also as a gift from Mr. Huntington in 1883, and is said to have been purchased that year by Huntington from a print dealer in Paris named Roblin, 23 Quai Voltaire, who claimed to have purchased this and other Saint-Mémin drawings from a member of the Saint-Mémin family named Baronne de Juigne.

When these two profiles are superimposed on one another, the outline is so closely identical as to lead us to conclude, as in the case of so many duplicate likenesses of Adams, that they cannot have been taken separately; one must be a copy or tracing of the other. One or two peculiarities suggest that the Metropolitan profile (Fig. 57) is the original and the other (Fig. 58) the copy. The Metropolitan example discloses a facial profile in a perfect unbroken line, in no way "touched up." This might be expected of a drawing made directly by the pantograph. The Zabriskie example, on the other hand, has a double line under the lower lip, chin, and double chin—the chin has in fact been redrawn, as if the artist in copying or making a tracing from the model made the chin too full and was obliged to reduce it. It is noticeable that the Metropolitan's example is more sketchily drawn, the hair and the shading of the collar and sleeve are roughed in, and the pupil of Adams' eye is not apparent. A fair conclusion from this might be that the second effort, the Zabriskie example (if it were the copy) would benefit from the artist's experience with the first and would show any improvement that he might have been able to make, even to modifying the fullness of the double chin. By the same token he might have been expected to sell or otherwise dispose of the better one and keep the first sketch himself. This would account for the Metropolitan's drawing having remained in the hands of Saint-Mémin's family until its acquisition by the dealer from whom Huntington bought it.

Although possibly lacking the quality of the traditional oil portrait, these striking sketches should not be scorned as being purely mechanical. Their origin, their exactness, and the vigor of the drawing, all guarantee a speaking likeness; they should be looked on as types or norms against which the other painted portraits of the day may fairly be judged.

58. JOHN ADAMS. PHYSIOGNOTRACE
BY C. B. J. FEVRET DE SAINT-MÉMIN, CA. 1800

123

XV

Primitives

Hanging in the John Adams Birthplace in Quincy are a pair of small likenesses of John and Abigail Adams (Figs. 59, 60) which, though they are apparently copies and primitive in execution, have an appealing charm. Measuring only 10 x 8 inches, they are framed under glass, broken glass in each case. That of John Adams, who appears in a gray-brown coat and with ruddy expression, bears the following inscription written in an unknown hand on a bit of paper pasted on the back of the picture:

The following data is from Wm. G. Spear. John and Abigail Adams, done in oil, life size, by Asa Pope who labored for them at the time. Mr. Pope was—God save the mark—a Natural Artist. They now are (July 1900) in the possession of Mr. Pope's daughter Sara A. or Susan C. Pope, 31 Elm St.

Those descendants of Asa Pope who have been found know nothing of the whereabouts of the original paintings, which have so far eluded discovery. No mention of Pope in the Adams family papers has so far come to light.

Of the two pictures, that of Abigail appears somewhat better drawn, the details of her hat and dress being more recognizable than, for example, John's waistcoat, the buttons and folds of which are confusing. The numbers and letters that appear upside down on the left side of Abigail's collar are presumably printed on the paper on which the picture is painted. From the style of Abigail's dress and hat, the pair can be dated about 1805.

For a likeness, Pope's Abigail should be compared with that by Brown (Fig. 21), which though painted years earlier reveals the same long face, sharp nose and chin, and piercing eyes. The likeness of John Adams is recognizable if compared with the next to be considered.

Of the same period and style is a third primitive (Fig. 61), showing John Adams, only 7¼ x 5½ inches in size, now belonging to Thomas Boylston Adams of South Lincoln. The similarity to Fig. 59 in both color and style is more than a coincidence. One must be a copy of the other, or else they must each derive from a common source. Fig.

61 is better drawn than Fig. 59 and is a readily recognizable likeness of Adams. The buttons and folds of the waistcoat are more intelligible and served as the model for the confused treatment in Pope's picture. The waistcoat collar and the shirt or stock, as well as the hair curls and pigtail, are almost identical. Where Pope, or his copyist, went awry was in the profile, this appearing as of a younger man with an indeterminate shaped nose. Nothing is known of the provenance of Fig. 61 except that it was presented to its present owner many years ago by a member of his wife's family. Its value to our inquiry is the consistency in the appearance of Adams it preserves when compared with other profiles.

59. JOHN ADAMS. OIL ON GLASS BY ASA POPE, CA. 1800

60. ABIGAIL ADAMS. OIL ON GLASS BY ASA POPE, CA. 1800

61. JOHN ADAMS. OIL ON PAPER BY AN UNKNOWN ARTIST,
CA. 1800

XVI

Silhouettes, 1809

"I think a profile cut in black
Would suit your style of face!"
Oliver Wendell Holmes,
"To the Portrait of 'A Lady' in the Athenaeum Gallery."

"I have . . . a Collection of profiles, taken in August 1809. My father and mother, my wife and myself; and my sons George and John, as boys, which I often look at with pleasure; all in one frame. It is a piece of family History." [1] This note in John Quincy Adams' diary was prompted by the visit on 25 March 1829 of Master Hankes, the profilist, who, as Adams added in the same entry, "cut me out and all the family in paper." The shades of John Adams and Abigail referred to (Figs. 62, 63) are now framed together with those of John Quincy Adams and his wife. The inscriptions that appear over their heads are in the hand of John Quincy Adams and are doubtless contemporary with the silhouettes.

The occasion of the taking of these profiles was the imminent departure in August 1809 of the younger Adamses for St. Petersburg, and it was but natural to have a picture made of the family to take away or leave behind as a keepsake. In his diary for 2 August 1809, John Quincy Adams had written, "This was the day we had fixed upon for our departure; but the difficulty of getting ready . . . detained me for a few days. We all dined at Mr. Gray's. . . . After dinner I went to the Miniature Painter Williams's for my wife's pictures, and had two profile shades taken of myself." He is silent about the rest of the family but from the inscriptions on the shades and the 1829 diary entry there can be little doubt but that the family were all taken together. Henry Williams, born in Boston in 1787, a well-known miniaturist and modeler-in-wax, is characterized by Dunlap as "a small, short, self-sufficient man; very dirty, and very forward and patronizing in his manner." [2] Of the group of silhouettes John Quincy Adams mentions, all appear to be on the same kind of old faded white paper.

[1] JQA, Diary, 25 March 1829.
[2] Dunlap, *Arts of Design*, ed. Bayley and Goodspeed, 3:30.

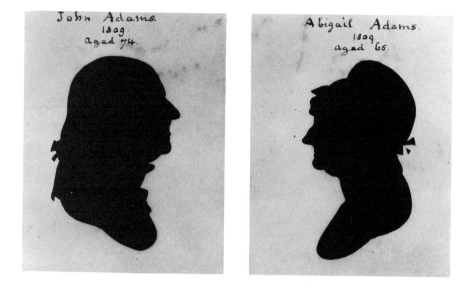

62. JOHN ADAMS. SILHOUETTE BY RAPHAELLE PEALE, 1809
63. ABIGAIL ADAMS. SILHOUETTE BY RAPHAELLE PEALE, 1809

His and his wife's each bear an embossed stamp "Williams." Those of John and Abigail, on the other hand, are embossed with the name "Peale," Abigail's, with the name reversed, appearing immediately under the bust and faintly visible in the illustration. The only explanation of this name that offers itself is that Raphaelle Peale, one of the talented sons of Charles Willson Peale, had by 1809 gone into the profile-cutting business and had for several years traveled extensively through the South and in New England before bad health overtook him. It is not unlikely that he had a business connection with Williams in 1809 which would account for the two names appearing on the group of silhouettes cut that evening. The two "Peale" shades cannot be confused with others cut at Peale's Museum in Philadelphia, as the latter, if marked at all, were embossed with the single word "Museum."

The likenesses, as shadows fall, are excellent if not flattering, and evidence the vigor and forthrightness so typical of this medium when under the hand of an expert. That of John is remarkably consistent with his other profiles, the Sharples (Fig. 38), Saint-Mémin (Fig. 57), and Binon (Fig. 91).

This pair, with those of John Quincy Adams and his wife and sons George and John, was at one time in the collection of Oliver Barrett of Chicago and with six others cut by Hankes was sold at auction for $225 at the Parke-Bernet Galleries on 10 February 1959. They are cut from white paper and set on a dark background. In the Adams Papers is a duplicate cut of John Adams, also embossed "Peale," together with several others of the younger generation cut at the same time.

XVII

The Early Stuarts—and Morse

"Trumbull for the figure, Stuart for the head, and Sharples
for the expression."
George Washington Parke Custis to
Thomas William Channing Moors, 1857.

From Stuart as from no other artist to whom Adams sat does the most commonly conceived public image of the second President so truly owe its origin. Although reproductions of Stuart's early work were often curiously distorted, even caricatured, they were widely circulated, have become familiar and popular, and are always clearly, though perhaps intricately, traceable to the original. To rationalize the almost innumerable reproductions is, in a sense, to solve a most complicated genealogical problem. So far as we can tell, there were only two originals of this period by Stuart, and two replicas, but there were several dozen copies in oil and scores of reproductions by engraving, lithograph, or woodcut. Many of those identifiable as to artist or publisher are listed later, in the Catalogue, yet they are but a fraction of the number that have been made. All that can be claimed for the Catalogue in this respect is that most of the significant copies and engravings made prior to the 20th century have been listed.

In 1798, at the instance of the Massachusetts legislature, Adams sat to Stuart for a portrait designed to be hung in the hall of the House of Representatives in Boston. The trials and vicissitudes surrounding the painting of this portrait are inextricably bound up with those of its pendant of Abigail. She, too, sat to Stuart, in 1800, and even took the great man's receipt for $100 for her prospective portrait,[1] fortunately as it proved. And then set in the procrastination and frustrating delay, so familiar to any one who in those days became involved with Stuart. For years, Adams tells us, he saw nothing of his portrait but the first sketch. Not until 1815 did the two finished portraits finally find their way into the hands of the Adamses. Flexner attributes Stuart's refusal to finish the portraits to Adams' condescension toward

---

[1] "Philadelphia May 20th 1800. Received of Mrs. Adams one hundred dollars in Payment for a Portrait painted by me. G. Stuart" (Adams Papers).

painters,[2] but a more likely explanation is simply Stuart's well-known procrastination and slipshod business habits. After all, it took him sixteen years to finish the "Edgehill" portrait of Jefferson! [3]

The efforts of the Adamses to have the two portraits completed and delivered safely into their own possession punctuate the family correspondence for fifteen years. By 1801 Stuart was in serious financial difficulty, and the sheriff was obliged to levy on him to satisfy the claims of his not unreasonable creditors. Thomas Boylston Adams wrote his mother from Philadelphia:

About three weeks ago I happened, by accident, to hear that an Execution had been levied upon the household furniture &c. of Stuart the painter, and also upon his paintings, and that the sale was to take place at Germantown, on the same day that the information was communicated. I felt alarmed for the safety of your portrait and my father's, so I resolved to set off on the pious and laudable expedition to redeem my parents from "durance vile" and ignominious bondage. I found however, upon my arrival, that my father's picture had not been seized or levied upon, but that your's had, and upon my assurance, that the picture was already paid for, the Sheriff consented to withdraw your representation, from the fangs of the law. I left the portrait in Stuart's hands, but I have no idea it will ever be finished, unless you should stimulate his attention by a letter. There is no appearance of any thing more having been done towards finishing the painting, than when I saw it twelvemonth, or more, ago. . . . It so happened, that your picture was the only one seized, as it was in his house and not in *his Stable,* which he occupies as his painting room. The debt for which the execution was taken out, was to an English Creditor and of long standing. How soon he may be served with similar process, for debts contracted here, is more than I can answer. I value your picture quite as much as any body in this part of the Country, and I shall endeavor to rescue it from future exposure in this way.

Abigail recognized the problem. Not long afterwards she wrote to her son: "I know not what to do with that strange man Stewart. The likeness is said to be so good, both of your Father and of me, that I shall regret very much if he cannot be prevaild upon to finish them as our Children may like to look upon our Likeness when the originals are no more seen." [4]

Adams himself wrote to his Dutch friend Van der Kemp in 1802: "Steuart has taken a Portrait of me, and intends I suppose to have it

[2] James Thomas Flexner, *American Painting: First Flowers of Our Wilderness,* Boston, 1947, p. 271.

[3] Bush, *Life Portraits of Jefferson,* p. 71.

[4] TBA to AA, 31 May 1801 (Adams Papers); AA to TBA, 12 June 1801 (Adams Papers).

engraved. . . . But nothing can be depended on, His Health and Motions are so precarious." [5] A year or so later Van der Kemp inquired, "Has Steward success been complete?—so that every one, who beholds the portrait, cries with exstatic joy, Hos habuit vultus: haec illi verba fuere / Hic decor, haec facies, hic color oris erat." [6] Adams could only reply: "I know nothing of Steuart's Success. I satt to him, at the request of our Massachusetts Legislature. But have never seen any Thing of the Picture but the first Sketch." [7] Later the same year Abigail urged her son John Quincy in Washington to do what he could with Stuart. Her son replied:

Stuart's receipt for the portrait was not enclosed in your former letter; but I hope you will find and forward it. Stuart is now here, and perhaps if I had the right to call on him for the picture he might be induced to finish it, under the apprehension, that it would be liable to injure his reputation by its being exhibited in the owner's possession, in its unfinished state. At any rate, it is so excellent a likeness, that being the only one extant of you, I am very anxious to have it in our own power; to whomsoever of us it may rightfully belong. [8]

After a short time Abigail replied:

I have found Stuart's receipt and now inclose it to you. I have thoughts of writing him a few lines when you call upon him for the portrait. I wish he could be prevaild upon to execute the one of your Father, which was designed for the State House in Boston. Genius is always eccentrick, I think. Superiour talents give no security for propriety of conduct; there is no knowing how to take hold of this Man, nor by what means to prevail upon him to fulfill his engagements. [9]

But he wasn't readily prevailed upon and the struggle continued. A half dozen years later John Quincy Adams wrote home from St. Petersburg:

This reminds me of the two portraits, of my father and mother, which that, I know not what to call him, Stuart has so shamefully kept, and which I wish you could get once more out of his hands, as you once rescued them from the Sheriff at Philadelphia. Among some of my papers which I left with you, is the receipt for painting that of my mother, but I

---

[5] 14 Dec. 1802 (PHi; LbC, Adams Papers).
[6] To JA, 15 Feb. 1804 (Adams Papers); quoting from memory from Ovid, *The Fasti*, bk. 2, lines 773–774; "Hos habuit voltus, haec illi verba fuerunt, / hic color, haec facies, his decor oris erat" (That was his look, those were his words, / That his color, his form, and his handsome face).
[7] 3 March 1804 (PHi, printed in JA, *Works*, 9:589).
[8] 19 Dec. 1804 (Adams Papers).
[9] 30 Dec. 1804 (same).

know not whether you can find it. If you can, I recommend to you to bring an action against Stuart, and make the Sheriff take it from him again.[10]

Writing a month later to Copley about his portrait of John Adams, John Quincy Adams said:

It is I believe the only full length picture of my father as large as life that ever has been painted, and perhaps the only one that will remain after him. Mr. Stuart was engaged by the Legislature of Massachusetts to paint one to be placed in the hall of the House of Representatives, and in pursuance of this engagement he actually took a likeness of his face. But Mr. Stuart thinks it the prerogative of genius to disdain the performance of his engagements, and he did disdain the performance of that. There is in America no other painter capable of executing a work, which I should wish to see preserved, and considering my father's age, it is more than probable that hereafter your portrait of him will be an *unique*.[11]

This pessimistic foreboding was happily not realized; Stuart himself would yet paint his greatest portrait of John Adams. John Quincy made a last effort with his brother a few days later:

I never think of this subject without feeling against Stuart an indignation, which I wish I could change into contempt. If there was another portrait painter in America, I could forgive him. I beg of you to try to get the portrait he has of my mother, and to buy of him that of my father for me. If he will finish it, I will gladly give him his full price for pictures of that sort for it. Perhaps you may tempt him by this offer, taking care to withhold the payment until the work is finished.[12]

In the end they prevailed and the portraits were finished. To be sure, genius exercised its prerogative, but the same genius set the palette and guided the brush that painted what were two of Stuart's great paintings of the time. On 9 December 1815 Stuart drew on William Smith Shaw, Mrs. Adams' nephew, for $100 in payment for Adams' portrait [13] (Fig. 64), and by 1816 the two portraits were safely in John Quincy Adams' possession (though for a time in Shaw's custody), where they remained for many years.

From J. Q. Adams the two portraits descended to his son Charles Francis Adams and from him to his son Brooks Adams, then to Brooks' niece Abigail Adams Homans. They hung for many years under the gaze of successive generations of Adamses in the Old House on Adams Street, Quincy, and later in the home of Mrs. Homans' brother, the

[10] To TBA, 29 March 1811 (Adams Papers, printed in JQA, *Writings*, 4:71).
[11] 29 April 1811 (LbC, Adams Papers, printed in JQA, *Writings*, 4:71).
[12] 13 May 1811 (Adams Papers, printed in JQA, *Writings*, 4:70–71).
[13] "Wm. S. Shaw, Esq. Sir: Please pay I. S. Davis or his order one hundred for my account for Mr. Adams portrait. Dec. 9. 1815. G. Stuart" (Adams Papers).

64. JOHN ADAMS. OIL BY GILBERT STUART, 1798 AND 1815

third C. F. Adams, at 177 Commonwealth Avenue, Boston. On the occasion of the Centennial Celebration, in 1889, of the inauguration of Washington as President, the pair was lent to the Loan Exhibition and later reproduced in Bowen's *Centennial.* In 1954 Mrs. Homans, aware of the hazards in the lives of family portraits and recognizing their value not only as works of art but as part of our national heritage, presented them to the National Gallery of Art in Washington.

The preliminary sketch of Abigail (Fig. 65), in some ways a more powerful human document than the finished work (Fig. 66), was fortunately preserved by Stuart and was bequeathed by the late John Adams of South Lincoln, her great-great-grandson, to his son John Quincy and by him given to the Massachusetts Historical Society in 1964. It had been bought in 1904 for $500 by his father, the second Charles Francis Adams, from Catherine Carlton Manson, daughter of the painter William T. Carlton of Dorchester.[14] Family tradition records that Abigail considered it beneath her dignity as an elderly lady to be painted bareheaded as Stuart wished, and thus even in the sketch she appears in the outline of her cap. How Carlton came by the sketch is not known, but it is not unlikely he purchased it from the Stuart family in the days when their straitened circumstances forced them to sell to the Boston Athenæum the unfinished portraits of George and Martha Washington that now proudly hang in the Museum of Fine Arts in Boston. In the years following her sitting to Stuart, Abigail came to lose interest in the portrait of herself. In 1815 she wrote to her son John Quincy: "He [Stuart] has promised to finish that which twenty [actually fifteen] years ago he took for me, but now, no more like me than that of any other person. I am sure my Grand children will never know it and therefore I cared not whether he ever finishd it. It has however a strong resemblance of you."[15] A contemporary and more acceptable judgment of the sketch is given in William Smith Shaw's letter to Abigail in 1800, only a few days after she had sat to Stuart: "Your likeness has attracted much company to Stewarts and has as many admirers as spectators. Stewart says, he wishes to god, he could have taken Mrs. Adams when she was young, he believes he should have a perfect Venus." Upon learning of this remark, President Adams emphatically agreed.[16]

Abigail's portrait, in its finished state (Fig. 66), has been engraved

[14] CFA2, Diary, 2 Dec. 1904: "Paid for the Stewart Sketch of Mrs. John Adams ($500)" (Adams Papers, Fourth Generation).
[15] 8 June 1815 (Adams Papers).
[16] Shaw to AA, 25 May 1800 (Adams Papers).

65. ABIGAIL ADAMS. OIL BY GILBERT STUART, 1800

138

66. ABIGAIL ADAMS. OIL BY GILBERT STUART, 1800—1812

139

a number of times, the earliest in 1839 by G. F. Storm for Longacre and Herring's *National Portrait Gallery of Distinguished Americans*.[17] Jane Stuart's copy in oil (Cat. No. 162), evidencing genuine inherited talent and characteristically true to the original, hangs as a pendant to that of her copy of John Adams in the Long Room of the Old House in Quincy.

Both the sketch of Abigail and the finished portrait undoubtedly portray Abigail as she appeared in 1800. But what of the portrait of John (Fig. 64)? He sat first to Stuart in 1798, and this portrait has always been supposed to represent him as he appeared in that year when still President. It is however entirely possible that the likeness is that of Adams as he appeared in 1815, not 1798. This possibility is suggested by two letters written in 1815 and 1816, one from Abigail to John Quincy Adams, already quoted in part above, and the other from Joseph Delaplaine to John Adams. Abigail wrote to her son:

> Your father is gone, to comply with a request made by you through your Brother, to sit to Stuart for his portrait. If he gets a good likeness, as I think it promises, you will value it more than if it had been taken, in youth or middle Age. He has promised to finish that which twenty years ago he took for me, but now, no more like me than that of any other person.[18]

What Abigail implies is that, while Stuart was simply going to finish the portrait he had many years ago started of her, her husband was posing again, and this likeness of him ("if he gets a good likeness") would be more acceptable to his family as being contemporary and not as in youth or middle age. We have to remind ourselves that in 1815 Adams was eighty years old!

Delaplaine's letter to Adams was primarily concerned with his efforts to borrow Stuart's original portrait for the purpose of having it engraved, and the letter is quoted at greater length hereafter. But it contains a few sentences bearing directly on the problem of dating this portrait. Delaplaine, purporting to be quoting from an anonymous writer, refers to the portrait of Adams as "a likeness lately taken of him by Stuart which is so strong that a child not two years old knew it. Age has given a softness and mellowness to the countenance which Stuart has happily caught without losing the characteristic vigor of former years." [19] This letter was written to Adams only a short time

[17] James B. Longacre and James Herring, *The National Portrait Gallery of Distinguished Americans*, Phila., 1834–1839, vol. 4.
[18] 8 June 1815 (Adams Papers).
[19] 27 Feb. 1816 (Adams Papers).

after the family had at last received the portrait from Stuart, and would not seem to have been referring to a likeness of Adams as he had appeared in 1798, eighteen years before! The expression "without losing the characteristic vigor of former years" would seem to be speaking, in 1816, of the earlier, Presidential years, not last year. The anonymous writer (undoubtedly Delaplaine himself) would hardly have used the expression "a likeness lately taken of him" to refer to a likeness taken so long ago. This then, with what is said below with reference to the Otis copy (Fig. 70) and the Morse original (Fig. 68), is the external evidence available for dating this early Stuart. Lawrence Park ascribed it to the year 1798 without question, but he lacked access to the family correspondence now available.[20] A comparison of this portrait with the Williams and Sharples portraits (Figs. 40, 31) of the 1790's, on the one hand, and with the Morse (Fig. 68), on the other hand, suggests strongly that this likeness, though conceived in 1798, presents Adams in some measure as he appeared in 1815, or at least is a compromise between the Adams of 1798 and the Adams of 1815.

There is no further mention of the 1798 "Sketch" of John Adams that was referred to in his letters to Van der Kemp. Perhaps it was thought to be only the first few brush strokes of what became the finished painting. Yet, if a new sitting were required for John's portrait in 1815, would it not have been because the 1798 sketch was considered inadequate? Very likely the 1798 sketch was entirely superseded. There is today, in the possession of John F. Seymour of Topanga, California (a sixth-generation descendant of John Adams through his son Charles), a handsome oil painting (Fig. 67), showing Adams considerably younger in appearance than in the National Gallery example. Although the head in this painting has been accepted as by the hand of Stuart, the rest of the portrait, clothes, and background is thought to be the work of another, unlike Stuart.[21] This circumstance is quite consistent with the history of this canvas.

Abigail Louisa Smith Adams, the daughter of John Adams' son Charles, married Alexander Bryan Johnson in 1814. At Johnson's death in 1867, he left a manuscript autobiography, written late in

---

[20] Park, *Gilbert Stuart*, 1:90.

[21] The present owner of the picture, John F. Seymour, wrote to the author on 19 Dec. 1963: "About twelve years ago the portrait was cleaned and restored by a woman on the staff of the Huntington Art Gallery. At this time it was examined by the Curator of Art, Marion Block, and after comparing it with the paintings shown in Lawrence Park's *Gilbert Stuart*, Mr. Block felt that only the features appeared to be the work of Stuart—the balance of the painting being unlike Stuart's work."

67. JOHN ADAMS. OIL BY GILBERT STUART, 1798

142

life, in which he recorded a meeting with Stuart shortly after his marriage:

> We, also, visited the Studio of Gilbert Stuart and saw the portrait he was painting of President Adams. He had completed all but the drapery and had long held it in this condition from a repugnance to paint drapery. I was surprised to see the tremulousness of the artist's hands, induced, as was supposed from a habit of excessive stimulation. He also took snuff in an immoderate quantity and was not over cleanly with it. He offered to make me a copy of President Adams' portrait for two hundred and fifty dollars, but he said his daughter would make me a copy for fifty dollars, and it would be as good as he could make—the difference being only in the imagination of the purchaser. The fame of the artist gave him no little interest to me and he was communicative and obliging.[22]

Johnson's memory played him false, and he has confused the date of his first visit to Stuart with a second visit or perhaps combined two visits into one. To be sure Stuart had not finished Adams' portrait in 1814, but neither could he have offered to Johnson a copy by his daughter Jane, then only two years old. In all probability Johnson saw Stuart in 1814 as he recalled and again perhaps in 1827 or 1828, by which time Jane had acquired some skill in painting. Nothing more is known of the origin of this Topanga portrait except that attached to the back of it by Johnson's granddaughter, Abigail Johnson Seymour, the paternal grandmother of the present owner, is a note in an unidentified hand stating that it was painted by Gilbert Stuart.

A reasonable explanation of this painting is that it was the first sketch of John Adams, which he refers to as having been done in 1798. Because of Adams' more youthful appearance in it, this likeness would not have satisfied Stuart by 1815, hence Adams' second sitting at that time, resulting in the later portrait. This would also account for the possibility of Johnson's having seen an unfinished portrait in Stuart's possession in 1814. Very likely it was Jane Stuart who completed the painting by adding the coat, shirt, and background. Any other hypothesis is hard to imagine. There is no other comparable likeness of Adams of which this could be a copy; it quite closely compares in style of hair, facial expression, and resemblance with the later portrait—only appearing younger—and the head is generally accepted as the work of Stuart. In respect of age, Adams in this picture has a greater resemblance to the Sharples and Williams portraits of the 1790's (Figs. 31, 40) than, for example, to the Morse of 1816 (Fig.

[22] "Autobiography of Alexander Bryan Johnson" (MS in the possession of Alexander Bryan Johnson of New Canaan, Conn., 1965)

68). The almost inescapable conclusion is that this is in fact the 1798 sketch in completed form and is therefore the earliest Stuart portrait of Adams. So far as we can tell, this portrait has never been engraved or copied and is reproduced here for the first time.

The replicas, copies, and derivative reproductions of Stuart's 1815 Adams, although at first glance so numerous and varied as to appear to have no recognizable relation to each other, have a genealogy of their own, shown graphically here. They divide themselves quite neatly into groups: (1) the Newton–Otis copies (Figs. 69, 70) and their sharp-faced offspring; (2) the lost Stuart (Doggett) replica (Cat. No. 108) and its round-faced descendants; (3) the Stuart (Gibbs) replica (Fig. 82) and its small family; and (4) a catch-all group embracing the few engravings traceable directly to the original with scarcely any identifiable descendants, and the numerous copies in oil. Many of the copies in oil are fine paintings, good likenesses, but most of the engravings, including the "round-faced" and "sharp-faced" families, are, to say the least, "unlike," but are yet so numerous and widespread as to make their origin and progress worth recording.

THE NEWTON–OTIS COPIES AND THEIR SHARP-FACED DERIVATIVES

The genesis of the descendants of the Newton–Otis copies of Stuart's Adams can be traced directly to the grandiose schemes of the Philadelphia bookseller Joseph Delaplaine. His dream, extravagantly advertised, was, to use his own words, "to publish a National Work, in perpetual commemoration of those illustrious men who have most distinguished themselves, by their virtue, talents, and public services; to be entitled *'Delaplaine's Repository of the Lives and Portraits of Distinguished American Characters.'* "[23] For the biographical part of this projected and unique encyclopedia we are told he had "called in gentlemen of well-tried and acknowledged talents, erudition and taste." But, better yet, he was to be "more fortunate than Plutarch in having the opportunity of subjoining a portraiture of the body to a delineation of the mind." To make good this boast required, of course, access to first-class original portraits of his "Distinguished American Characters" to serve as models for his engravers. The work was to extend for many years and many volumes. How far he succeeded is plain, and

[23] Broadside prospectus of Delaplaine's *Repository,* an example of which is bound in with the first thirty-three pages of the *Repository* and endorsed, in Delaplaine's hand, "Presented to Benjamin West Esquire, President of the Royal Academy of London as a token of respect by his most obedient humble servant Joseph Delaplaine. Philadelphia June 2d, 1814" (NHi).

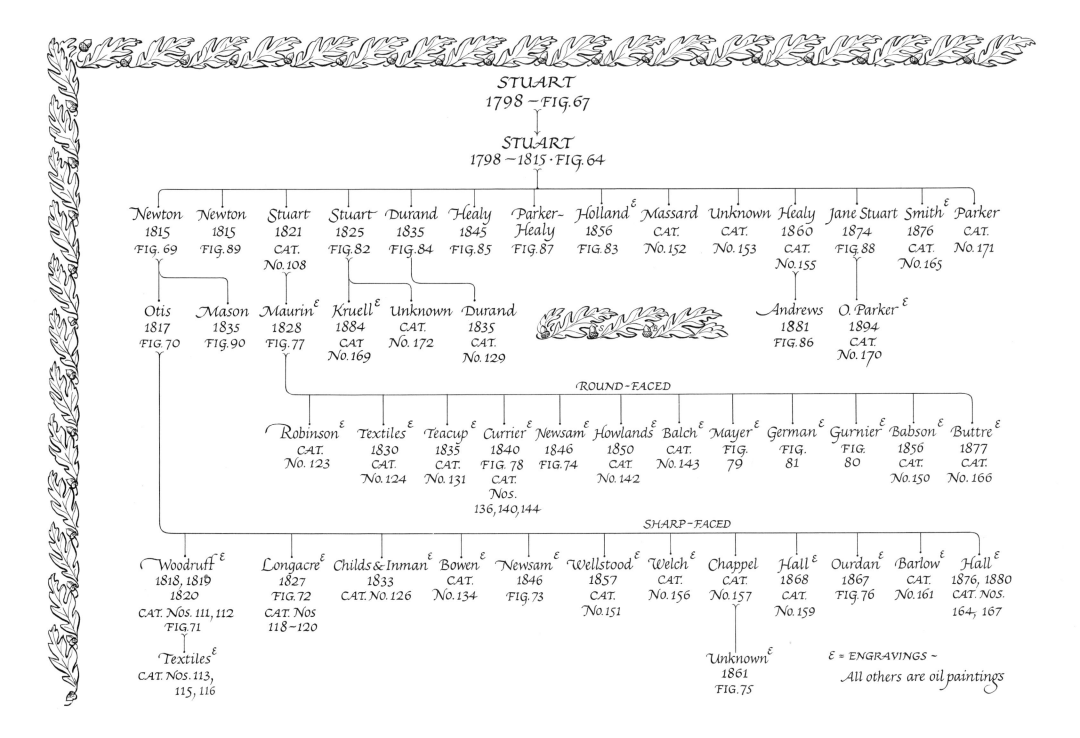

STUART
1798 – FIG. 67

STUART
1798 – 1815 · FIG. 64

Newton
1815
FIG. 69

Newton
1815
FIG. 89

Stuart
1821
CAT.
No. 108

Stuart
1825
FIG. 82

Durand
1835
FIG. 84

Healy
1845
FIG. 85

Parker-
Healy
FIG. 87

Holland ᴱ
1856
FIG. 83

Massard
CAT.
No. 152

Unknown
CAT.
No. 153

Healy
1860
CAT.
No. 155

Jane Stuart
1874
FIG. 88

Smith ᴱ
1876
CAT.
No. 165

Parker
CAT.
No. 171

Otis
1817
FIG. 70

Mason
1835
FIG. 90

Maurin ᴱ
1828
FIG. 77

Kruell ᴱ
1884
CAT
No. 169

Unknown
CAT.
No. 172

Durand
1835
CAT.
No. 129

Andrews
1881
FIG. 86

O. Parker ᴱ
1894
CAT.
No. 170

ROUND-FACED

Robinson ᴱ
CAT.
No. 123

Textiles ᴱ
1830
CAT.
No. 124

Teacup ᴱ
1835
CAT.
No. 131

Currier ᴱ
1840
FIG. 78
CAT.
Nos.
136, 140, 144

Newsam ᴱ
1846
FIG. 74

Howlands ᴱ
1850
CAT.
No. 142

Balch ᴱ
CAT.
No. 143

Mayer ᴱ
FIG.
79

German ᴱ
FIG.
81

Gurnier ᴱ
FIG.
80

Babson ᴱ
1856
CAT.
No. 150

Buttre ᴱ
1877
CAT.
No. 166

SHARP-FACED

Woodruff ᴱ
1818, 1819
1820
CAT. Nos. 111, 112
FIG. 71

Longacre ᴱ
1827
FIG. 72
CAT. Nos
118~120

Childs & Inman ᴱ
1833
CAT. No. 126

Bowen ᴱ
CAT.
No. 134

Newsam ᴱ
1846
FIG. 73

Wellstood ᴱ
1857
CAT.
No. 151

Welch ᴱ
CAT.
No. 156

Chappel
CAT.
No. 157

Hall ᴱ
1868
CAT.
No. 159

Ourdan ᴱ
1867
FIG. 76

Barlow ᴱ
CAT.
No. 161

Hall ᴱ
1876, 1880
CAT. Nos.
164, 167

Textiles ᴱ
CAT. Nos. 113,
115, 116

Unknown ᴱ
1861
FIG. 75

ᴱ = ENGRAVINGS ~
All others are oil paintings

from our vantage point not unexpected. The first half-volume of the *Repository* was published in 1816 and was castigated, even ridiculed, in an entertaining review appearing in the *Analectic Magazine and Naval Chronicle* for September 1816.[24] Delaplaine was badly stung by what he termed a "feeble and unfounded attack," and joined the lists in his own defense in a pamphlet published in Philadelphia on 23 September 1816, entitled *The Author Turned Critic, or the Reviewer Reviewed.*[25] For thirty-four pages he defended himself and his *Repository* and for five more pages advertised his wares, assuring the public that "from the extensive arrangements he has made, and the large sums of money he has expended in it already (upwards of eleven thousand dollars) he is enabled to state, positively, that the permanent continuance of the Repository may be relied upon." The outcome was probably a foregone conclusion; the second half-volume was produced in 1817 and that was the end, although Delaplaine continued for some years to gather portraits for his Gallery in Philadelphia.[26]

Adams' likeness did not appear in the first two half-volumes of the *Repository,* but its absence was not due to any lack of effort or ingenuity on the part of Delaplaine, who first wrote to Adams in May 1813:

> I have commenced the publication of engraved portraits of the eminent men of our country, by Mr. Edwin and Leney, in their best style.
>
> Have the goodness to inform me, whether there is an approved likeness of you, by whom painted, and in whose possession it is. And be pleased also to grant me permission to have it engraved.
>
> The portrait of Dr. Rush, from a painting by Mr. Sully, is in the hands of Mr. Edwin, and will appear on the 10th of June next.[27]

To this letter Adams replied from Quincy, characteristically belittling any portraits of himself:

> Sir:
> There are several things abroad which are reported to have been intended as pictures of me; some of them drawn by persons who never saw me, others by persons to whom I never 'sat and others by painters who [never] requested me to sit.

[24] Published by Moses Thomas in Philadelphia; the review appeared in vol. 8:193–209.

[25] *The Author Turned Critic or the Reviewer Reviewed being a Reply to a Feeble and Unfounded Attack on Delaplaine's Repository in the Analectic Magazine and Naval Chronicle, for the Month of September 1816,* Phila., 1816, sometimes attributed to Dr. Charles Caldwell.

[26] In the *Prospectus of Delaplaine's National Panzographia for the Reception of the Portraits of Distinguished Americans,* Phila., 1818, p. 16, Delaplaine was able to report that his collection of more than two hundred portraits, including one of John Adams, would be open for visitors on 1 July 1819.

[27] 29 May 1813 (Adams Papers).

I pretend not to be a judge of the merit of any of them. But there is not an approved likeness among them. The least approved of all is one that was taken by a Roman Catholic Priest who was preaching to me while I was sitting mute before him, on transubstantiation and the incarnation of God. This he had engraved and as Mr. Stewart informed me, sold two and twenty thousand of them at a dollar a peice.

My head has been so long the sport of painters, as my heart has been of libellers, that I shall make no objection to any use that may be made of either.

It would rejoice my soul to see a real portrait of Dr. Rush or Mr. Jay.[28]

For a while Delaplaine turned his efforts in other directions and gradually gathered together sufficient portraits and engravings for his first half-volume. How well his engravings turned out is indicated in an entry in the diary of John Quincy Adams for 4 December 1815 when he was in England:

A Mr. Wolford came here; lately arrived from Philadelphia. He is an Englishman, by Birth, and has relations in this neighbourhood; but is settled in America, and intends to return there. He brought with him several Prints, of the Collection, now publishing by Mr. Delaplaine. Among them one of Commodore Perry's victory on Lake Erie; which with Portraits of President Washington from Houdon's bust, of Mr. Jay, Mr. King, R. Fulton and DeWitt Clinton, I took of him. He had also those of President Madison, Dr. Rush, General Harrison, and a Dr. Wilson, but so badly executed that I declined taking them.

That same month Delaplaine took up again his correspondence with John Adams, recalling their exchange two years earlier and sending him engravings of Mr. Jay and Dr. Rush. He also enclosed a prospectus of the first half-volume of the *Repository,* and renewed his appeal for a portrait:

I am desirous of obtaining your portrait for the purpose of having an engraving taken from it for the Repository. A respectable young gentleman, Mr. Morse lately from London, son of the Reverend Dr. Morse is an excellent artist I learn, and I beg you to do me the honour of sitting to him at my expence. I have written to him on the subject, and he will wait to receive from you a letter in which have the goodness to state the place and time where and when it will be most agreeable for you to sit.[29]

Adams was grateful for the engravings of his two friends. That of Jay he thought a likeness, but what could he say of Rush?

[28] 8 June 1813 (LbC, Adams Papers). For the "Roman Catholic Priest" see Chapter XXI.
[29] 6 Dec. 1815 (Adams Papers).

Dr. Rush the last time I saw him in March 1801, was as upright as a Reed, and his Countenance no less animated than intelligent. But his portrait now exhibits not only the decripitude of old age worn out by long labours in the cause of humanity; but a costume of democratical plainness which my excellent friend sometimes too much affected.

Adams went on to say that he had received from Dr. Morse some weeks since a request to sit to his son and that he would be glad to oblige, adding that "it seems not worth while to take a bald head, on which fourscore Winters have snowed." [30] To Morse he had already written: "The Proposal of taking my bust can only make me Smile. If your son had proposed it I would have written him a Letter too ludicrous for you to read, describing the Portraits and Busts which have already transmitted me to Posterity." [31] A further exchange between Delaplaine and Adams arranged for the sitting and elicited from Adams a brief autobiography.

Morse's young son, Samuel Finley Breese Morse, set to work at once and in a short time finished his portrait (Fig. 68). He was at the time but twenty-four years old, having at the age of twenty gone to London to study under Benjamin West. His opinion of the portrait painters of the day is revealing. From London in 1813 he wrote:

The American character stands high in this country as to the production of artists. . . . Mr. West now stands at the head. . . . Mr. Copley next, then Colonel Trumbull. Stuart in America has no rival here. As these are now old men and going off the stage, Mr. Allston succeeds in the prime of life. . . . After him is a young man from Philadelphia by the name of Leslie, who is my room-mate. [32]

Charles Robert Leslie at the time was only nineteen and within three years was to paint his well-known portraits of John Quincy Adams and his wife.

As time was to show, Morse unquestionably had remarkable talents, but his reputation as a portrait painter could not have been advanced by his portrait of Adams, which today belongs to the Brooklyn Museum. [33] Inscribed on the back of the painting, and stated to be copied from the original inscription when the painting was relined in

[30] 17 Dec. 1815 (LbC, Adams Papers).
[31] 20 Nov. 1815 (RC in PHi:Gratz Coll.; LbC, Adams Papers; printed in JA, *Works*, 10:180).
[32] *Samuel F. B. Morse: His Letters and Journals,* ed. Edward L. Morse, Boston and N.Y., 1914, 1:102–103.
[33] Oliver W. Larkin, in *Samuel F. B. Morse and American Democratic Art,* Boston, 1954, describes this portrait as a "graceless revelation of New England character," painted "with a dry and overcautious hand" (p. 39).

68. JOHN ADAMS. OIL BY SAMUEL F. B. MORSE, 1816

1888, are the words "Original portrait of John Adams late President of the U. States, painted by S. F. B. Morse in 1816 for Joseph de la Plaine." It was reproduced in Bowen's *Centennial* and there described as then belonging to Alexander M. White of Brooklyn; it was presented to the Museum in 1932 by Miss Harriet H. White. Abigail Adams saw it early in February 1816 and correctly pronounced it "a stern unpleasing likeness." [34] In a postscript to a letter to John Quincy Adams a year later, Delaplaine added, "I have just received from Boston, the portrait of your worthy father, painted by young Mr. Morse, but its execution is so unsatisfactory, that I shall not have an engraving from it." [35] As a matter of fact, he had long since decided not to have it engraved.

Here was an impasse; but the resourceful Delaplaine was not entirely nor for long at a loss. He tried a new approach, ingenious though not too subtle. Early in 1816 he wrote to John Adams reporting the receipt of an anonymous letter reading:

Sir:
As you have lately requested a likeness of the ex-President Adams, I presume you would wish the best likeness which is to be obtained of him. Mr. Morse has taken a portrait of him which I cannot deny is sufficiently a likeness to be known, but is by no means a pleasing one. It is austere and fails in character. I regret this the more as I consider Mr. Morse a rising genius whom I should wish to encourage and a gentleman I highly esteem; but the portrait he has taken will rather injure than promote his interest, which will not be the case with some others I have seen of his. There is at the Ex-President's house a likeness lately taken of him by Stuart which is so strong that a child not two years old knew it. Age has given a softness and mellowness to the countenance which Stuart has happily caught without losing the characteristic vigor of former years. If you obtain a copy of that you would then have the likeness you wish for. I am not alone in the opinion I have expressed.

Emerging from behind this smokescreen, Delaplaine then spoke for himself:

I respect Mr. Morse so highly, that I am particularly desirous that the contents of this letter from Boston should be kept entirely from him. I can receive his picture of you and thereby give no offence. But as it appears he has failed in a characteristic likeness, so well obtained by Stuart, I am very desirous to have the engraving executed from that picture.[36]

[34] To JQA, 10 Feb. 1816 (Adams Papers).
[35] 28 March 1817 (Adams Papers).
[36] 27 Feb. 1816 (same).

Adams saw through this, replying immediately that he had no knowledge of the writer of the anonymous letter, that the "Stewart" portrait belonged to John Quincy Adams, and that he would never let it be out from under his roof until he gave it to its rightful owner. In any event he wouldn't want it copied without "Stewart's" consent. He could offer Delaplaine no solution, only sympathy for his expense and labors. One remark in his letter causes us some speculation: "Mr. Stewart possesses another portrait as like it as any two objects in nature or art are alike." [37] He may have been referring to the Doggett replica (Cat. No. 108), or to the Newton copy (Fig. 69). But his hesitancy didn't stop the persistent Delaplaine—only delayed him for a space during the publication of the first half-volume of the *Repository,* its review and defense. In March 1817, as already mentioned, Delaplaine told John Quincy Adams that the Morse portrait was unsatisfactory. In May he wrote again to John Quincy asking him to become a contributor to the *Repository.* Adams demurred. Delaplaine then approached Adams' cousin, William Smith Shaw, writing on 21 August 1817:

> I had the honor of writing to you yesterday, on the subject of the portrait of the venerable Mr. Adams which is in your possession   that I should have the portrait on loan for the purpose of causing an engraving to be executed from it for my national work, the Repository of the Lives and Portraits of Distinguished Americans. . . . I need scarcely mention how essential it is that my engravings should be executed from *original* pictures. I pledge to you my honor that the moment my engraver has done with the portrait, it shall be returned with the utmost care and safety.[38]

On 16 September 1817 John Quincy Adams recorded in his diary that he had called at Delaplaine's gallery, and afterwards met him on the street, giving him a verbal answer to the letter he had received from him in London as well as his letter to Shaw asking for a biographical memoir of John Adams and the loan of Stuart's portrait. In December he wrote to Delaplaine: "I regret the utter impossibility I am under of furnishing the Memoir which you desire. Mr. Shaw will I do not doubt send you the Portrait, if you can indicate to him any mode of conveying it safely." [39] Although this ends the correspondence on this subject, and we can only turn to the portraits and engravings themselves to discover the outcome of Delaplaine's efforts, this ex-

[37] 5 March 1816 (LbC, Adams Papers).
[38] Joseph B. Felt, *Memorials of William Smith Shaw,* Boston, 1852, p. 316–317.
[39] 15 Dec. 1817 (LbC, Adams Papers).

change between Delaplaine and J. Q. Adams and the reference to a portrait in Shaw's possession are very significant.

Stuart had a talented nephew and namesake, Gilbert Stuart Newton, who was born in 1794 in Halifax, Nova Scotia, and brought to Cambridge in 1803 after his father's death. In Cambridge young Newton's talents developed, and he was fortunate enough to be able to study under his uncle until 1817, when he went to Italy and then to London for the rest of his life, except for a short visit to Boston in 1832. While under his uncle's tutelage he made a copy of the portrait of Adams, probably during the year 1815. This copy (Fig. 69) is now owned by the Boston Athenæum. It came to its present owner from the estate of William Smith Shaw, who had been Librarian of the Athenæum, by agreement with the Reverend Joseph B. Felt, Shaw's administrator. Shaw's successor as librarian, Seth Bass, records the portrait in his Report of 1825 as "Adams by Stuart—belongs to Shaw, but not the *frame*—paid by the Athenæum." [40] By 1834 it was described in the Athenæum list of paintings as "after Stuart by Newton," and from 1877 to 1900 it was on loan to the Museum of Fine Arts in Boston. It is but a poor copy, differing from the original in several significant respects: the hand and chair arm are missing, Adams is given a pointed chin and lips pursed in a way that produces a weak, silly expression, the ruffles of his shirt front and his jabot are sketched in roughly, perhaps because the original itself had not yet been completed in this respect, and a dark shadow appears behind Adams' left ear not present in the original. The significance of these differences will be appreciated in considering the copy by Bass Otis.

Although Delaplaine never succeeded in borrowing Stuart's original portrait, it becomes quite clear that he did borrow the Newton copy that was in Shaw's possession. Before many years elapsed, engravings began to appear inscribed variously as "Engraved by Longacre, from a Painting in Delaplaine's Gallery, from Stuart," or "Engraved by J. B. Longacre from a Painting by B. Otis after the Portrait by G. Stuart," or "Drawn and Engraved by J. B. Longacre from a Portrait by Otis after Stuart." But no trace of Otis' copy itself could ever be found.

Born in Bridgewater, Massachusetts, in 1784, Bass Otis in his youth was apprenticed to a scythemaker, but as early as 1808 he appeared in New York as a portrait painter and was later one of the pioneer American lithographers. Delaplaine discovered him and employed him to take Jefferson's portrait for the *Repository*. That portrait appeared in

[40] Letter from David McKibbin, of the Boston Athenæum, to the author, 25 Feb. 1964.

69. JOHN ADAMS. OIL ON WOOD PANEL BY GILBERT STUART
NEWTON, CA. 1815

70. JOHN ADAMS. OIL ON WOOD PANEL BY BASS OTIS, 1817

153

the second half-volume, engraved by Neagle. The engraving is unsatisfactory, but the portrait, now belonging to the Thomas Jefferson Memorial Foundation, is a warm, sympathetic, gentle representation of Jefferson. As this and other portraits attest, Otis was an artist of no little skill. Yet the Longacre engravings of Adams "after Otis" are not satisfactory representations of Stuart's original and raised the question as to what Otis' copy might have been like. And then it turned up (Fig. 70), hanging in prominent anonymity in the gallery of The New-York Historical Society. The portrait was given to the Society in 1867 by its great benefactor Thomas Jefferson Bryan and had for years been catalogued as a replica by Stuart. It is so listed in Lawrence Park's Register.[41] In 1942, however, when The New-York Historical Society's catalogue of its American portraits was being prepared, William Sawitzky, then the Society's Advisory Curator of American Art, refused to accept the painting as by Stuart and it has since then been described as a copy of Stuart "by an unknown hand."[42] How Bryan acquired the copy is not known, perhaps on the breakup of Delaplaine's Gallery.

That this portrait (Fig. 70) is the source of Longacre's engravings and is therefore the Otis copy is evident from a comparison of the painting with any of the Longacre group, or for that matter with any of the sharp-faced family. The real clue, in addition to the pointed chin and pursed lips, is in the peculiar treatment of the jabot and shirt front, the folds of which are reproduced in the closest detail by Longacre. The same is true of the shadow behind Adams' left ear. Compare it, for example, with Longacre (Fig. 72). The handling of these details is so minutely exact as to be beyond the realm of coincidence.

Finding the Otis prototype did not of itself solve all questions. There was still the perplexing problem of how such an able artist could have painted such a poor copy of Stuart, so poor as to lose not only the style of the clothes Adams wore but also all individuality and character of the subject. This was not in keeping with an artist of Otis' ability.

The solution of the problem was influenced by the order in which the various copies were first photographed and taken into consideration. One of the last to be studied was Newton's copy (Fig. 69), and when it was viewed side by side with Otis' it became apparent that the peculiarities of the two versions and the aspects in which they differed from Stuart were such that they could not be independent cop-

[41] Park, *Gilbert Stuart*, 1:90.
[42] *Catalogue of American Portraits in The New-York Historical Society: Oil Portraits, Miniatures, Sculptures*, N.Y., 1941, p. 5.

ies of one original; one must have stemmed from the other. The logical progression from that point was simple. Newton's copy was painted in 1815 and he went abroad in 1817. In September 1817 Delaplaine was still trying to borrow the original; after corresponding with Shaw and J. Q. Adams, he undoubtedly succeeded in borrowing Shaw's portrait (the Newton copy, Fig. 69), possibly believing it to be Stuart's original, and set Otis to work to make a copy. Otis, being a better artist than the youthful Newton, understandably improved on the face, though without changing its shape or expression, and formalized Newton's sketchy treatment of the shirt front and jabot. Being a faithful copyist, he repeated the dark left-ear shadow. If these two paintings are considered side by side, this explanation is almost inescapable. The order of descent from the Stuart original (Fig. 64) can then be fairly established as commencing with Newton's copy (Fig. 69) then followed by Otis' copy after Newton (Fig. 70) and then the numerous engravings after Otis.

The earliest known engraving after Otis is that by William Woodruff, published in 1818 (Cat. No. 111), one of three diminutive portraits of Washington, Adams, and Jefferson and the arms of the original thirteen States surrounding a facsimile of the Declaration of Independence. It has not been possible to locate a copy of Woodruff's engraving, but it has been several times reproduced on textiles, one of the most striking being that produced by H. Brunet et Cie. of Lyons about 1820, printed on silk (Fig. 71). Even in miniscule, the folds of Adams' jabot clearly follow Otis. The engraving that served to establish The New-York Historical Society's copy "by an unknown hand" as being by Otis appeared in 1827 in volume 8 of Sanderson and Gilpin's enormously popular *Biography of the Signers,* and in several other states, drawn by Longacre (Fig. 72). It is but a short step in time from Longacre to Albert Newsam's frontispiece to a new edition of John Wood's *Suppressed History of the Administration of John Adams* in 1846 (Fig. 73), by which time Adams had been fairly transformed into a sort of toothless likeness of Washington. Newsam, a deaf-mute, is the only artist encountered who drew for his model of Adams on both the sharp-faced prototype by Otis and the round-faced source by Maurin (Fig. 77). Newsam's lithograph (Fig. 74), one of a series of the twelve Presidents, published in 1846, 13 x 10 inches in size, was sold in color as well as black and white. It shows Adams within an elaborately carved frame, his head after Maurin and his coat and collar after Newsam's own earlier lithograph (Fig. 73), which had

71. JEFFERSON, WASHINGTON, AND ADAMS.
PRINTED SILK, LITHOGRAPHED BY H. BRUNET ET CIE., CA. 1820

156

72. JOHN ADAMS. ENGRAVING BY J. B. LONGACRE, 1827

73. JOHN ADAMS. LITHOGRAPH BY ALBERT NEWSAM, 1846

JOHN ADAMS.
2ᵈ PRESIDENT OF THE UNITED STATES.

PHILADELPHIA.
Published by C.S.WILLIAMS, N.E. corner of Market & 7ᵗʰ St.

74. JOHN ADAMS. LITHOGRAPH BY ALBERT NEWSAM, 1846

followed Otis. A firsthand comparison of these two prints (Figs. 74, 73) would never lead to the conclusion that they were of the same sitter, nor for that matter that either was supposed to be a representation of Stuart's original.

Probably also traceable to Otis is Alonzo Chappel's 1861 familiar "free translation" (Cat. No. 157) of Stuart's Adams engraved for Duyckinck's *National Portrait Gallery of Eminent Americans* (Fig. 75). In a way it is a caricature, yet it revived Adams' stubborn petulance in a manner in which Newton, and hence Otis, failed.

75. JOHN ADAMS. ENGRAVING BY AN UNKNOWN ARTIST, 1861

76. JOHN ADAMS. ENGRAVING BY JOSEPH PROSPER OURDAN, 1867

In 1867, Joseph Prosper Ourdan, who, as his father had been, was employed by the Bureau of Engraving and Printing, and who later became head of it, engraved a little vignette (Fig. 76) of Adams after Otis, or perhaps Longacre, only 2 inches in size, which very likely has had the largest circulation of any engraving of Adams. It is an excellent reproduction of his model and it is only to be regretted that he lacked access to a portrait likeness of Adams. The vignette was reproduced in 1898 as a decorative device on $162,315,400 of 4 percent thirty-year bonds, and again in 1900 on $646,250,150 of 2 percent Consols of 1930. Of this aggregate of some $800,000,000 of bonds, only $9,900 remain outstanding, but the Bureau of Engraving and Printing is still selling the little Adams unlikenesses at 25 cents each.[43] They are now reproduced on a die-stamping press by the intaglio process from a plate made from a roll that had been transferred from the original hand-engraved die. Now that Stuart's original portrait (Fig. 64) belongs to the National Gallery, it is not too much to hope that the time will come when the Bureau of Engraving and Printing will offer as an official likeness of Adams an engraving made directly from the original.

[43] Letter from the United States Bureau of Engraving and Printing to the author, 14 Feb. 1964.

THE DOGGETT REPLICA AND THE ROUND-FACED SERIES

Stuart's own first copy or modified replica was painted in 1821 (Cat. No. 108), with copies of his portraits of four other Presidents, Washington, Jefferson, Madison, and Monroe, for John Doggett, a well-known Boston dealer. The price is reported to have been $50 each. Doggett retained the set until 1839, when he sold all five to Abel Phillips of Boston for $2,861.50 at what must have been a closely driven bargain.[44] Phillips had a plan. He took the portraits to Washington and devoted much time and effort in an attempt to sell them to the Government for hanging in the White House. Would that he had succeeded! They were offered first for $4,500, and later, more hopefully, for $6,000, but without takers. In 1846 a bill was introduced in Congress to provide for the purchase of the set at not to exceed $1,000 each, but, though favored by Caleb Cushing and Martin Van Buren, it was defeated. For years the paintings remained in Washington, in safe-keeping, ironically enough in the Library of Congress. But in 1851, alas, the Library rooms in the Capitol burned! The portraits of Adams, Washington, and Jefferson were destroyed. Those of Madison and Monroe, badly burned, were saved and subsequently passed into the hands of Seth Low, Mayor of the City of New York; the portrait of Monroe was bequeathed by him to the Metropolitan Museum of Art in 1929, but the present location of that of Madison is unknown.

The painting of this replica is mentioned by John Quincy Adams in his diary: "W. S. Shaw came out with Stewart the painter, who brought with him the copy he had made of Shaw's portrait of my father, and to whom my father gave a sitting of two or three hours. They returned this afternoon to Boston. Stewart paints this picture for a Mr. Doggett, as one of the five Presidents of the United States. He is to paint them all for him."[45] Louisa Catherine Adams describes the same visit:

George went into Town and Mr. Shaw and Mr. Stewart the Painter came out to take a sitting of the old Gentleman for a Picture. He looked remarkably well and was in fine spirits. Mr. S. dined with us and contrary to expectation was a perfect lump from whom it was impossible to extract any thing unless the snuff he was continually scattering about in the very eyes of the company may be counted as an agréement. In this case he must be superlative for he certainly was an Emblem of abundance. He is so noted for brilliancy that it could only be accounted for by supposing that he was so intent on procuring a good likeness his thoughts could not be

[44] Park, *Gilbert Stuart*, 1:90.
[45] Entry of 27 September 1821.

161

77. JOHN ADAMS. LITHOGRAPH BY MAURIN, 1828

called from his subject. The personal appearance of this man is if possible more than disgusting, he is literally one of those Persons that one would select to point out to youth the dangers of dissipation.[46]

The extent to which Stuart may have modified the likenesses of his subjects in the Doggett replicas is not known, but we do know that he deliberately varied the background. John Doggett Jr., in a letter to Charles Beaumont, 28 December 1837, revealed, "In the picture of Washington which I heard Stuart pronounce to my father as the best portrait he ever painted of that illustrious man, a sheathed sword and

[46] Diary (M/LCA/4), 27 Sept. 1821.

78. JOHN ADAMS. LITHOGRAPH BY NATHANIEL CURRIER, CA. 1840

a rainbow are represented, signifying that war and strife had ceased, and the storms of the Revolution passed away. In each of the pictures tassels are introduced appended to the draperies; they were intended to illustrate the number of terms that each served." [47] Although we can never know just what the Doggett replica of Stuart's Adams looked like, we have a clue from this letter and other clues from the many engravings that followed.

Late in the 1820's a series of five engravings of the Doggett replicas that became known as "The American Kings" series was lithographed

[47] Bowen, *Centennial of Washington's Inauguration,* 2:505.

79. JOHN ADAMS. ENGRAVING BY CARL MAYER

and published by John B. Pendleton, one of the founders of lithography in this country. Doggett's son-in-law Jonathan Cobb reveals in his diary that in 1825 he undertook to sell such a series, but that Pendleton could not "perform the workmanship as had been represented" even though he offered to go to France to procure the prints to be executed. For a time Cobb lost all confidence in Pendleton, and it seemed the project was doomed to failure. Finally in 1828, after a trip to France for Doggett, Pendleton returned bearing with him the lithographs. He had succeeded in procuring Maurin, the French lithographer and engraver, to draw the portraits on stone, and the stones had been brought back to Boston with a press for the printing. The price was two dollars each, or two dollars and a half on India paper.[48] In one advertisement of the time they were described as a series of six, but only the first five were ever producd. Today they are scarce and

[48] Mabel M. Swan, "The American Kings," *Antiques*, 19:281 (April 1931); Harry T. Peters, *America on Stone*, N.Y., 1931, p. 314.

80. JOHN ADAMS. LITHOGRAPH BY H. GURNIER

coveted. The lithograph of Adams (Fig. 77) was the prototype of all
the other round-faced engravings, those by Currier, Newsam, Casilear,
and others listed in the Catalogue. However faithfully Maurin may
have reproduced the Doggett replica, it is but a shadow of a likeness
of the Stuart original. The engravings of four of the five "Kings" portray them as facing in the same direction as in the original Stuart
prototype and we therefore can assume that the Doggett replicas of
those four originals faced the same way. But the Maurin engraving of
Adams shows him facing three-quarters right rather than left, which
suggests that Stuart for variety had reversed the image in this replica
of Adams. The peculiarities of facial expression, however, have been
perpetuated in successive engravings taken from Maurin. Currier (Fig.
78) portrays an ageless man, devoid of character, and with a bland,
vacant expression. This was no King! Babson, years later, added a

165

John Adams.
— Präsident von 1797 bis 1801. —

81. JOHN ADAMS. ENGRAVING BY A GERMAN ARTIST

somewhat more mature expression (Cat. No. 150). Carl Mayer, the German engraver, reverses Maurin's pose and transforms Adams into a young German (Fig. 79). Gurnier, the French artist, preserves the odd twist of Adams' mouth so noticeable in Maurin's lithograph, and in his slavish copying of Maurin overlooks the fact that Adams' buttons end up on the wrong side of his coat (Fig. 80). Casilear's minute engraving of the seven Presidents in a group (Cat. No. 127), done for the *New York Mirror,* is a modification of Maurin that has been followed many times. Another example (Fig. 81), by an unidentified engraver, shows the second President as a stolid, solemn-faced, middle-aged German. Newsam's conglomerate (Fig. 74) is immediately recognizable. The round-faced Doggett series are interesting in their va-

166

riety as well as in the consistency with which they preserve the characteristics of Maurin's lithograph, which he in turn had derived from the Doggett replica. Mostly they face to the right, all are round-faced and far younger-looking than the Adams of the Stuart original. And they are not likenesses!

THE STUART (GIBBS) REPLICA

In 1825 at the instance of Colonel George Gibbs of Newport, Rhode Island, the mineralogist, Stuart painted his second and somewhat modified replica of the original portrait, at the same time also producing a new series of replicas of his portraits of the same four other Presidents. This new series of five portraits was ultimately bought by Jefferson's grandson, Thomas Jefferson Coolidge, at the sale of Colonel Gibbs' estate, following his death in 1853, and today belong to his descendants. The so-called "Gibbs" replica of Adams (Fig. 82) is like but not exactly like the original. The hand and chair arm are missing, the coat collar now comes up almost to Adams' cheek, and the hair at the top of his head stands up more pertly than in the original. These little differences are perpetuated in the few reproductions that were made of this replica in a way that makes them readily recognizable. A copy in oil of the "Gibbs" replica, by an unknown hand (Cat. No. 172) was presented by Mrs. B. A. Beale to the American Embassy in London some years ago; a vivid white-line wood engraving (Cat. No. 169) was done in 1884 by G. Kruell for *Harpers Magazine;* but, except for these few public appearances, this replica has not had much influence in shaping the public image of Adams. The Gibbs collection of the five Stuart replicas does, however, constitute a group of inestimable value, both intrinsically and extrinsically, as being not only each by the hand of Stuart but also with a history of always having been owned as a group.

THE MISCELLANEOUS ENGRAVINGS AND THE COPIES IN OIL

That the Stuart original was long kept in the family's own possession accounts for the fact that only a few engravings have been made directly from it. Two have come to light in the course of the present inquiry: one by Holland and Stinson in 1856 (Fig. 83) done expressly for Charles Francis Adams' edition of *The Works of John Adams*,[49] and the other (Cat. No. 165) in 1876 by the Scottish engraver H. Wright Smith of New York. Neither of these is impressive

[49] Vol. 1 (Boston, 1856), frontispiece.

82. JOHN ADAMS. OIL BY GILBERT STUART, 1825

83. JOHN ADAMS. ENGRAVING BY T. R. HOLLAND
AND W. H. STINSON, 1856

but each is a better representation of Adams than any of those derived
from Newton or Maurin.

Two fine copies in oil of Stuart's original were made in 1835 by the
capable Asher B. Durand (who had made his reputation engraving
Trumbull's *Declaration of Independence* in 1823) at the instance of
the well-to-do merchant Luman Reed, then busily engaged in forming
a duplicate collection of portraits of the first seven Presidents.[50] On
completion, one set (including Cat. No. 129) was presented by Reed
in December 1835 to the Brooklyn Naval Lyceum, whence on the dis-
establishment of the Lyceum in 1892 it passed to its present owner,

[50] Durand wrote on 10 June 1835: "I have four paintings begun; . . . a third
[is] the head of President John Adams (after Stuart) which is almost done" (John
Durand, *The Life and Times of Asher B. Durand*, N.Y., 1894, p. 109). "I lent Mr.
Durand the Portrait of my father, painted by Stuart in 1799 for him to copy" (JQA,
Diary, 1 June 1835).

84. JOHN ADAMS. OIL BY ASHER B. DURAND, 1835

the United States Naval Academy at Annapolis. The other set (including Fig. 84) Mr. Reed retained for himself to supplement his already famous collection of paintings. But he had not long to enjoy them. In June 1836 he died, greatly lamented, a "man whose equal we never shall see again," as Durand, who had painted many portraits for him, feelingly wrote.[51] His collection was seen some years later by John Quincy Adams, who recounts in his diary going "to the home of the late Mr. Luman Reed whose collection of pictures is still kept by his widow and family. . . . The first seven presidents of the United States are ranged in their order, myself and Jackson painted by Durand, and the rest good copies by him from Stuart." [52] Through the affectionate enthusiasm and generosity of Reed's friends, the collection was acquired for the newly formed New York Gallery of the Fine Arts, and in 1858 passed forever into the hands of The New-York Historical Society. Durand's two copies of Stuart's Adams are of the highest order of merit as copies, preserving all that a strange hand could preserve of Stuart and adding something of Durand himself.

George P. A. Healy, a prolific copier of both his own and others' works, and an artist of skill and imagination (known especially for his gigantic canvas *Webster's Reply to Hayne,* hanging in Faneuil Hall), produced several copies of Stuart's Adams. The first, painted in 1845 at the command of Louis Philippe, now hangs in the Musée de Blérancourt (Fig. 85). Another (Cat. No. 155), executed in 1860, is in The Corcoran Gallery of Art in Washington and has been often reproduced in gravure or by photograph for hanging in the many "Presidents' Rooms" of hotels and clubs. Eliphalet F. Andrews in 1881 copied the Corcoran Healy, reversing the image, and his painting (Fig. 86) now hangs in the main corridor of the Senate Wing of the Capitol Building in Washington.[53]

In the Blue Room of the White House, facing Rembrandt Peale's first portrait of Jefferson, is an excellent copy of the Stuart Adams bearing on its frame the inscription "G. P. A. Healy, 1864." In 1888 this same portrait (Fig. 87) hung in a different frame and was ascribed to Edgar Parker and said to have cost $150.[54] On the back of the canvas is written "J. Adams / From the portrait by Stuart / by Edgar Parker." Healy's granddaughter, however, writing in 1930 of

[51] Durand, *Life and Times of Asher B. Durand,* p. 124.
[52] Entry of 20 Nov. 1840.
[53] Eliphalet F. Andrews to Edward Clark, 21 March 1881 (Records of the Office of the Architect of the Capitol, Washington, D.C.).
[54] De Benneville Randolph Keim, *Illustrated Handbook: Washington and Its Environs,* Washington, 1888, p. 124.

85. JOHN ADAMS. OIL BY G. P. A. HEALY, 1845

86. JOHN ADAMS. OIL BY ELIPHALET F. ANDREWS, 1881

87. JOHN ADAMS. OIL BY G. P. A. HEALY OR EDGAR PARKER

88. JOHN ADAMS. OIL BY JANE STUART, CA. 1874

175

this portrait, said that it "is, I am pretty sure, a copy of the Gilbert Stuart ordered for the White House," [55] meaning that it was by her grandfather.

A copy unquestionably by Edgar Parker (Cat. No. 171), painted about 1874 and belonging to the Bostonian Society, now hangs in the rotunda on the second floor of the Old State House in Boston. It bears a striking resemblance to the copy painted by Stuart's daughter Jane in 1874 (Fig. 88) and could perhaps be a copy of that. Jane's copy, in the Long Room of the Old House in Quincy, was engraved by Otto Parker in 1894 for *Scribner's Magazine* (Cat. No. 170).

A miniature copy (Cat. No. 152), only 4 inches in size and a poor likeness, painted by J. M. R. L. Massard, who is known especially for his many posthumous portraits, was sold in New York at the Erskine Hewitt sale in 1938 for $3.00 and now belongs to the Metropolitan Museum of Art.

G. Stuart Newton, whose youthful effort was responsible for such a large progeny of Adams likenesses, painted a second copy of Stuart's original which, after he went to England, remained in the United States in the hands of his family until 1862, when it was presented to the Massachusetts Historical Society by Newton's brother Edward A. Newton. In his letter of gift Newton wrote:

It is a copy by my brother Mr. G. Stuart Newton, of the original by Mr. Gilbert Stuart.

The coloring, for which both the artists are so highly distinguished, has been well preserved in the copy; and due allowance will be made for any defects in the execution of the work in other respects, when it is understood that it was painted when the copyist was under twenty years of age.

The likeness is an admirable one as all who have seen Mr. Adams will recognize.[56]

A formal resolution accepting the portrait was adopted by the Society welcoming "it to its walls, both as an excellent likeness of an illustrious statesman, and as one of the earliest works of a most accomplished artist." [57] This painting (Fig. 89) now hangs in the Old House in Quincy, on loan from the Historical Society. On comparison with Stuart's original, it does not live up to Newton's claim. It is but a poor copy, perpetuating the peculiarities of Newton's first effort (Fig. 69)

[55] Mme. Marie de Mare to the Frick Art Reference Library, 4 June 1930.
[56] Edward A. Newton to Chandler Robbins, Secretary of the Massachusetts Historical Society, 7 April 1862, printed in MHS, *Procs.*, 6 (1862–1863):3.
[57] Resolution of the Massachusetts Historical Society, 10 April 1862 (same).

89. JOHN ADAMS. OIL ON WOOD PANEL BY GILBERT STUART
NEWTON, CA. 1815

—the pointed face, the pursed lips, the unfinished shirt front, and
the dark shadow behind the ear. This time, however, the shadow is
somewhat shorter than in the earlier copy, and it is this difference
which makes it possible to distinguish which of the two Newtons was
the prototype of the "Adams" now belonging to the New England Historic Genealogical Society (Fig. 90). The latter was painted by Jonathan Mason Jr., the son of the Senator from Massachusetts who had

90. JOHN ADAMS. OIL BY JONATHAN MASON, CA. 1835

been responsible for Stuart's moving to Boston, and was presented to the Society by the artist in 1879. Mason's copy preserves not only Newton's strange facial expression, but also the telltale long shadow behind Adams' left ear, establishing quite clearly that the early New-ton (Fig. 69) served as Mason's model.

XVIII

J. B. Binon

Adams entered his eighty-third year in October 1817. Though an old man he was not forgotten by his fellow citizens. "A resolution has passed the legislature of Massachusetts," *Niles' Weekly Register,* published in Baltimore, reported early in the following year, "requesting John Adams, late president of the United States, to consent that a model of his bust be taken for the purpose of being sculptured in marble, and placed in the public halls of the state house. The bust is to be formed of American marble, if any can be found of suitable quality." [1] The next issue of the *Register* disclosed that "the resolve that passed the house of representatives to procure a marble bust of Mr. Adams, has been indefinitely postponed." [2]

The events referred to had taken place early in February. William Tudor Jr., who had proposed the original resolution, wrote, with some concern, to Adams on 19 February to say that he had had reason to presume upon a certainty of success but that objection has been raised that it was "an improper testimony to a living character." He concluded his letter by saying, "as I trust through the favor of Providence that their objection will long exist, I hope you will meet the wishes of your fellow citizens to place your bust in Faneuil Hall, while the legislative Committee are maturing their plan." [3] With his letter Tudor enclosed a copy of excerpts from a letter he had received from Harrison Gray Otis dated 9 February:

As to the fate of your motion respecting Mr. Adams's bust, I am too full to speak with propriety, and if I don't say something, I shall die of apoplexy. . . . Can there be a doubt that John Adams deserves from Massachusetts not merely a bust of marble but a statue of bronze. . . . Who among us of the present generation has seen the like of the man "take him for all in all". . . . I know of no person in whom so many great and rare qualities are combined, and I truly believe that the remnants of information hoarded in his iron memory, and the embers of his imagination which remain after the fires of fourscore winters, constitute at this moment an intellectual stock of which any man of any age might be justly proud.

[1] 13:436 (21 Feb. 1818).
[2] 14:15 (28 Feb. 1818).
[3] 19 Feb. 1818 (Adams Papers).

Otis' veneration and enthusiasm were catching. A public subscription was quickly set on foot, and, as Abigail Adams reported to her granddaughter, was "soon filled, although no person was allowed to subscribe more than two dollars." [4] A Committee waited on Adams to obtain his consent:

Sir:

In behalf of a numerous body of Citizens of Boston, we request your consent, to set for *a Bust,* in Marble, to be executed by an eminent Artist, now resident in that Town, to be placed in Faneuil-Hall.

In soliciting your assent to this tribute of our high respect and veneration, we are particularly influenced by a desire of transmitting to our Children the Features of the Man, whose patriotic energies were so strenuously exerted for the Independence of our common Country:—and that future Ages, while contemplating the object, may recall the Virtues, Talents and Courage of one of the Founders of the American Republic.

March 16th, 1818

Arnold Welles
Henry Dearborn
William Tudor
William Spooner
Josiah Quincy [5]

There is today attached to this letter (perhaps originally delivered with it) the subscription list, the preamble to which reads:

As an evidence of the Gratitude of the Subscribers for the eminent Public Services of the

Honorable John Adams

late President of the United States, we agree to pay the sums set against our names respectively, for the purpose of procuring by an Artist from Europe now in this Town, an elegant marble Bust of him, to be placed in some suitable situation in Faneuil Hall.

N.B. No subscriptions will be received for more than *Two* Dollars.

Boston   Feby 16th 1818. [6]

There then followed the signatures of 215 subscribers, all of whom subscribed two dollars, some even signing the names of their children and other members of their families in order to be allowed to swell their contributions. All are marked "paid."

Adams replied to the Committee the same day:

[4] To Caroline Amelia (Smith) de Windt, 22 March 1818, printed in AA2, *Jour. and Corr.,* 1:238.
[5] MS in MHi, in folder labeled "John Adams, Bust at Faneuil Hall, 1818."
[6] Same.

J. B. Binon

Gentlemen

As I owe to the town of Boston all the opportunities I ever had of performing any public service, this mark of the benevolence of her Citizens, excites all my sensibility.

At the same time it reminds me of many characters among whom I can have no pretensions to have merited so honourable a distinction.

To you Gentlemen, my thanks are due for the obliging manner in which you have executed the will of your fellow citizens, which shall be obeyed by their, and your obliged friend, John Adams [7]

This exchange was followed in March by a letter from Tudor introducing the artist:

At the Request of General Welles, I write this Letter to introduce Mr. Binon the Artist we yesterday mentioned in the Committee's Address and whose Services you so kindly condescended to encourage, for the Public Purpose of gratifying the Citizens of this Town, and Posterity.

From the Specimens of his Abilities as an Artist of which we have a satisfying Proof in a Bust of General Dearborn, we confide in a successful Obtainment of a much desired Purpose, not lessened by the interesting Interview which took Place yesterday at Quincy. [8]

It was Dearborn to whom Adams graciously replied, through an amanuensis:

I am obliged to borrow a hand to thank you for your favour of March 11th and for introducing to me Mr. Binon whom I find to be a Gentleman of Sense and Letters, as well as Taste and skill in All the fine Arts. He has been an agreable Companion—and we have been fortunate enough to procure the best accommodations for him. Excuse me for I can barely write the name of your Friend and humble Servant, John Adams [9]

Family interest in the project ran high. "He will have an admirable likeness," Abigail wrote to her granddaughter.[10] "Let me know what you think of the Bust," she asked Harriet Welsh.[11] John Quincy Adams' wife wrote from Washington to her fifteen-year-old son John:

You tell me that your Grandfather has been sitting for his *Bust,* and that will prove a good likeness; I am glad to hear it; and it does honour to the Citizens of Boston, who by this handsome voluntary tribute of respect, shame the narrow and mean policy of their Legislature.

In a postscript she added, "Remember the word *Bust* is spelt without an e." [12]

[7] Same.
[8] To JA, March 1818 (Adams Papers).
[9] To Henry Dearborn, 25 March 1818 (LbC, Adams Papers).
[10] To Mrs. de Windt, 22 March 1818, printed in AA2, *Jour. and Corr.,* 1:238.
[11] 7 April 1818 (Adams Papers).
[12] LCA to JA2, 5 April 1818 (Adams Papers).

Dr. Benjamin Waterhouse, who had been a friend of the family since their days in Holland almost forty years since, added his report in a letter to John Quincy Adams:

> This weather and increasing years seem to have affected your father more than I ever before observed. His signature to a note, which he dictated, to General Dearborn, shewed to my eyes that the "quiveration" of his hand was extreme. I cannot but regret that the Sculptor should be employed at this late period of his life. His age ought to be engraven on the pedestal of the bust. Should not a bust, to be placed in so large a room as Faneuil hall, be made much larger than life? [13]

But all proceeded as hoped for, and only a few months later Adams could report to his old friend at Monticello:

> Mr. Binon a French Artist from Lyons who has studied Eight Years in Italy has lately taken my Bust. He appears to be an Artist and a Man of Letters. I let them do what they please with my old head.[14]

What they did with the old head we can judge for ourselves by studying Binon's bust (Fig. 91). The shattering of the nose is distracting, but if we overlook the fracture, the representation is truly impressive. What looks out on us is an old man, over fourscore years in age, bald and toothless, but with, what is still evident, more than a remnant of the character and force that made up that impetuous, stubborn, pugnacious, courageous patriot.

Two contemporary artistic judgments of Binon's skill are preserved, though they relate to his busts of Washington. An 1818 entry in John Quincy Adams' diary tells of his visit with William Smith Shaw to Binon in Boston:

> I went with Shaw to Binon's workshop. Binon is the French Sculptor who made the marble bust of my father which is in Faneuil Hall. He is now at work upon a Bust of Washington of the same size. The original from which he works, is a cast from the Bust of Houdon, taken from the life; incomparably the best likeness ever taken of Washington, and an ad-

---

[13] 13 April 1818 (Adams Papers). "Quiveration" was not a new complaint. Seven years earlier Adams had written to Benjamin Rush: "My hearing for any thing that I perceive or my Friends have remarked to me, is as good as ever. So much for the bright side: On the other I have a 'Quiveration.' What in the Name of the Medical Dictionary, you will say, is a 'Quiveration?' A wild Irish Boy who lives with my son TBA, let a horse run away with a chaise. One of the Family ran out and cried out Nat! why did you not scream and call for help. Sir! Sir! said Nat, I was seized with such a *Quiveration* that I could not speak. Nat's Quiveration is the best word I know to express my Palsy" (JA to Benjamin Rush, 21 June 1811, LbC, Adams Papers; printed in Biddle, *Old Family Letters*, p. 285).

[14] JA to Thomas Jefferson, 29 May 1818 (DLC: Jefferson Papers, printed in Cappon, ed., *Adams-Jefferson Letters*, 2:526).

91. JOHN ADAMS. MARBLE BUST BY J. B. BINON, 1818

mirable work of art. Mr. Binon is spoiling his work, by departing from his original. He was not at his shop, having been confined these three weeks with an ague or abscess in the jaw. Shaw sent for him however, and he came. I shewed him where and how his likeness was defective, solely from his having varied from his original; he promised to return to it with all possible exactness.[15]

To have put up with such advice, Binon must have shared Job's virtue!

The following contribution appears in the *Columbian Centinel* of about the same date:

He [Binon] has made the model of the bust of the immortal Washington from the original portrait of him by Mr. Stuart, aided by the condescending instructions of this great master, whose "mind's eye" still beholds the countenance which his immortal pencil has saved from the grave to transmit to posterity. Mr. Binon appears to have caught a share of the Promethean fire in his attempt, and we venture to predict that he will obtain sufficient encouragement to execute the bust in marble of George Washington to be placed in Faneuil Hall.

Mr. Binon was a pupil of the celebrated Chinard, and has hitherto done great honour to his instructor. One of the first proofs of his genius is to be seen in the statue, fifteen feet in height, of the Carabinier, in the Place de Carrousel in Paris. Since his arrival in this town he has completed the marble busts of Mr. Adams and of General Dearborn, and is now giving the last touches to the one of General Humphreys destined for Yale College.[16]

Binon's bust of Adams still stands in Faneuil Hall, in the Speaker's hall, under Healy's expansive canvas depicting *Webster's Reply to Hayne,* and across the platform from John Crookshank King's bust of John Quincy Adams. On the base, under the elder Adams' left shoulder, is incised the inscription: "Binon. Boston 1818." In profile the likeness is surprisingly familiar and compares closely with the earlier profiles. In full face it most resembles Morse's "stern unpleasing likeness" though with less apparent acidity.

The artist himself was well pleased with his work and proceeded to reproduce it in plaster, as the following letter attests:

J'ai l'honneur de vous annoncer que je viens de faire mouler votre buste; le premier exemplaire vous est destiné, le Second à l'honnorable y'hon Quincy Adams, votre fils et le troisième à l'Athéneum.

Comme plusieurs personnes m'ont témoignés le desirs d'en avoir, avant de le rendre public, je crois de mon devoir de vous demander si vous n'y trouvez aucun inconvénient, ainsi je n'en délivrerai aucun autre avant que

---

[15] Entry of 22 Sept. 1818.
[16] Quoted in William T. Whitley, *Gilbert Stuart,* Cambridge, 1932, p. 162–163.

vous ne m'ayez autorisé à le faire; Veuillez je vous supplie derober quelques instants à vos occupations et me transmettre votre intention à ce Sujet.[17]

Consistently derogatory of likenesses of himself, Adams replied in a friendly if not complimentary tone:

I have received your polite favour of the 3d of this month. I am afraid that you are engaged in speculations that will never be profitable to you. The age of sculpture and painting have not yet arrived in this country and I hope it will not arrive very soon. Artists have done what they pleased with my face and eyes, head and shoulders, stature and figure and they have made of them monsters as fit for exhibition as Harlequin or Punch. They may continue to do so as long as they please. I would not give sixpence for a Picture of Raphael or a Statue of Phidias. I am confident that you will not find purchasers for your bust and therefore I am sorry that you are engaged in so hopeless a speculation, because I believe you to be a great artist and an amiable man.[18]

Despite such uncomplimentary remarks, Adams thought well of Binon and gave him a letter of recommendation in 1821 in which he characterized him as "very much of a gentleman, and a Manly, candid and generous Man . . . eminent in the fine Arts—especially in sculpter and statuary which are his professional occupations," adding that he had "given universal satisfaction." [19]

The plaster reproductions were made, in the face of Adams' warning to the contrary, and are somewhat more pleasing in appearance than the marble, though lacking any spark of Promethean fire. Figure 92 shows the copy presented by Binon to the Boston Athenæum on 18 March 1819. The two given to John Adams and his son are now in the Old House in Quincy, and in Adams House, Harvard, respectively. A fourth belonged for some time to the Peabody Museum of Salem and is now owned by Lyman H. Butterfield of Cambridge; a fifth belongs to the author.

Still another copy was given to Thomas Jefferson in 1825, the gift being preceded by a letter from Benjamin A. Gould:

Sir:

I have sent by the Schooner Virginia, Capt. Otis, a Box containing a plaister Bust of Mr. Adams, which I beg you will do me the favour to accept. It is taken from the marble bust of Binon, which was made for the City of Boston and is placed in Faneuil Hall. The likeness is considered most striking. No one can hesitate an instant in recognizing it, who has

[17] J. B. Binon to JA, 3 Feb. 1819 (Adams Papers).
[18] JA to J. B. Binon, 7 Feb. 1819 (MBBS:Colburn Coll., on deposit in MHi; LbC, Adams Papers).
[19] JA: "To all who may see this letter," 11 Oct. 1821 (LbC, Adams Papers).

92. JOHN ADAMS. PLASTER BUST BY J. B. BINON, 1819

seen the original within ten years. The Box is directed to Col. Bernard Peyton, Richmond, for you. I hope it will reach you safely.[20]

Jefferson acknowledged the gift with appreciation:

I am much indebted to you, Sir, for your present of the bust of my friend Mr. Adams. Without knowing exactly the precise period at which it was taken, I think it a good likeness of what he was a little after he had past the middle years of life. It received a little injury by fracture, but the parts are preserved, and being in the back part, can be repaired without disfiguring it. I place it with pleasure in the line in my cabinet of his predecessor and successors.[21]

These remarks are significant when we reflect that the bust was taken and Jefferson's letter written more than eighteen years since he had last laid eyes on Adams. The flame that had guided these two patriots through the early days of their republic yet burned, and still kept alight in Jefferson's "mind's eye" the image of his old friend, though now long past the middle years of life.

Jefferson's copy of the bust has long since disappeared; it is no longer at Monticello, though a modern copy fills its place. In 1875 the Athenæum gave permission to John T. Gibson to have casts made from its bust of John Adams, but whether Gibson ever took advantage of the opportunity we do not know. Henry B. McLellan, recounting a visit to Lafayette at La Grange in July 1833, described the scene on entering the great hall: "On this side you see busts of Adams and Jackson . . . portraits of Washington and Franklin."[22] Possibly this bust of Adams was a seventh plaster copy of Binon's marble, but it is no longer at La Grange. A chalk copy of Binon's marble was made in the summer of 1818 by his pupil, Horatio Greenough, but it, too, is lost.[23]

Glimpses of the early history of one of the Binon plaster busts are furnished in two entries in the "Waste Book" of Peter Chardon Brooks,[24] the Boston insurance magnate whose daughter Abigail later married Charles Francis Adams. Under date of 1 May 1819 Brooks recorded the purchase for $10 of "a Bust of Hon. John Adams in Plaster by Binon." On 10 July 1827 he recorded its sale, at no great appreciation, as follows: "3 images, casts, Flora, Ceres & Presidt. Adams sold to Sam May . . . $20."

[20] Gould to Jefferson, 14 July 1825 (DLC: Jefferson Papers).
[21] Jefferson to Gould, 5 Aug. 1825 (FC, DLC: Jefferson Papers).
[22] Henry B. McLellan, *Journal of a Residence in Scotland,* Boston, 1834, p. 261.
[23] Nathalia Wright, *Horatio Greenough: The First American Sculptor,* Phila., 1963, p. 22.
[24] MS in MHi.

XIX

The Last Stuarts

A happy combination of filial affection with a sense of history and the value of portraits as historical documents, prompted Secretary of State John Quincy Adams, when at home in Quincy in 1823 for the first time in two years, to engage Stuart to paint the aged former President once more. It had been a quarter of a century since Adams had first sat to Stuart.

"I then called with Mr. Cruft upon Stewart the Painter," Secretary Adams wrote, "and engaged him to go out to Quincy and there paint a Portrait of my father. More than twenty years have passed since he painted the former portrait, and time has wrought so much of change on his countenance that I wish to possess a likeness of him as he now is. Stewart started some objections of trivial difficulties—The want of an Easel, of a room properly adapted to the light; but finally promised that he would go, and take with him his best brush, to paint a picture of Affection, and of curiosity for future times," a picture "that should be admired as long as the materials would hold together." [1]

This time Stuart lived up to his engagement and, if possible, surpassed himself. When he began, or how many sittings Adams gave him, we don't know. William Winston Seaton, visiting Boston with his wife in the autumn of 1823, drove out to Quincy to see Adams. Seaton, co-editor of the *National Intelligencer* of Washington and a strong supporter of John Quincy Adams, found Adams, he recalled, "sitting to the famous Stuart for his portrait, to be completed on his eighty-ninth birthday [30 October 1824]. His son led me to him and said a few words aside, when I was quite affected by his rising from the sofa and, affectionately kissing my cheek, bidding me welcome to Quincy." [2] On 9 September 1824, young Charles Francis Adams, at home in Quincy reading the newspaper and studying the Presidential election, was interrupted by a visit from Mrs. Thomas L. Winthrop and others who came in to look at Stuart's portrait of his grandfather.[3] By then it must have been nearly completed. Only two weeks later the young Adams wrote in his diary: "Mr. Stuart the painter came out here this morn-

[1] JQA, Diary, 3, 11 Sept. 1823, printed in JQA, *Memoirs*, 6:175–176, 177.
[2] William T. Whitley, *Gilbert Stuart*, Cambridge, 1932, p. 172–173.
[3] CFA, *Diary*, 1:318.

188

ing for a final sitting for my Grandfather. I saw the portrait which is a remarkably fine one." He added, "Stuart is a singular man, a wag, but rather a disgusting object than otherwise. He is said to be habitually intemperate and his appearance confirms it." [4] Anson Dickinson's miniature of Stuart, painted in 1825 and now owned by The New-York Historical Society, bears out this view.

Adams had found it tiring to sit to most artists, and he had had a wealth of experience in that respect, but he now felt differently with Stuart. "I should like to sit to Stuart," he told young Josiah Quincy, "from the first of January to the last of December, for he lets me do just what I please and keeps me constantly amused by his conversation." [5]

The portrait (Fig. 93) presumably was finished in time for Adams' eighty-ninth birthday. The last portrait of Adams, it stands today as a monument to the longevity and high quality of Stuart's skill. Dr. Benjamin Waterhouse recognized the abiding presence of genius in the artist. "The child Gilbert betrayed very early signs of genius, and the only reason for doubting it is the fact that his talents continued bright over three score years and ten: witness his portrait of the venerable President Adams and that of his son John Quincy Adams . . . in both of which Mr. Stuart far exceeded any other of his portraits. Van Dyck himself might have been proud of either, especially that of the elder Adams." [6]

Josiah Quincy, who saw the portrait, almost *in limine*, remembered that "Stuart caught a glimpse of the living spirit shining through the feeble and decrepit body. He saw the old man at one of those happy moments when the intelligence lights up its wasted envelope, and what he saw he fixed upon his canvas." [7] Except for Stuart's own waggish comment on the portrait,[8] all who have seen it have been enthusiastic in their praise and admiration. "It is the privilege of genius alone," wrote Mason in his life of Stuart, "to measure at once the highest and the lowest. In his happiest efforts, no one ever surpassed him in embodying (if we may so speak) those transient apparitions of the soul. Of this not the least admirable instance is his portrait . . . of the late President Adams, whose then bodily tenement seemed rather to pre-

---

[4] Same, p. 331 (22 Sept. 1824).
[5] Quincy, *Figures of the Past*, p. 71.
[6] Dunlap, *Arts of Design*, ed. Bayley and Goodspeed, 1:196.
[7] Quincy, *Figures of the Past*, p. 71.
[8] Showing the finished portrait to a friend, Stuart is reported (probably apocryphally) to have said: "Look at him. It is very like him, is it not? Do you know what he is going to do? He is just going to sneeze" (James Thomas Flexner, *Gilbert Stuart, A Great Life in Brief*, N.Y., 1955, p. 189).

93. JOHN ADAMS. OIL BY GILBERT STUART, 1823

190

sent the image of some dilapidated castle than that of the habitation of the unbroken mind; but not such this picture; called forth, as from its crumbling recesses, the living tenant is there,—still ennobling the ruin and upholding it, as it were, by the thought of his own life. In this venerable ruin will the unbending patriot and the gifted artist speak to posterity of the first glorious century of our Republic." [9]

Not long after the tragic death of his son George in 1829, John Quincy Adams, recognizing that the family tradition and genius were to pass to Charles Francis Adams, presented him with three family portraits. The young man, about to be married, records the gift in his diary with evident pleasure. "Morning to town, Conversation with my father upon his property. Many very heavy calls upon it just at present. Then upon my Marriage. He made me a present this morning of three portraits. One of my Grandfather painted by Stuart and exceedingly valuable, and those of my father and Mother by the same artist but not so good. I was surprised and pleased. They are now in the possession of Mr. Cruft and I must attend to their being shortly transferred." [10] Charles went next day to claim the pictures, but Cruft was away from home. Failing to find him the following day also, he left with Mrs. Cruft a letter of instructions for their delivery. The following week he notes, "But I accomplished my purpose of having the pictures hung which belong to me. They now form quite a goodly collection. That of my Grandfather is invaluable both as a Painting and as a correct likeness of what he was in those times." [11] Although we scarcely need it, the comment on Stuart's having obtained a "correct likeness" is not only contemporary with the portrait, but comes from one who had spent much time with Adams during his last years and was in a position to know what was a likeness of the man.

The painting has been handed down through the generations as one of the most valued Adams possessions and now belongs to Charles Francis Adams of Dover, Massachusetts. At the George Washington Bicentennial Historical Loan Exhibition held in The Corcoran Gallery of Art in 1932, it was one of the great historical documents.

That this painting should have been many times reproduced is to have been expected, but it is worthy of note how soon the process was commenced. John Quincy Adams himself, only a few months after his father's death, commissioned Stuart for the purpose. The first notice

[9] George Champlin Mason, *Life and Work of Gilbert Stuart*, N.Y., 1894, p. 33.
[10] 2:426 (27 Aug. 1829).
[11] Same, p. 429 (31 Aug. 1829).

of this replica (Fig. 94) which has come to light is John Quincy Adams' letter from Washington to his son George, late in 1826: "You have mentioned . . . that Mr. Stewart had finished the Portrait of your Mother, and the copy of that of my father: Whereupon I wish you to receive them immediately from him, and to pay him for them. Take care also to obtain the *original* of my fathers Portrait, which if Mr. Cruft is willing may again be suspended in his parlour. . . . And send the copy of my father's Portrait, packed in the manner that Mr. Stewart shall direct, by a Coasting vessel, as occasion may offer to this place."[12]

The replica exhibits minor variations from the original; Lawrence Park noticed the difference in the curve of the back of the sofa,[13] and some have referred to the replica as the portrait of the "unfinished hand," yet it compares favorably with the original. At his death John Quincy Adams bequeathed the replica to his granddaughter Mary Louisa Adams, who later married her cousin William Clarkson Johnson. It descended to Mary Louisa Adams Clement and at her death in 1950 passed under the terms of her will to the Smithsonian Institution with many other Adams portraits and memorabilia, together forming the Adams-Clement Collection.

Less than a year after the elder Adams' death, Charles Bird King painted a copy (Fig. 95) which met with John Quincy Adams' approval. "I called at C. B. King's the Painter's," he notes, "and saw the Portrait he is painting of my Son Charles, which was much improved since I saw it last Sunday.—He has also made a very good copy of Stewart's last Portrait of my father which he borrowed."[14] King, born in 1785, a native of Rhode Island, is perhaps best known for his series of portraits of Indian Chiefs painted in the 1820's and 1830's. He was a distinguished portrait painter and, following the custom of the day, painted copies of many well-known portraits by other artists. In his youth he studied under Edward Savage in New York, and later under Charles Robert Leslie and Washington Allston in London. Although he established his studio in Washington in 1822, he frequently spent the summer in Newport, Rhode Island, where he became one of the patrons and benefactors of the Redwood Library, contributing not only money but books, prints, and paintings. Today some forty-three of his portraits hang in the Library. By his will, King gave the library the right of selecting portraits from his estate, and George Champlin Ma-

---

[12] 19 Nov. 1826 (Adams Papers).
[13] Park, *Gilbert Stuart,* 1:92.
[14] Diary, 22 April 1827.

94. JOHN ADAMS. OIL BY GILBERT STUART, 1826

95. JOHN ADAMS. OIL BY CHARLES BIRD KING, 1827

son, the annalist of Redwood, charged with the choice, selected, among others, King's copy of Adams (Fig. 95).[15]

Although King's copy is usually thought of as a copy of Stuart's original (Fig. 93), it is in fact copied from the replica (Fig. 94) which, as John Quincy Adams notes, King had borrowed for the purpose. And he must have borrowed it soon after its arrival in Washington. In late November 1826 young George Adams was instructed to send the replica to Washington, and by April 1827 King had finished his copy. Careful comparison of the three paintings will reveal that King's model must have been the replica: note, for example, the curves of the back and arm of the sofa.

Four other copies in oil show what can be expected from a copyist: those by Healy (Fig. 96); by Jane Stuart (Fig. 97); by John Cranch (Fig. 98); and by Henry Inman (Fig. 99). It is not known for certain just when each was painted or whether the artists had access to the original Stuart or only to the replica, but by comparing each of the four with the original and the replica we can form some opinion. Healy's copy, owned by the Chicago Historical Society, is believed to have been painted about 1855, not long after Healy at the request of Louis Philippe painted John Quincy Adams and a diminutive copy of Stuart's earlier John Adams. Access to the earlier painting would undoubtedly have afforded him an opportunity also to copy the later one. The similarity in detail between the two paintings confirms this view. Note the position of the fingers of Adams' right hand and the shape of the arm of the sofa.

Jane Stuart's copy, now in the Old House in Quincy, was painted probably about 1850, toward the end of her artistic career. She, too, had copied the earlier Stuart of Adams, and her two copies will support her reputation as a faithful copyist of her father's works. Not only does her copy of the last Stuart follow the treatment of Adams' fingers and the sofa arm but it also repeats in exact detail the folds of the ruffled shirt front.

A close look at Cranch's and Inman's copies, on the other hand, indicates that they must have been made from the replica. Both betray the telltale deeply curved sofa back and broad curved arm and the same fingers. Cranch's copy (Fig. 98) belonged many years since to Henry Ware Eliot, by whose widow it was presented to Washington University, St. Louis; but it is now unlocated. Cranch, a descendant of Abigail Adams' sister Mary Cranch, painted a life portrait of John

---

[15] George C. Mason, *Annals of the Redwood Library and Athenaeum*, Newport, R.I., 1891, p. 233.

96. JOHN ADAMS. OIL BY G. P. A. HEALY, 1860

97. JOHN ADAMS. OIL, PERHAPS BY JANE STUART

98. JOHN ADAMS. OIL BY JOHN CRANCH

99. JOHN ADAMS. OIL BY HENRY INMAN

100. JOHN ADAMS. ENGRAVING BY THOMAS GIMBREDE, 1831

Quincy Adams in 1843 and several posthumous ones eight years later which perhaps give a clue to the date of this one. Inman's copy (Fig. 99) is part of the Lynton-Surget Collection at Tulane University, having been acquired in June 1889 by gift of Mrs. C. B. Sarget (or Surget) of Bordeaux, France. Little is known of it except that it had been painted for her father. It fails of a likeness but there can be little doubt that it follows the replica or perhaps one of the other copies of the replica.

Although the Catalogue includes several engravings of Stuart's last Adams, most of them of little merit, only one received any notice from the family. John Quincy Adams' diary entry for 4 October 1831 mentions one:

My nephew [Thomas Boylston Adams Jr.] the Lieutenant was here, and took with him Gimbrede's drawing from Stewart's last Portrait of my father. That Portrait was painted at my special desire, about two years before

200

my father's decease and when he was in his ninetieth year. My purpose was
to have a likeness of him in his last days by the first Painter in this Country. It has been a source of much gratification to me that this was effected.
The picture is an excellent likeness and one of the best that Stewart ever
painted. After my father's death I had a copy of it painted by Stewart himself which is at Washington. Charles has the Original in his house at Boston.

At the time John Quincy Adams was living in Washington, and there
can be little doubt that Gimbrede's drawing and engraving followed
the replica which was at that time in Washington. Like the painted
copies of the replica, Gimbrede's engraving (Fig. 100) exhibits the
same characteristics—the deep curve of the sofa back, the shape of the
arm, and the folds of the shirt front. Gimbrede, then instructor of
drawing at the Military Academy at West Point, had not long since
made a fine engraving of Stuart's portrait of John Quincy Adams and
would have been welcomed for the purpose of trying his art on the
elder Adams. Though it is a finer engraving than the others listed, it
is an unsatisfactory, unpleasant likeness.

XX

John Henri Isaac Browere

The last portrait taken of Adams was to be more than a likeness; it was to be a facsimile, made by the sculptor and painter John Henri Isaac Browere by a secret process of his own invention which, though handed down to the next generation, died with it. Browere was born in New York City in 1790 and spent most of his life there. He studied with Archibald Robertson and, like so many of his era, spent some years studying in Europe. During the last decade of his life, he traveled about the country taking life masks of distinguished Americans and building up his own National Gallery. It was from his bust of Lafayette that he received the nod of fortune, and with that example at hand was enabled to take life masks of all he approached.

His process is eloquently, if not technically, described by Jefferson, who submitted to it only a few weeks after Madison and his wife had been cast. "I was taken in by Brower," Jefferson wrote soon afterward:

He said his operation would be of about 20 minutes and less unpleasant than Houdon's method. I submitted therefore without enquiry but it was a bold experiment on his part on the health of an Octogenary, worn down by sickness as well as age. Successive coats of thin grout plaistered on the naked head, and kept there an hour, would have been a severe trial of a young and hale person. He suffered the plaister also to get so dry that separation became difficult and even dangerous. He was obliged to use freely the mallet and chisel to break it into pieces and get off a piece at a time. These thumps of the mallet would have been sensible almost to a loggerhead. The family became alarmed, and he confused till I was quite exhausted and there became real danger that the ears would separate from the head sooner than from the plaister. I now bid adieu forever to busts and even portraits.[1]

Yet, despite Jefferson's discomfort, the finished bust itself was found by S. F. B. Morse to be a "perfect facsimile." [2]

Less than two weeks after his experience with Jefferson, Browere, nothing daunted, approached President John Quincy Adams to add his head to his collection. In Washington he took Adams and his son

[1] To James Madison, 18 Oct. 1825 (DLC). This famous letter has often been printed and occasionally facsimiled.
[2] Bush, *Life Portraits of Jefferson*, 1962, p. 96.

Charles, the latter finding the "Operation of making a bust from the head, disagreeable."[3] Late in November he journeyed to Quincy and there with some difficulty persuaded the former President to submit to his process, fortunately completing the task with none of the pain and fright suffered by Jefferson. As proof of that fact, on 23 November Adams signed a statement certifying, "that John H. I. Browere, Esq. of the City of New York has yesterday and today made two portrait bust moulds on my person and made a cast of the first which has been approved of by my family." As a further precaution Browere persuaded Adams' son Judge T. B. Adams to add to the certificate: "P.S. I am authorized by the ex-President to say that the moulds were made on his person without injury, pain or inconvenience."[4]

A glimpse of Adams as he appeared only a few months before this event is preserved in a letter from Dr. Waterhouse to John Quincy Adams:

I found your Father better, much better than when I saw him last Novr. Indeed, I then, tacitly, took, as I thought my final leave of him. I thought it next to impossible that he should ever recover strength enough to sit upright and converse freely and easily. But physicians do not always consider how much the powers of the mind, and what is called good spirits can recover the lost energies of the body. I really believe that your Father's revival is mainly owing to the demonstration that his Son had not served an ungrateful public. He can raise himself up from a supine posture in bed, relate anecdotes, and laugh heartily, and what is more, eats heartily, more than any other at table. We staid until he smoked out his cigar after dinner.[5]

Browere's secret process required several steps. First the making of the plaster impression or mold of grout applied directly to the "naked head." From the mold was made the cast mentioned by Adams in his certificate and illustrated here (Fig. 101). The bust (Fig. 102) would have been completed some time later—a veritable facsimile of the old patriot in his ninety-first year. Whether Browere's process be an art or purely mechanical, whether it be considered inartistic because lacking the imaginative conception of the artist or sculptor, we can almost echo Hart's opinion that it produced an historical human document that "outweighs all the portraits ever limned or modelled."

Today Browere's gallery of life masks is recognized as a great treasure. Yet he himself was subject to great disappointment. He spent

[3] CFA, *Diary*, 2:12 (17 Oct. 1825).
[4] Charles Henry Hart, "Unknown Life Masks of Great Americans," *McClure's Magazine*, 9:1059 (Oct. 1897).
[5] 4 July 1825 (Adams Papers).

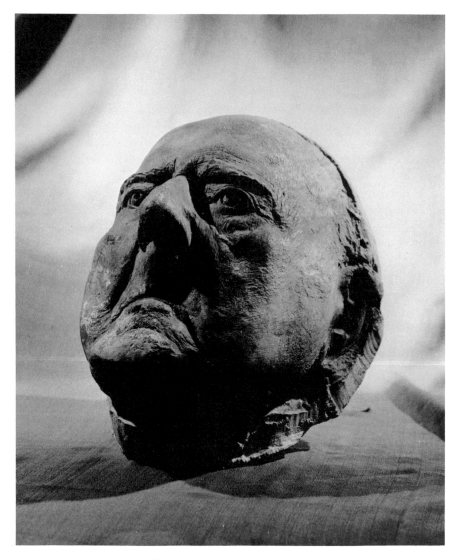

101. JOHN ADAMS. PLASTER LIFE MASK
BY JOHN H. I. BROWERE, 1825

102. JOHN ADAMS. PLASTER BUST BY JOHN H. I. BROWERE, 1825

$12,087 in collecting his specimens, but he had constant fear of being plagiarized. "I have been hindered from completing the gallery," he wrote, "fearful of having the collection pirated." [6] He was not only attacked by his brother artists but was kept out of the American Academy. Trumbull criticized his manner of executing his work, considering it but a process, not an art. He in retaliation turned on Trumbull: "Remember what was said on the floor of Congress in reference to your four celebrated pictures: 'Instead of being worth $32,000 they were not worth 32 cents.' In remembering this remember that 'nemo me impune lacessit.' And by attending to your own concerns you will retain a reputation or name of being an able artist and not a slanderer." On receipt of this outburst, Trumbull endorsed the letter, "Browere. Poor man! too much vanity hath made him mad." [7] But shortly afterward they healed the breach.

Not having received the recognition he thought his busts entitled him to, Browere on his deathbed, and about to be separated from his wife and eight children, instructed his family to detach the heads of the principal busts, box them up, and lay them away for forty years. By good fortune only the latter part of his instructions was followed. They were brought to light for a brief moment on the occasion of the Centennial celebration, when Browere's grandson Albertus Browere tried unsuccessfully to sell them, and again in 1897 by Hart. With his genuine interest in historical portraits, and fired by his trading instinct, Hart tried to persuade the United States Government to purchase the entire collection. But the Government was consistent; just as it had parsimoniously rejected the opportunity to acquire Stuart's five American Kings many years before, so it passed up the chance to acquire this, the greatest single collection of likenesses of great Americans. For a third time they went back into limbo. Forty years later they came to light again, and on this occasion the larger part of them was purchased by the late Stephen C. Clark, and then duplicated in bronze. The excellence of the bronze reproductions is apparent from a glance at that of Adams (Fig. 103). First placed on permanent loan to the New York State Historical Association at Cooperstown, the collection, both plaster and bronze, at Mr. Clark's death in 1940, was bequeathed to the Historical Association with the stipulation that neither the originals nor their replicas should ever leave Cooperstown. With the fifteen busts Mr. Clark purchased, he acquired

[6] Charles Henry Hart, *Browere's Life Masks of Great Americans*, N.Y., 1899, p. 18.
[7] Same, p. 20.

103. JOHN ADAMS. BRONZE BUST MADE FROM BROWERE
PLASTER BUST, 1938

a typewritten biography of Browere written by Everett Lee Millard, Browere's great-grandson. From this account it appears that seven of the original series, including the bust of young Charles Francis Adams, were bought by Fowler and Wells, the phrenologists, and have disappeared from sight. What a find to uncover that group: C. F. Adams, Dr. Valentine Mott, Fannie Wright, Dr. Samuel Latham Mitchill, Richard Rush, Philip Barbour, and Samuel Southard!

XXI

Paralipomena

Miniatures

Although the record is conflicting, there is little doubt that one or more miniatures were taken of Adams. In 1809 he himself denied it. "I have no Miniature," he wrote, "and have been too much abused by Painters ever to sit to any one again."[1] By this time he was seventy-four years old and had sat so often to artists that it would not be surprising if he had forgotten two or three instances. Abigail mentioned one example in 1780:

> I have a request to you which I hope you will not dissapoint me of, a minature of Him I best Love. Indulge me the pleasing melancholy of contemplating a likeness. The attempt here faild, and was more the resemblance of a cloisterd Monk, than the Smileing Image of my Friend. I could not endure the sight of it.—By Sampson will be a Good opportunity, should he be taken none but a Savage would rob a Lady, of what could be of no value, but to her. Let him put it into his chest, and it will come safe I dare say. Let it be set, it will be better done with you than here.[2]

The "attempt" has not come to light, although her husband apparently complied with her request. The following year, still bravely holding the family together in Quincy after John's absence of three long years, Abigail wrote in her loneliness, "Do you look like the Miniature you sent? I cannot think so. But you have a better likeness I am told. Is that designd for me? Gracious Heaven restore to me the original and I care not who has the shadow."[3] The whereabouts of this miniature is also unknown, nor can we tell what is the "better likeness" to which Abigail referred, unless it is that by Vinkeles (Fig. 5), or possibly the presently unknown original from which the printed textile likeness (Fig. 105) was derived.

There is, however, one miniature, said (though without any known

---

[1] To Skelton Jones, 11 March 1809 (LbC, Adams Papers, printed in JA's *Works*, 9:613).

[2] To JA, 24 July 1780 (Adams Papers).

[3] To JA, 25 Oct. 1782 (Adams Papers).

104. JOHN ADAMS(?). MINIATURE IN OIL, POSSIBLY
BY JOHN SINGLETON COPLEY

supporting evidence) to be of Adams, which has made a brief appearance and then dropped from sight. In the Frick Art Reference Library
is a photograph of a tiny locket-size painting of a young lad (Fig.
104), framed in the back of which was said to have been a lock of
Adams' hair twisted into a golden rope forming the word "Copley." We
could wish the lock had formed the word "Adams." At the time it was
last examined it was thought to have been painted about 1753; it
couldn't have been later and show Adams so young in appearance, and
it couldn't have been earlier and still have been painted by Copley.
There appears to be no proof of the date. In 1753 Adams was a junior
at Harvard College. Copley, aged sixteen, was then living in Boston
with his mother and half-brother Henry Pelham in what is now (or
was but a while since) known as Scollay Square, having already embarked on his career as an artist. It is difficult to imagine how the
youthful artist would have been drawn to paint the young Harvard
junior, but it is not impossible. It might be possible to form a more acceptable judgment of the picture if ever the original should come to
light.

The Roman Catholic Priest

In 1813 when Joseph Delaplaine, the Philadelphia bookseller, was
at work on his *Repository,* he had written to Adams to inquire if there

were an approved likeness of him that might be engraved for his forth-coming volume. Adams replied from Quincy:

> There are several things abroad which are reported to have been in-tended as pictures of me, some of them drawn by persons who never saw me, others by persons to whom I never sat . . . and others by painters who requested me to sit.
>
> I pretend not to be a judge of the merit of any of them. But there is not an approved likeness among them. The least approved of all is one that was taken by a Roman Catholic Priest who was preaching to me while I was sitting mute before him, on transubstantiation and the incarnation of God. This he had engraved and as Mr. Stewart informed me, sold two and twenty thousand of them at a dollar a piece.[4]

The conversation with Stuart might very likely have taken place in 1798 when Adams was sitting to Stuart for the first time. This would help date the likeness referred to (Cat. No. 200), and it could be expected that if 22,000 were sold, one would have turned up for identification. Yet no record has come to light that any of the artists who painted Adams, whether before or after 1798, was a Roman Catholic priest, though Saint-Mémin was a Roman Catholic and Wil-liam J. Williams became one long after painting Adams. The only like-nesses of Adams dating before 1813 by unknown artists are the so-called Jenings portrait, known only through the engraving that appeared in the *European Magazine* of August 1783 (Fig. 7), and the original engraving or painting from which the early textile prints were taken (Fig. 105). No other candidate suggests itself.

Giuseppe Ceracchi

The tale of the frustrated and unhappy life of the Italian sculptor Ceracchi has been well told by Ulysse Desportes[5] and needs only to be outlined here. With a reputation as an able sculptor already estab-lished in Europe, Ceracchi arrived in Philadelphia at some time be-tween October 1790 and March 1791, to try to bring to fruition his dream to have the Congress commission him to execute on a grand, heroic scale a "Monument Designed to Perpetuate the Memory of American Liberty." As proof of his ability and to further his course by flattery, he set about to model, in terra-cotta, some thirty-six busts of

[4] 8 June 1813 (LbC, Adams Papers).
[5] "Giuseppe Ceracchi in America and his Busts of George Washington," *The Art Quarterly,* 26:141–178 (Summer 1963); and "Ceracchi's Medallic Portrait of James Madison," *The Princeton Univ. Libr. Chronicle,* 24:108–120 (Winter 1963).

prominent Americans, including Washington, Adams, Jefferson, Madison, Hamilton, and Rittenhouse. These he sent to Italy when he returned the following year and in due course carved marble busts or alabaster medallions from at least six of them. Returning to America in 1794, he made gifts of his works to Washington, Jefferson, Adams, and other men of prominence and influence. When the Congress failed, however, to accept and finance his design for the monument, his "donations" changed their complexion, and he drew in large amounts on those who thought they had been favored by his generosity. Failing payment in most cases, disillusioned and hard up, he at last returned to Europe in June 1795, and, after a stormy artistic and political career there, lost his head in Paris by the guillotine on 31 January 1801.

Ceracchi's several busts of Washington and his medallion of Madison are well known and have been illustrated in *The Art Quarterly*.[6] They are executed with such a striking degree of excellence as to make us regret the more the loss of all trace of the bust and medallion of Adams. All that is known of the medallion, presumably comparable to that of Madison, is what follows. Late in 1794 the sculptor wrote to Adams:

Mr. Ceracchi's respectfull compliments to the Wiss President, and takes the Liberty to beg him to present the annexed Medal to Mrs. Adams, he hopes that this Respectable Lady in honor him with her acceptance, will tink it as a very small degree of the high estime that he intertanes for the Sobjet roppresented in the Medal, as well as for his family.[7]

To this note Adams replied with characteristic modesty:

The Vice-president of the United States presents his compliments to Mr. Ceracchi: he has received and will transmit to Mrs. Adams a medallion in marble in an elegant gilded frame. While he admires the durability of the material and the delicacy of the art, he regrets that they do not immortalize some other head more worthy of being transmitted to posterity.

Philad. Dec. 2, 1794 [8]

The medallion "as brittle as it is elegant" was sent to Abigail by Adams who declared the likeness was "as grave, as sad, as anxious, as severe as the marble is hard, and the work fine." [9] She in turn thought

[6] In the first of Desportes' articles cited in the preceding note.
[7] 25 Nov. 1794 (Adams Papers).
[8] 2 Dec. 1794 (printed in A. G. Montanari, *Della vita e delle Opere di Giuseppe Ceracchi*, Rimini, 1841, p. 41; translation supplied to the editors of the Adams Papers by Ulysse Desportes, 1959).
[9] To AA, 25 Dec. 1794, 2 Dec. 1794 (Adams Papers).

it would be more suitable to send it to the American Academy of Arts and Sciences; that to keep it would suggest vanity. She was also undoubtedly suspicious of Ceracchi's motives. In February 1795 she herself wrote to him:

> Will you Sir do me the favour to present this Medallion to the Accademy of Arts of whom the original is their President. It may be addrest to their Vice President. I will take Charge of the conveyance, and any further information you may wish for will be communicated to you by applying to Mr. Adams.[10]

What became of the medallion is a mystery; the Academy has no record of it. But Abigail's suspicions were confirmed. Not long afterward Adams received the following letter from Ceracchi written from Philadelphia:

> The confidence I put in the permotion of the most high Caracters of this Country, which have all at once retracted from there promises of promoting the plan of a National Monument puts me in the necessity of taking the prudent step to return to Europe directly.
> My expences having been of great consideration, and moved by my application in the Noble monumental plan I am in the necessity of calling for the sommes of my works, which I cant give them as a donation as I had proposed to do for the said circumstances.
> An immoral man would [. . .], for the same reason and upon the same principles of which those high caracteristic Gentilmen have acted in withdrawing themself from promoting the plan, as they had constantly promised.
> Therefore I shall take the Liberty to draw upon you and in favour of Mr. George Meade the somme of 350 Dollars price of your medallion in Alabaster Originaly performed by me. Reckoning upon your discharge with honoring your Signature, I am with consideraton.[11]

There the record ends; there appears to have been no reply from Adams nor any evidence that he paid the draft. Within a short time afterward Ceracchi returned to Europe.

The fate of the original terra-cotta busts, of which there were twenty-seven cases, is clouded. Before Ceracchi left Florence for Philadelphia in 1794 he had put them in the care of the Pisani brothers, Florentine sculptors. After Ceracchi's death the Pisanis made overtures to his widow to purchase some of the busts.[12] At one time it appears that suit was threatened to recover all of them for the widow,

[10] 12 Feb. 1795 (Dft, Adams Papers).
[11] 8 May 1795 (Adams Papers); Madison was dunned $250 for his medallion and Washington and Jefferson $1,500 each for their large busts (Desportes, "Ceracchi's Medallic Portrait of James Madison," p. 117).
[12] Arsenne Thiebaut to Giovanni Fabbroni, [15 Sept. 1802] (PPAmP).

who was then destitute. All further trace of them is lost. Recent "extensive search in Florentine collections" has been fruitless.[13] Yet somewhere, hidden away in some shop in Florence, there may await the perceptive art historian a treasure trove of immeasurable moment.

Waxwork

In the 18th century as today, there was scarcely any great man who was not reproduced in wax, and Adams was no exception. The *Weekly Museum,* published in New York, carried the following information on 9 December 1797:

Moulthrop and Street Respectfully inform the Ladies and Gentlemen of New York that their New Exhibition of Wax Figures, is opened at the house of Mr. William Treadwell, No. 5 Courtland street, this exhibition consists of thirty-two figures, as large as life, among which are the following characters. 1. His excellency George Washington, late President of the United States. 2. His Excellency John Adams, now President of the United States. 3. Dr. Ezra Stiles, late President of Yale College. 4. King Saul, in his extremity, consulting with the witch of Endor, and Samuel raised. . . . The Exhibition will be opened from 9 in the morning until 9 in the Evening. Admittance one quarter of a dollar for grown persons, children half price.[14]

Early in the following month the ladies and gentlemen of Baltimore were similarly alerted.[15]

Reuben Moulthrop, born in 1763, died in East Haven, Connecticut, in 1814. He was both an artist and a modeler in wax. Whatever he may have known of the appearance of Saul in his extremity, or the witch of Endor, he had firsthand knowledge of the likeness of President Stiles, having painted his portrait. Whether he modeled Adams from life or from one of the portraits of the day—Trumbull's, Winstanley's, or perhaps Sharples'—we cannot tell; by now the life-sized figure has surely melted away. That it received as much notice as it did is an indication of the interest of the people in the likeness of the great men of the age.

Transparent Painting

On 1 July 1797, only a few days before Independence Day, the public was advised by the *Weekly Museum* of the opening in New York of a new exhibition:

[13] Bush, *Life Portraits of Jefferson,* p. 29.
[14] Quoted in Rita Susswein Gottesman, *The Arts and Crafts in New York, 1777–1799,* NYHS, *Colls., Pubn. Fund Ser.,* 81 (1954):393.
[15] *Federal Gazette & Baltimore Daily Advertiser,* 3 Jan. 1800, p. 3.

Transparent Painting.—Independence, 4th July 1776 a new beautiful Transparent Painting will be exhibited at the Panorama in Greenwich street, on the evening of 4th July, the principal characters of which will be our late worthy President G. Washington, the present President Adams, and the Vice-President T. Jefferson, executed by a celebrated artist from original Paintings. The Museum will be illuminated on the same evening, and a patriotic Transparent Painting exhibited, and other decorations, admittance to the Panorama 2s. to the Museum 2s.

G. Baker Proprietor.[16]

Two years later the same or a similar exhibition was advertised to take place at Columbia Garden, with the added advice that the "Proprietor flatters himself that the superior elegance and style in which the Transparencies are executed and the well known abilities of the artist, cannot fail to secure the general approbation of the public." [17] The exhibition apparently lasted until the end of August.

It is to be regretted the public were not informed as to who the celebrated artist was. The paintings, presumably on glass shown with the light behind, do not appear to be mentioned again and have undoubtedly long since disappeared or been destroyed.

Figureheads: Rush–Train

In the Yale University Art Gallery in New Haven, stands a carved wooden bust of Benjamin Franklin executed by the talented carver William Rush of Philadelphia. It has been reproduced in Sellers' *Franklin in Portraiture* and furnishes us with a fine example of the state of the art of wood carving at the end of the 18th century. Rush also carved a figurehead of Adams (Cat. No. 197), described as a "striking likeness . . . from memory alone," and giving "full proofs of the powers of his mind, and the success of his chisel." [18] *The Philadelphia Daily Advertiser* on 5 June 1799 reported Rush's Adams in glowing terms:

Charlestown [Mass.], May 20. We are informed, that Monday the 3rd of June is the day appointed for the launch of the frigate; she is to be called the JOHN ADAMS; her head [which] is said to be a great likeness of the President of the United States arrived from Philadelphia some days ago and now is placed in the frigate; it is from the masterly Chissel of Mr. Rush of that city whose elegant productions have long since placed him at the head of his profession.[19]

[16] Quoted in Gottesman, *Arts and Crafts in N.Y.*, 1777–1799, p. 32.
[17] New York *Commercial Advertiser*, 3 July 1799, quoted in same, p. 34.
[18] James Mease, *The Picture of Philadelphia*, Phila., 1811, p. 79.
[19] Quoted in Henri Marceau, *William Rush*, 1756–1833, *The First Native American Sculptor*, Phila., 1937, p. 73.

On 13 June the same newspaper announced that the launching had in fact taken place on 3 June. It is only to be regretted that the figurehead has disappeared, no mention of it having come to notice after 1831.

Two other carved figures of Adams were made in 1799 by Rush's pupil Daniel N. Train: one (Cat. No. 198), all trace of which is lost, was carved for the frigate *Boston* launched shortly before 25 May 1799; [20] the other (Cat. No. 199) for the ship *Adams* launched in June of that year at Walabout, Long Island. An account of the latter appeared in the *New York Gazette and General Advertiser* for 23 May 1799:

Mr. Daniel N. Train, a young gentleman of genius and abilities, late a pupil of Rush, the famous Carver of Philadelphia, some time since arrived in this City, has lately completed the ornaments of the Ship *Adams'*, soon to be launched at the Walabought, Long Island.

The following is a sketch of these ornaments: On the head of the ship is a figure of the President, represented in the attitude of addressing both Houses of Congress. In his left hand is a scroll, supposed to be his address —his right is raised in a spirited position, as if in the act of bidding defiance to the enemies of America. At his side, is a branch of oak, springing from a rock, emblematic of his firmness and patriotic virtues, in support of the rights of his country.[21]

Whether Train drew upon his imagination or memory alone, or was prompted by such representations as Copley's likeness (Fig. 9), or Graham's (Fig. 50), cannot be known, but Adams would surely have approved the figure with its striking pose and supporting ornaments. The fate of the ship *Adams* is known. During her fifteen years afloat she captured some sixteen prizes in the West Indies, along the Atlantic Seaboard, and off Ireland. In 1814, when returning from a voyage to Ireland, she put in to Penobscot Bay where, on the approach of a strong British force, her captain was forced to burn her on 3 September 1814.[22]

FROM UNKNOWN SOURCES

Textiles

One of the most perplexing engraved likenesses of Adams is that which appears on several examples of late 18th-century textiles printed both in France and in England. The earliest known example of these prints (Cat. No. 201) shows, in red on a fine white linen handker-

[20] *Gazette of the United States* (Phila.), 25 May 1799.
[21] Quoted in Gottesman, *Arts and Crafts in N.Y., 1777–1799*, p. 37.
[22] *Dict. Amer. Fighting Ships*, 1:9.

chief, a bust portrait of Washington surrounded by four labeled medallions or oval portraits of Adams, Franklin in Cochin's fur cap, General Lincoln, and General Greene. The print is inscribed "George Washington / Commander in Chief of the forces of the thirteen united provinces of North America." Largely on the basis of Franklin's fur cap and the reference to the thirteen "united provinces," this print, thought to have been made in England though derived from French sources, has been dated as not earlier than 1777 nor later than 1778.[23] A somewhat later textile example, dated about 1783, exhibits a larger number of individual medallion portraits, including one of Adams, most of which are believed to have been pirated from Du Simitière's engravings. In the latter instance the profile of Adams (Fig. 105) follows closely (is unquestionably derived from the same source as) that appearing in the 1777–1778 print (Cat. No. 201). Though Hart had apparently not seen the 1777–1778 print, he had noticed the later one and expressed the view that the portrait of Adams was derived from Trumbull, meaning, of course, Adams as he appears in Trumbull's *Declaration* (Fig. 22). The only difficulty with this view is that Trumbull's Adams was not painted until 1787, and all the known likenesses done before that date are full or three-quarter face. The textile likeness may, to be sure, have been fanciful, yet it bears more than a superficial resemblance to the Trumbull detail (Fig. 23) and is not at all at odds with what we would expect the Adams of Vinkeles' or Jenings' portraits (Figs. 5, 7) to look like if in profile. A perfect solution to the problem, so simple as to be suspect, is that, like so many of the other textile likenesses, Adams' oval portrait was also derived from an earlier engraving by Du Simitière but from one that has since disappeared.

Though born in Geneva, Pierre Eugène Du Simitière had come to America in 1765, and had lived in Philadelphia from about 1770 until his death in 1784, painting portraits there and for a while serving as Curator of the American Philosophical Society. During the session of the Continental Congress he would have had ample opportunity to have produced a likeness of Adams which could have served as the source for the textile print (Fig. 105). Failing this, we can only posit another unknown original Adams portrait or change our views of the date of the print and accept Hart's view that Adams' likeness is after Trumbull.

[23] Edwin Lefevre, "Washington Historical Kerchiefs," *Antiques,* 36:14 (July 1939).

105. JOHN ADAMS AND OTHERS. COPPERPLATE ENGRAVING
PRINTED ON LINEN, CA. 1783

Medals

Long before the American Revolution, the custom had been established by the Spanish, French, and British of distributing medals to
the more prominent Indian Chiefs as tokens of friendship. It was, as
Jefferson said, "an ancient custom from time immemorial," and was
simply a "mark of friendship to those who come to see us, or who do

218

105A. JOHN ADAMS: DETAIL OF FIGURE 105

us good offices." [24] Early in its establishment the United States took steps to procure medals for distribution to the Indians. During Washington's administration large medals, oval in shape and four to six inches in size, were executed. Though none was made during Adams' term, the practice was revived in the succeeding administration, and the Jefferson medal became the model for a long series. On the obverse appeared a likeness of the President, on the reverse two hands, clasped, one with a cuff showing stripes and buttons, the other a bare wrist, and, above, a crossed calumet and tomahawk; above and below, separated, appeared the words "Peace and Friendship." Hence, the medals early became known as Indian Peace Medals.

During the Presidency of Monroe, the Superintendent of Indian Trade procured the services of Moritz Furst as diesinker. Furst, born in Hungary in 1782, had been diesinker to the Imperial Mint of Vi-

[24] To Messrs. Carmichael and Short, 30 June 1793, printed in Jefferson, *Writings*, ed. Lipscomb and Bergh, 9:157–158.

106. JOHN ADAMS. MEDALLIC PORTRAIT BY MORITZ FURST,
AFTER 1819

enna but came to the United States from Leghorn, Italy, in 1808, remaining until 1841, when he returned to Europe. After making the medals voted by Congress to the Army and Navy for the War of 1812, Furst undertook to execute from life peace medals of Monroe, John Quincy Adams, Jackson, and Van Buren. In order to make the series complete, he also executed medals of John Adams, at some time during the incumbency of Monroe, although, unlike many of the medals, those of Adams were not signed. As was usual, the Adams peace medals were made in three sizes, 76 mm., 62 mm. and 51 mm., the larger ones to be distributed to the more distinguished chiefs.

Furst was a skillful medalist and took great care to get a satisfactory likeness. In the case of John Quincy Adams, many attempts were made before one was accepted. The likenesses of John Adams differ slightly on the several sizes, the smallest one (Fig. 106) being the best. What he used for a model we cannot be sure. Monroe's medals were struck in 1819 and it would have been after them that Furst set to work to fill in the series by adding Adams. Possibly he used as a model Binon's bust (Fig. 91), which in profile resembles the Adams peace medal head, though the latter is made to appear somewhat younger as though Furst was attempting to get an 1800 likeness. The medal has been once engraved, by Jules F. Jacquemart.[25]

Another medallic likeness of Adams was issued with a companion of John Quincy Adams, showing on the reverse the Old House in

[25] Joseph F. Loubat, *The Medallic History of the United States of America, 1776–1876*, N.Y., 1878, vol. 2, plate xxi.

Quincy (Cat. No. 205). These are signed "G.H.L., N.Y." and done by G. H. Leonard some time after 1848. The head of the elder Adams is not unlike that by Furst.

King–Gerard–Couché

An interesting iconographic problem is presented by the three likenesses of Adams described below, widely different in medium but stemming from the same, though an unknown, source, and all done some time after 1820. What is believed to be the first of the three in point of time (Fig. 107) was painted, probably in the 1820's, by Charles Bird King, who, except for Stuart, was the most prolific portrayer of the Adamses, having also painted J. Q. Adams in both 1819 and 1828, C. F. Adams in 1827, a copy of Stuart's replica of the 1823 John Adams (Fig. 95) in 1827, and, in 1835, J. Q. Adams' granddaughter Fanny Adams. The portrait illustrated here as Fig. 107 was presented by King to the Redwood Library and Athenaeum in Newport and is there recorded as a copy after Stuart, though it resembles none of the known Stuarts. King was, however, a faithful copyist, as many of his works attest, and there is no reason to suppose this to be other than a faithful reproduction of some original. But of which? Some of the engravings after Williams' portrait of Adams come readily to mind, for example Houston's (Fig. 43) or Scole's (Fig. 44), but it has so far been impossible to point to King's model with any assurance.

The second of this series is the small, lightly tinted drawing (Fig. 108) belonging to the Franklin D. Roosevelt National Historic Site at Hyde Park, New York. This drawing, hanging over Roosevelt's bed, shows John Adams and his son J. Q. Adams facing each other. Although not dated, the drawing bears an inscription in French, partly undecipherable; all that can be made out for certain being, "J. Adams, teint coloré, couleur (Gerard)." Nothing is known of the identity of Gerard or of the provenance of the drawing, but of the source of the likenesses of the two Adamses, father and son, there can be no doubt. Hanging in adjoining galleries in the Redwood Library are King's portrait of John Adams (Fig. 107) and his 1819 portrait of John Quincy Adams, the latter a familiar and readily recognizable likeness. The Gerard sketch of J. Q. Adams is very closely like King's Redwood portrait; that of John Adams, coupled as it is with his son, is undoubtedly taken from King's Redwood copy. In other words, it would appear that Gerard, if he be the artist who drew Fig. 108, must at some time have

107. JOHN ADAMS. OIL BY CHARLES BIRD KING

108. JOHN ADAMS. TINTED DRAWING BY GERARD

seen King's portraits of the two Adamses, either in his studio at Washington or in the Redwood Library.

The last of the series (Fig. 109) is more puzzling. This small engraving is inscribed "Couché fils," the usual signature of François Louis Couché, son of Jacques Couché, a better-known French engraver. Had it not also been inscribed "Adams Père," Couché's engraving of what is patently a Frenchman would never have been recognized as of Adams. Yet on close scrutiny we are obliged to conclude that Couché had as his model either King's Redwood portrait of John Adams or the Gerard drawing. How he would ever have come to see either is a mystery. Perhaps Gerard's sketch found its way back to France, or perhaps all three were taken from a common source. Curiously enough, Couché also engraved a likeness of J. Q. Adams, surely taken from either King's Redwood portrait of the younger Adams or from the Gerard drawing. The J. Q. Adams trilogy presents no problem, as the likeness is a familiar one, stemming from King's portrait of the younger Adams known to have been taken from life. The perplexity is with respect to the likenesses of the elder Adams. King's, which is undoubtedly the source of the other two, could not have been a life portrait, and yet such meager record as there is describes it as a copy after Stuart.

Only one possible original Stuart portrait of John Adams suggests itself, namely the Doggett replica (Cat. No. 108), the source of Maurin's engraving (Fig. 77). King was active in Washington from 1816 until his death in 1862, and there he would have had access to the Doggett replica, one of the original "American Kings," when they were offered for sale to the Congress. It is not beyond the realm of possibility that Maurin and King copied the same model; if so, we would expect the engraver to have taken greater liberties and the painter to have been more strictly accurate. King's copy therefore may furnish a clue to the appearance of the Doggett replica.

Schussele–Russell–Silhouette

Three likenesses of Abigail Adams remain to be considered. In 1854 there appeared in Griswold's *The Republican Court* [26] an engraving (Fig. 110) bearing the inscription "Mrs. John Adams (Abigail Smith) From an original picture by C. Schessele in possession of the Publishers. On steel by John Sartain   Phila." Christian Schessele, or Schussele as his name is more usually spelled, was an Alsatian, born in 1826,

[26] Rufus Wilmot Griswold, *The Republican Court*, N.Y., 1854, facing p. 169.

ADAMS PÈRE.

109. JOHN ADAMS. ENGRAVING BY FRANÇOIS LOUIS COUCHÉ, CA. 1820–1825

110. ABIGAIL ADAMS. STEEL ENGRAVING BY JOHN SARTAIN, 1854

226

who emigrated to America in 1848, settling in Philadelphia. It is reported of him that, in 1854, "he made a popular success with a historical painting which was engraved by John Sartain and thereafter he devoted himself entirely to painting." [27] This appears to be the historical painting referred to. What the artist used as his model can only be conjectured, possibly some combination of the Blyth (Fig. 2), and the Brown (Fig. 21), though where the latter was in 1854 is unknown. There is some suggestion of a likeness. The original painting by Schussele is unlocated.

The Society for the Preservation of New England Antiquities, of Boston, possesses a portrait of Abigail Adams (Fig. 111) that is probably the last portrait taken. The likeness is recognizable, revealing the familiar piercing eyes and pointed nose and chin, and shows the sitter aged perhaps sixty, seated at her writing desk engaged in carrying on the correspondence for which she has become celebrated. The canvas is unsigned, but pasted on the back is a paper on which is written, in an old handwriting style, "Painted, from life by Miss Lydia Smith afterwards Mrs. Russell, G.R.R.R." The painting was a gift from Miss Mary Thacher to the Society, whose records describe it as: "Portrait of Mrs. John Adams (Abigail), wife of John Adams, President of the U.S. Painted in 1804 by Lydia Smith Russell. This is an original." Lydia Smith Russell was the daughter of Barry Smith, the Boston importer who for a time occupied the former residence of Governor Thomas Hutchinson in Milton. In 1817 she married Jonathan Russell, then United States Minister to Sweden, formerly J. Q. Adams' colleague at Ghent and later his opponent in a bitter political controversy. That she was known to be a painter is evident from a letter John Adams wrote in 1817 in which he inquired, "Are you acquainted with Miss Lydia Smith, who I am . . . credibly informed is one of the most accomplished Ladies, and a Painter?" She is cryptically described in a letter from Elijah Hunt Mills to his wife, 15 January 1822: "Here for the first time I became acquainted with Mrs. Jonathan Russell. She seems to me to be fantastical in nothing but her dress and appearance." Her own portrait was painted by Stuart.[28]

What is probably the only likeness of Abigail Adams in her old age

[27] Groce and Wallace, *Dict. Amer. Artists*, p. 565.
[28] JA to William Tudor Sr., 29 March 1817 (LbC, Adams Papers, printed in JA, *Works*, 10:244–249). On Jonathan Russell, see *DAB*; Bemis, *JQA*, 1:190–194, 498–509; Lydia Smith was his second wife. Mills' letter about Lydia (Smith) Russell is in MHS, *Procs.*, 1st ser., 19 (1881–1882):32. Stuart's extremely attractive portrait of her as a young woman is in same, vol. 48 (1914–1915), facing p. 508, accompanying extracts printed from an epistolary journal she kept in London, 1805–1806 (p. 508–534).

III. ABIGAIL ADAMS. OIL BY LYDIA SMITH RUSSELL, CA. 1804

112. ABIGAIL ADAMS. SILHOUETTE BY AN UNKNOWN
ARTIST, AFTER 1809

is the little silhouette (Fig. 112) which hangs in the White House. The silhouettist is not known, although the White House Historical Association states that the inscription ("Mrs. Adams") is "apparently in the hand of the artist." [29] Nothing of its date or provenance has been found. Despite its crude execution there is a suggestion of a likeness, but of a far older person than, for example, the 1809 Peale silhouette (Fig. 63).

Unknown, 1800–1816

In the files of the Library of Congress there is a photograph of a painting of John Adams (Fig. 113) with no apparent provenance and

[29] Letter from the White House Historical Association to the author, 2 March 1964.

113. JOHN ADAMS. OIL BY AN UNKNOWN ARTIST

no explanation on the photograph of its source except a highly questionable notation that it represents "John Adams by G. Stuart." The likeness is, however, inescapable and bears comparison with those by Sharples (cf. Houston's engraving, Fig. 33), Savage (Fig. 53), and Morse (Fig. 68). It could be assigned a date somewhere between 1800 and 1816, probably nearer the latter. The photograph, itself approximately 8 x 10 inches, offers no external evidence of the size or medium of the original, but from the curious markings, brush marks perhaps, appearing on the lighter part of the background, and the shape and cut of the oval frame, so rare in life-sized portraits of this period, it appears that the original was painted in oil on ivory, probably not more than 2 or 3 inches in size. Except for the notation on the photograph, there is no clue to the artist. No mention of Adams' sitting to Stuart for such a picture has come to light; if it is a miniature it is unlikely that it was painted by Stuart, whose only known miniature is that of General Knox.[30]

[30] Harry B. Wehle, *American Miniatures, 1730–1850*, N.Y., 1927, p. 65.

Horatio Greenough

In the spring of 1828, after John Quincy Adams had given the sculptor Horatio Greenough several sittings for his bust, he commissioned Greenough to execute a bust of John Adams during the coming summer. The bust of the elder statesman (Cat. No. 215), when completed, was to be placed above a tablet to be erected in the First Church of Quincy in memory of John and Abigail Adams, who had been buried in the adjoining churchyard. The new building of the ancient church was largely financed by funds given to the town by John Adams before his death.

Many years later Greenough declared, "the sketch of Mr. Adams [as a basis for the model] was made at Washington from a Daguerreotype." [31] This of course could not have been the case; Daguerre's magic black box was not perfected and made public until 1839. We can, then, only conjecture what likeness or likenesses of Adams were availed of by Greenough to serve as a model. Possibly some combination of a Trumbull, Brown, and Stuart. The marble itself was executed in Italy during the summer of 1828 and shipped to Boston the following year, arriving in June. John Quincy Adams entered in his diary for 20 June 1829:

> Mr. Quincy now President of Harvard University was also here. He brought me a Letter from Horatio Greenough the Sculptor to him written at Rome and a Bill of Lading for my father's Bust in Marble, which Greenough has executed for me, and which Mr. Quincy has received, with one of himself. He mentioned that Greenough's father was desirous of having the Busts opened and exhibited at the Athenaeum, to which I consented, as respected that of my father, on condition that the subsequent repacking of the Bust and its delivery to me here at Quincy undamaged shall be at Mr. Greenough's risk.

On 2 July 1829 the elder Greenough sent out a bust to Quincy but it proved to be of John Quincy Adams. It was not until 17 July that the bust of the elder Adams was delivered. The memorial, of which the bust was the crowning portion, was unveiled on 25 October 1829.[32]

At some time not known, Greenough made a second bust of John Adams, half-sized (Fig. 114), which was bequeathed to the Museum

---

[31] To Robert C. Waterston, 25 March 1845 (MHi:Waterston Coll.).

[32] See JQA, Diary, 20 June–25 Oct. 1829, *passim*. "[T]he Tablet which my Father has caused to be erected to the memory of his Father and Mother . . . is very pretty and quite ornamental although in the utmost simplicity. The inscription was written by him" (CFA, Diary, 25 Oct. 1829). Both of the Adams Presidents and their wives are now buried in a crypt beneath the Stone Temple.

114. JOHN ADAMS. MARBLE BUST BY HORATIO GREENOUGH, 1828

115. JOHN ADAMS. MARBLE BUST BY DANIEL CHESTER
FRENCH, 1889

116. JOHN ADAMS. LINE ENGRAVING
BY DANIEL CHESTER FRENCH, 1938

of Fine Arts in Boston by the sculptor's widow on her death in 1891.[33]
It is now on loan to the Old House (Adams National Historic Site) in
Quincy.

Daniel Chester French

Under resolutions adopted by the Senate of the United States on 27
January 1885, 13 May 1886, and 6 January 1898, some thirty-five
marble busts of Vice Presidents, from John Adams to Harry S. Tru-
man, were acquired and placed in niches in the gallery of the Senate
Chamber and the adjacent corridors. That of Adams (Fig. 115) is
behind the press box, almost directly over the Speaker's chair. Adams'
bust was purchased in 1890 from the sculptor Daniel Chester French,
best known for his *Minute Man* which stands near Concord Bridge
and his *Lincoln* in the Lincoln Memorial in Washington. The bust
may have been made in New York, as the second Charles Francis Adams records in his diary for 26 March 1889, "New York . . . to
French's studio to see bust of John Adams." No sure record has come
to light as to what French used for his model but it was probably some
combination of the Brown, Peale, and Trumbull portraits (Figs. 21,
23, 29), all of which were in 1889 readily available.

French, whose father, Henry Flagg French, was for many years As-
sistant Secretary of the Treasury, was born in 1850, and was con-
nected with the families of Daniel Webster and John Greenleaf Whit-
tier. He lived to be eighty-one years old, dying in 1931. One of the last
of his works was the small engraving of John Adams (Fig. 116) used
on the rose-colored two-cent postage stamp of the 1938 Presidential series. The profile is a fair likeness and not unlike, though younger in
appearance than, Binon's marble (Fig. 91).

[33] Illustrated in Nathalia Wright, *Horatio Greenough: The First American Sculptor*, Phila., 1963, between p. 304–305.

A LIKENESS NEVER TAKEN

William John Coffee

John Adams only narrowly missed having his bust taken in plaster by the English sculptor Coffee, who had also modeled Jefferson's granddaughter Cornelia Jefferson Randolph.[34] Coffee modeled Jefferson himself in April 1818, and in the following month Jefferson wrote to Adams:

There is now here a Mr. Coffee, a sculptor and Englishman, who has just taken my bust, and is going on to take those of Madison and Monroe. He resides at New York and promises me he will ask permission to take yours and send me one. I hope you will permit him. He is a fine artist. He takes them about half the size of life in plaster.[35]

Although he had just finished sitting to Binon, Adams was game for more and replied, "Mr. Coffee has been mentioned to me by my Son. He will be welcome. But though Robin is alive he is not alive [*i.e.* long?] like to be. Mr. Coffee must be very quick or Robbin may die in his hand." [36]

It would have been rewarding to have been able to compare a bust of Adams by Coffee with the marble just made by Binon, but Coffee was not quick enough. He wrote 16 October 1818, seeking permission to take the bust and stating his terms to be thirty-five dollars for a model and ten dollars each for copies. When he failed to get a prompt response he wrote twice again. But time had claimed at least part of its own. The partnership of fifty-four years with that "choice Blessing of a Wife," was terminated. Abigail died in Quincy on 10 November 1818. Until with the passage of time the old tree could begin to grow bark over the wound left by the loss of its main branch, Adams would have no patience for busts or portraits. Eight days after Abigail's death, he wrote to Coffee, commenting on Jefferson's recent illness and on his own loss and concluding:

I pray you Sir not to think of coming this way to take my Bust. I have no loose Coins to waste in pictures or Statues.
"All worldly vanities be gone!
I would be silent and alone."
I am Sir your humble Servant,   John Adams [37]

[34] Reproduced in Bush, *Life Portraits of Jefferson*, p. 86.
[35] 17 May 1818 (Adams Papers, printed in Cappon, ed., *Adams-Jefferson Letters*, 2:524–525).
[36] 29 May 1818 (DLC:Jefferson Papers; LbC, Adams Papers; printed in same, p. 526).
[37] 18 Nov. 1818 (LbC, Adams Papers).

Catalogue

Catalogue

All known original portraits, busts, and silhouettes of John and Abigail Adams and most of the more significant replicas, copies, engravings, and other reproductions of them that have come to light are listed below. Likenesses known to be irrecoverably lost, as well as those currently unlocated, are included when records indicate their sometime existence. But no claim to exhaustiveness can be made, for the number of woodcuts and engravings of the Adamses appearing in periodicals and textbooks since the middle of the 19th century is almost limitless. I believe, however, that most of the significant and typical reproductions are recorded.

The Catalogue, like the chapters of text, is divided by artists, approximately in the order in which they delineated John Adams, with a catchall or paralipomena at the end. Within each division the separate items are listed chronologically. Each listing includes the name (and, where first mentioned, the dates) of the artist, the size of the picture (the first dimension being the vertical), its date if known, any inscription it bears, and a list of known owners, the last mentioned being the present owner. In many instances there are gaps in the record of ownership which diligent inquiry has been unable to fill. The source or sources of each representation, if a copy, replica, or engraving, and its derivatives, if any are known, are also indicated. When ascertainable, the location of engravings or other reproductions of original portraits in the first published work in which they appear, or in some known collection, is included. Wherever possible, engravings are identified by their numerical designation in David McN. Stauffer, *American Engravers upon Copper and Steel,* 2 vols., New York, 1907, in Mantle Fielding's supplement to that work under the same title, Philadelphia, 1917, or in Charles Henry Hart, *Engraved Portraits of George Washington,* New York, 1904. In a few instances items are listed which are known only from Stauffer, Fielding, or Hart but which appear to be significant; here, necessarily, the entry is silent on the question of location.

The items in the Catalogue are numbered consecutively from 1 to 218, and are referred to by their numbers within the Catalogue itself. For example, the entry under No. 74 (Houston's engraving, 1797) indicates that it is derived from No. 71 (Williams' oil portrait, 1795), and that its own derivatives are Nos. 75, 76, 79, and 80.

In the right-hand column appear the numbers of those items that are illustrated in the text, designated as "Fig. —." For example, Catalogue item No. 74 (Houston's engraving after Williams) is illustrated in the text as Fig. 43, and since the illustrations appear in strictly numerical order, they can be readily located by their "Fig." numbers alone as given in the right-hand column of the Catalogue. Because of the complex pedigrees of some of the derivative likenesses, there are occasional but necessary discrepancies between the order of the items illustrated and that of the items as catalogued; this is why equivalents are given both in the List of Illustrations (p. xix–xxviii, above) and in the present Catalogue.

For items in the Catalogue that are *not* illustrated (and therefore have no "Fig." numbers), the right-hand column of the Catalogue furnishes a reference to the text page where the item is introduced if it is discussed. In this way the right-hand column of the Catalogue, being a master cross-reference list connecting illustrations and text with all the items catalogued, forms a sort of subsidiary index to the volume as a whole (except for those items which are neither illustrated nor discussed in the text and therefore have no reference in the right-hand column).

Within the text itself, it should be pointed out, references to items in the Catalogue are to "Fig. —" if the item is illustrated (and it is always illustrated close to the primary mention in the text); otherwise to "Cat. No. —."

The last division of the Catalogue, the Paralipomena, includes items which have disappeared and a few, including posthumous likenesses, whose source or date or artist is unknown.

I. Benjamin Blyth (1746?–1787?)

CAT. NO.

1. JOHN ADAMS. Pastel; Salem, 1766. Size: 23×17½ in. Owners: (a) Thomas Boylston Adams (TBA); (b) Elizabeth C. Adams (ECA); (c) Charles Francis Adams (CFA); (d) Henry Adams (HA2); (e) John Adams, South Lincoln, Massachusetts; (f) the Massachusetts Historical Society. Derivatives: Nos. 3–7.   FIG. 1

2. ABIGAIL ADAMS. Pastel; Salem, 1766. Size: 23×17½ in. Provenance the same as its pendant, No. 1. Derivatives: Nos. 8–10.   FIG. 2

3. JOHN ADAMS. Engraving by G. F. Storm, after No. 1; 1840. Size: 8½ × 8 in. *Letters of John Adams, Addressed to his Wife,* ed. Charles Francis Adams, Boston, 1841, vol. 1, frontispiece. FIG. 3

4. JOHN ADAMS. Engraving by Stephen Alonzo Schoff (1818–1904), after No. 1; 1850. Size: 4 × 3 in. *The Works of John Adams, Second President of the United States,* ed. Charles Francis Adams, Boston, 1850–1856, vol. 2, frontispiece.

5. JOHN ADAMS. Engraving by Samuel Wallin, after No. 1. Size: 6 × 4 in. Example in the New York Public Library, Prints Division.

6. JOHN ADAMS. Engraving on wood by John William Orr (1815–1887), after a drawing by Samuel Wallin from No. 1; 1853. Size: approx. 6½ in. in height. A. D. Jones, *Illustrated American Biographies,* New York, 1853, 1:59.

7. JOHN ADAMS. Pastel by May Hallowell Loud, after No. 1; December 1904. Size: 23 × 18½ in. Owner: the Quincy Historical Society (John Quincy Adams Birthplace), Quincy, Massachusetts. P. 12

8. ABIGAIL ADAMS. Engraving by Oliver Pelton (1798–1882), after No. 2; 1840. Size: 4⅛ × 3¹¹⁄₁₆ in. *Letters of Mrs. Adams, the Wife of John Adams,* ed. Charles Francis Adams, Boston, 1840, frontispiece (and in subsequent editions through 1848). Stauffer No. 2477. FIG. 4

9. ABIGAIL ADAMS. Engraving on wood by John William Orr, after drawing by Samuel Wallin from No. 2; 1853. Size: approx. 6 in. in height. A. D. Jones, *Illustrated American Biographies,* New York, 1853, 1:71.

10. ABIGAIL ADAMS. Pastel by May Hallowell Loud, after No. 2. Date, size, and provenance the same as its pendant, No. 7. P. 12

II. Reinier Vinkeles (1741–1816)

11. JOHN ADAMS. Engraving; Amsterdam, 1782. A variant of No. 12. Size: 5⅜ × 3¹¹⁄₁₆ in. Frontispiece to the Dutch translation of Adams' "Novanglus" essays published by William Holtrop in Amsterdam, 1782; and in John Adams, *Diary and Autobiography,* 3:32. FIG. 5

12. JOHN ADAMS. Engraving; Amsterdam, 1782. Size: 5⅝ × 3½ in. Example at The New-York Historical Society. FIG. 6

13. JOHN ADAMS. Engraving by an unknown artist, after No. 11. Size: 3 in., round. Justin Winsor, *Narrative and Critical History of America,* Boston, 1884–1889, 6:36.

III. Unknown Artist

14. JOHN ADAMS. Painting by an unknown artist, in the possession of Edmund Jenings, London, 1783. Unlocated; known only from No. 15.   P. 19

15. JOHN ADAMS. Engraving by an unknown artist, after No. 14; 1783. Size: 6×3½ in. Inscribed: "His Excellency John Adams / From an Original Portrait in the Possession of Edmund Jennings Esq. / Publish'd Sep. 1, 1783 by J. Fielding, No. 23 Pater noster Row." *European Magazine* (August 1783), facing p. 83.   FIG. 7

16. JOHN ADAMS. Engraving by John Norman (about 1748–1817), probably after No. 14; Boston, 1784. Size: 4×3½ in. *The Boston Magazine* (February 1784), facing p. 125. Stauffer No. 2327.   FIG. 8

IV. John Singleton Copley (1738–1815)

17. JOHN ADAMS. Preliminary drawing for No. 18; London, 1783. Size: 18¾ × 14¼ in. Owners: (a) Copley; (b) Lord Lyndhurst; (c) Edward Basil Jupp; (d) Martha Babcock or Charles Amory; (e) Linzee Amory; (f) Charles D. Childs and Harry Shaw Newman; (g) the Metropolitan Museum of Art, New York City.   FIG. 11

18. JOHN ADAMS. Oil on canvas; London, 1783. Size: 7 ft. 9¾ in.×4 ft. 10 in. Owners: (a) John Adams (JA); (b) Ward Nicholas Boylston; (c) the Fogg Museum of Art, Harvard University. Derivatives: Nos. 19–34. See Prown, *Copley*, 2:300, 411.   FIG. 9

19. JOHN ADAMS. Detail of Adams from No. 18.   FIG. 10

20. JOHN ADAMS. Engraving by [George?] Noble, bust only, after No. 18; London, 1786. Size: 3⅞×2½ in. *The New London Magazine* (March 1, 1786). Example in the Princeton University Library, André deCoppet Collection.   FIG. 12

21. JOHN ADAMS. Engraving by Hall, bust only, after No. 18; London, 1794. Size: 4×3½ in. Inscribed: "Painted by Copley–Engraved by Hall / John Adams, L.L.D. / Vice President of the United States of America / Publish'd Feby. 15, 1794 by John Stockdale." John Adams, *A Defence of the Constitutions of Government of the United States of America*, London, 1794, vol. 1, frontispiece. Derivatives: Nos. 22, 27, 31–33.   FIG. 13

22. JOHN ADAMS. Engraving, bust only, by James Smither (d. 1797), derived from No. 21, after No. 18; Philadelphia, 1797. Size: 3¹⁵⁄₁₆×3⅜ in. Inscribed: "Painted by Copley–Engraved by J. Smither / John Adams / President of the United States of America / Philadelphia. Published Feby. 15, 1797 by William Cobbett." Stauffer No. 2971. John Adams, *A Defence of the Constitutions of Government of*

the United States of America, Philadelphia, 1797, vol. 1, frontispiece.   P. 31

23. JOHN ADAMS. Engraving, bust only, surrounded by the seals of sixteen states, by Amos Doolittle (1754–1832), after No. 18; New Haven, 1799. Over-all size: 19×15½ in. Owner: the Massachusetts Historical Society. Stauffer No. 509. Derivatives: Nos. 25, 28.   FIG. 14

24. JOHN ADAMS. Oil on canvas; replica, or copy by an unknown artist, after No. 18; London, about 1800. Size: 20×13½ in. Owners: (a) Martin Colnaghi; (b) Knoedler & Co.; (c) A. Meeker; (d) the Museum of Fine Arts, Boston.   FIG. 17

25. JOHN ADAMS. Engraving by Amos Doolittle, bust only, derived from No. 23, after No. 18; 1801. Size: 3 in. Inscribed: "A. Doolittle Sculp / John Adams / Late President of the United States." *The Connecticut Magazine* (May 1801), frontispiece. Stauffer No. 508.   P. 31

26. JOHN ADAMS. Engraving, bust only, by Thomas Gimbrede (1781–1832), derived from No. 21, after No. 18; New York, 1812. Size: 4×3⅜ in., oval; Adams with Washington, Jefferson, and Madison. Inscribed: over, "American Star"; under, "Copy Right secured / Printed by Andw Maverick – Thomas Jefferson – James Madison – John Adams – N. York Design'd, Engrav'd & Publish'd by Thos. Gimbrede Jany. 30th, 1812." In a second state, "Andw Maverick" and "& Publish'd" erased and "Shelton & Kensett, Cheshire Conn." substituted. Example in the Princeton University Library. Hart Nos. 794, 794a. Derivative: No. 27.   FIG. 15

27. JOHN ADAMS. Oil on wood panel, bust only, by an unknown artist, after No. 26; date unknown, probably early 19th century. Size: 24×19¾ in. Owners: Mr. and Mrs. Bertram K. Little, Essex, Massachusetts.

28. JOHN ADAMS. Engraving by Ralph Rawdon: Adams with Washington, Jefferson, and Madison. Size: 11½×9⅛ in. Inscribed: "American Star / Published & Sold by Shelton & Kensett Cheshire Con. Jan. 16th 1814–Engraved by Ralph Rawdon / Gen. George Washington." Hart No. 795.

29. JOHN ADAMS. Engraving, bust only, by William S. Leney (1769–1831), derived possibly from No. 23, after No. 18; New York, 1819. Size: 3¹¹⁄₁₆×3¼₆ in. *State Papers and Public Documents of the United States from the Accession of George Washington to the Presidency . . . ,* 3d edn., Boston, 1819, p. 3. Stauffer No. 1706.

30. JOHN ADAMS. Engraving after No. 18, engraver unidentified; about 1850; full-length figure. Size: 6½×3⅞ in. *The Works of John Adams,* ed. Charles Francis Adams, Boston, 1850–1856, vol. 5, frontispiece.   FIG. 16

31. JOHN ADAMS. Engraving, bust only, by Henry Bryan Hall (1808–1884), derived from No. 22, after No. 18; about 1850. Size: 4×3½ in. Example at the Boston Athenæum.

32. JOHN ADAMS. Engraving, bust only, by Stephenson, derived from No. 22, after No. 18; about 1856. Size: 4×3½ in. William H. Bartlett and B. B. Woodward, *History of the United States of North America,* New York, 1856, 2:190.

33. JOHN ADAMS. Engraving by Frederic T. Stuart (1817–1913), derived from No. 21, after No. 18. Size: 1⅞×1⅝ in., oval; one of a group of five Presidents surrounding a view of The White House. Inscribed: "Engraved expressly for Abbott's Lives of the Presidents." J. S. C. Abbott, *Lives of the Presidents,* Boston, 1867, p. 97.

34. JOHN ADAMS. Oil on canvas by John M. Carpenter, after No. 18; 1946. Size: 48×36 in. Owner: the Bostonian Society, Old State House.   P. 38

V. Benjamin West (1738–1820)

35. JOHN ADAMS. *American Commissioners at the Preliminary Peace Negotiations with Great Britain,* oil on canvas; about 1783. Size: 28½×36½ in. Owners: (a) West; (b) Joseph Strutt; (c) Edward Strutt, M.P., the first Lord Belper, nephew of (b); (d) Henry Strutt, the second Lord Belper; (e) J. Pierpont Morgan; (f) the Henry Francis du Pont Winterthur Museum. Derivatives: Nos. 36–37.   FIG. 18

36. JOHN ADAMS. Oil on canvas; replica or copy by an unknown hand, of No. 35. Size: 36)(27½ in. Owners: (a) George Grote, the historian of Greece; (b) John Jay, grandson of one of the Commissioners; (c) Mrs. Dorothy Iselin Paschal, New York City.   P. 43, 45

37. JOHN ADAMS. Oil on canvas, artist unknown, copy of No. 35. Size: 28×36 in. Written at lower right-hand corner: "Unfinished sketch by Benjamin West." Owners: (a) Lewis Cass, American Minister to France (1836–1844); (b) Mrs. Frank Gray Griswold; (c) Cass Canfield; (d) The Department of State, Washington.   P. 45

38. JOHN ADAMS. Detail of No. 35.   FIG. 19

VI. Mather Brown (1761–1832)

39. JOHN ADAMS. Oil portrait; July–August 1785. Unlocated. Known only from a letter from young Abigail Adams (AA2) to her brother John Quincy Adams, 4 July–11 August 1785.   P. 47

40. ABIGAIL ADAMS. Oil on canvas; London, 1785. Size: 30¼×26½ in. Owners: (a) H. A. Hammond Smith; (b) Erskine Hewitt; (c) Frances J. Eggleston; (d) the New York State Historical Association, Cooperstown.   FIG. 21

41. JOHN ADAMS. Oil on canvas; London, 1788. Size: 34½×27¼ in. Owners: (a) Thomas Jefferson; (b) George Francis Parkman of Boston; (c) the Boston Athenæum.   FIG. 20

42. JOHN ADAMS. Marble statue by Randolph Rogers (1825–
    1892); about 1859; Mt. Auburn Cemetery, Cambridge.
    American Architect and Building News, 19 (1886):280–
    281.

43. JOHN ADAMS. Bronze bust by John Francis Paramino; 1924.
    Size: 20 in. in height. Examples at the Hall of Fame for Great
    Americans, New York University, and the State House, Bos-
    ton. *Outlook,* 137:129. (28 May 1924).   P. 52

VII. John Trumbull (1756–1843)

44. *Declaration of Independence.* Oil on canvas; 1787–1796.
    Size: 20¾ × 30⅞ in. Owner: the Yale University Art Gal-
    lery. Derivatives: Nos. 50–57.   FIG. 22

45. JOHN ADAMS. Detail of No. 44.   FIG. 23

46. JOHN ADAMS. Oil on mahogany panel; Philadelphia, 1792.
    Size: 4×3 in., oval. Inscribed: "John Adams / first Vice
    President of / the United States of America / & one of her
    Ministers at / the conclusion of peace / with G. Britain in
    1783. / Painted by J. Trumbull / at Philadelphia 1792."
    Owner: the Yale University Art Gallery.   FIG. 26

47. JOHN ADAMS. Oil on canvas; Philadelphia, 1793. Size:
    30½×24½ in. Owners: (a) John Jay; (b) Col. William
    Jay; (c) Estate of Eleanor Jay Iselin, Katonah, New York
    (John Jay Homestead).   FIG. 27

48. JOHN ADAMS. Oil on canvas; Philadelphia, 1793. Size:
    30×25 in. Owners: (a) Andrew Craigie; (b) the Fogg
    Museum of Art, Harvard University.   FIG. 28

48a. JOHN ADAMS. Oil on canvas; presumably Philadelphia, 1793.
    Size: 30×25 in. Perhaps a replica of No. 48 or the original
    of which No. 48 is a replica. Label on frame reads: "John
    Adams by Gilbert Stuart." Came to light after the present vol-
    ume was in page proof. Owner: Alexander P. Morgan, by
    descent, Princeton, New Jersey.

49. JOHN ADAMS. Full-length portrait, presumably oil on canvas;
    about 1802 or earlier, possibly as a study for No. 44. Known
    only from the catalogue of the 1802 exhibition of the Co-
    lumbian Gallery, New York City.   P. 65–66

50. JOHN ADAMS. Oil on canvas, modified replica of No. 44; New
    York, 1818. Size: 12×18 ft.; in the rotunda of The Capitol,
    Washington.   P. 58, 60

51. *Declaration of Independence.* Engraving by Asher B. Durand
    (1796–1886), after No. 44; 1820–1823. Size: 29¹¹⁄₁₆ ×
    30¼ in. Inscribed: "Painted by John Trumbull. Copy Right
    secured according to the Act of Congress Decr. 20th 1820.
    Engraved by A. B. Durand / The Declaration of Independ-
    ence of the United States of America / July 4th, 1776."

Stauffer No. 679. Example at The New-York Historical Society. FIG. 25

52. JOHN ADAMS. Engraving by Thomas Illman, after No. 44. Size: 4×6 in. Inscribed: "Painted by Trumbull–Engraved by Illman & Pilbrow / Declaration of Independence." Charles A. Goodrich, *Lives of the Signers of the Declaration of Independence,* New York, 1829, frontispiece.

53. *Declaration of Independence.* Oil on canvas; modified replica of No. 44; after 1831. Size: 72½ × 108¹¹⁄₁₆ in. Owner: the Wadsworth Atheneum, Hartford. FIG. 24

54. JOHN ADAMS. Oil painting by Edward Hicks (1780–1849); a copy of No. 44; about 1840. Size: 24×31½ in. Owners: (a) Edward Hicks; (b) Isaac Hicks; (c) Edward Hicks, son of (a); (d) Mrs. Mary B. Hicks Richardson, daughter of (c); (e) Captain Richard A. Loeb; (f) the Abby Aldrich Rockefeller Folk Art Collection, Williamsburg. Another version, owned by Col. and Mrs. Edgar W. Garbisch, is in Alice Ford, *Edward Hicks,* Philadelphia, 1952, p. 144.

55. JOHN ADAMS. Engraving after No. 44 by John F. E. Prud'homme (1800–1892); 1842. Size: 8⁷⁄₁₆×12¹¹⁄₁₆ in. Inscribed: "Painted by John Trumbull Esqr. Engraved On Steel By J. F. E. Prud'homme / The Declaration Of Independence / Printed by D. Fanshaw / Engraved expressly for the New York Mirror 1842." Stauffer No. 2622.

56. JOHN ADAMS. Engraving by Denison Kimberly (1814–1863), after No. 44, showing, within an elaborate border, the *Declaration of Independence* and a facsimile of the Declaration with accompanying signatures. Size: of the "Declaration," 4×6 in. Inscribed: "Engraved by D. Kimberly–Lettered by J. B. Bolton 1844." Example at the Library of Congress.

57. JOHN ADAMS. Engraving by J. P. M. Jazet (1788–1871), after No. 44. Size: 29½×19½ in. Inscribed: "Gravé par Jazet Paris Publié par Jazet et par Thre. Vibert, Editeur rue de Lancry 7 et Chez Bance et Schroth rue du Mail 5."

VIII. Charles Willson Peale (1741–1823)

58. JOHN ADAMS. Oil on canvas; Philadelphia, about 1794. Size: 23×19 in. Owners: (a) Peale's Museum Collection; (b) Independence National Historical Park, Philadelphia. Derivative: No. 59. FIG. 29

59. JOHN ADAMS. Engraving by an unknown artist, after No. 58. Size: 3×2½ in., oval. John Fiske, *The Critical Period of American History,* Cambridge, 1898, p. 23. P. 72

IX. James Peale (1749–1831)

60. JOHN ADAMS. Oil portrait; about 1795. Size: 10¾×8¾ in. Unlocated; photograph in the Frick Art Reference Library. FIG. 30

Catalogue

X. The Sharples

61. JOHN ADAMS. Tempera on paper by James Sharples (about 1751–1811); Philadelphia, 1796–1797. Size: 9×7 in. Owner: Miss Ima Hogg, Houston, Texas. FIG. 31

62. JOHN ADAMS. Tempera on paper by James Sharples; Philadelphia, 1796–1797. Size: 9×7 in. Owners: (a) Ellen Sharples, widow of James Sharples; (b) the City Art Gallery, Bristol, England. FIG. 32

63. JOHN ADAMS. Engraving by H. Houston, after No. 61 or No. 62; 1797. Size: 3½×2¹⁵⁄₁₆ in. Inscribed: "For the American Universal Magazine / Houston Sculpt. / John Adams / President of the United States." *American Universal Magazine,* 1:361 (20 March 1797). Stauffer No. 1455. FIG. 33

64. JOHN ADAMS. Tempera on paper by James Sharples; about 1797. Size: presumably 9×7 in. Unlocated. Source for Nos. 68, 69; but see No. 65. Owners: (a) Judge William Cushing; (b) Henry Bowers. P. 82

65. JOHN ADAMS. Tempera on paper, probably by James Sharples; about 1797. Size: 7×5½ in. This is possibly the same as No. 64. Owner: the City of Quincy, Massachusetts (John Quincy Adams Birthplace). FIG. 39

66. JOHN ADAMS. Pencil drawing by Ellen Sharples (1769–1849), after No. 62; 1804. Size: 3×2½ in. Inscribed: "Hon. Mr. Adams." Owners: (a) Ellen Sharples; (b) the City Art Gallery, Bristol, England. FIG. 37

67. JOHN ADAMS. Pencil drawing by Ellen Sharples; about 1804, after unlocated original, possibly No. 64. Size: 3×2½ in. Owners: (a) Ellen Sharples; (b) the City Art Gallery, Bristol, England. FIG. 38

68. JOHN ADAMS. Copy in oil by Edward D. Marchant (1806–1887) of No. 64; 1843. Size: 10×7¾ in. Owners: (a) John Quincy Adams (JQA); (b) Mary Louisa Adams; (c) Mary Louisa Adams Clement; (d) the Smithsonian Institution, Adams–Clement Collection. FIG. 35

69. JOHN ADAMS. Copy in oil, by an unknown artist, of No. 64; 1854. Size: 10×8 in. Owners: (a) Henry Bowers; (b) Samuel Wetmore; (c) William H. Bliss; (d) Mrs. Charles Warren; (e) Mrs. Graham L. Russell, Upper Montclair, New Jersey. FIG. 36

70. Subject unknown. Tempera on paper by James Sharples; about 1800. Size: 9×7 in. Since 1876 said (in error) to be of John Adams. Owner: Independence National Historical Park, Philadelphia. FIG. 34

XI. William Joseph Williams (1759–1823)

71. JOHN ADAMS. Oil on wood panel; Philadelphia, about 1795. Size: 15×12½ in. Owners: (a) John Frederick Lewis;

(b) The Pennsylvania Academy of the Fine Arts. Derivatives: Nos. 71, 73, 74. FIG. 40

72. JOHN ADAMS. Oil on wood panel, replica of No. 71; about 1795. Size: 17×14 in. Owners: (a) Charles Henry Hart; (b) Henry Adams (HA); (c) the Adams National Historic Site. FIG. 41

73. JOHN ADAMS. Engraving by H. Houston, after No. 71; about 1797. Size: 11⅞₁₆×9 in. Inscribed: "Drawn & Engrav'd by H. Houston / His Excellency John Adams President / of The United States of America / Respectfully Dedicated to the Lovers of their Country / and Firm Supporters of Its Constitution. / Published by D. Kennedy, 228 Market St. Philada." Stauffer No. 1454. Example at the Massachusetts Historical Society. Derivatives: Nos. 76–78, 81. FIG. 42

74. JOHN ADAMS. Engraving by H. Houston, after No. 71; 1797. Size: 5¹⁵⁄₁₆×4¹³⁄₁₆ in. Appears in three states, inscribed: (1) "W. Williams pinxt–T. B. Freeman Excudit–H. H. Houston Sculpt. / His Excellency / John Adams, Esqr. / President of the United States of America / Published, September 1st 1797"; (2) painter erased and relettered "Houston Sc."; (3) as illustrated, the same as (2) with the year erased. Stauffer No. 1453. Example at the Massachusetts Historical Society. Derivatives: Nos. 75, 76, 79, 80. FIG. 43

75. JOHN ADAMS. Sanguine drawing on paper, after No. 74, or possibly working drawing for No. 74. Artist unknown, possibly Houston. Size: 21½×16½ in. Owner: Andrew Oliver, New York City. FIG. 46

76. JOHN ADAMS. Engraving by H. Houston, after No. 74 or No. 73; 1798. Size: 5³⁄₁₆×4⅜ in. Inscribed: "John Adams Esqr. L.L.D. / President of the United States / Publish'd by T. Condie Booksr. Philada." Fielding No. 727. *Philadelphia Monthly Magazine, or Universal Register of Knowledge and Entertainment*, vol. 2, no. 8 (July 1798). P. 98

77. JOHN ADAMS. Engraving by John Scoles, after No. 73; about 1800. Size: 3×2⁷⁄₁₆ in. Inscribed: "Engraved by Scoles. / John Adams." Stauffer No. 2768. James Hardie, *The New Universal Biographical Dictionary and American Remembrancer of Departed Merit*, New York, 1805, 1:68. Derivatives: Nos. 81, 82. FIG. 44

78. JOHN ADAMS. Engraving by John Scoles; profiles of Washington and Adams (after No. 73) in outline of an apple tree, the letters of their names on the apples. Size: 4½×2⅞ in. Inscribed: "The Portraits of George Washington and John Adams / Scoles sculp." Stauffer No. 2813.

79. JOHN ADAMS. Engraving by Cornelius Tiebout (about 1773–1832), after No. 74. Size: 8¹⁵⁄₁₆×7 in. Inscribed: "C. Tiebout Sct. / John Adams / Published by A. Day No. 33 Chesnut St. Philada." Stauffer No. 3161. Example at The New-York Historical Society. P. 98

80. JOHN ADAMS. Engraving by Benjamin Tanner (1775–1848), derived from No. 74; 1804. Size: 5½×4½ in. Inscribed: "B. Tanner, Sc., / John Adams Esqr." Stauffer No. 3080. *Literary Magazine and American Register,* vol. 2, frontispiece (August 1804).   FIG. 45

81. JOHN ADAMS. Engraving by Asaph Willard (1786–1880), derived from No. 77, after No. 73. Vignette, 2½ in. Inscribed: "A. Willard, / John Adams, / Inaugurated President, 1797"; also appears without inscription. *History of the United States,* Hartford, 1823. Stauffer No. 3366. Derivative: No. 82.

82. JOHN ADAMS. Engraving by unknown artist after No. 77 or No. 81. Size: 3 in. height. Facing right, buttons appearing on left side of coat. Example at the Metropolitan Museum of Art, New York City.

XII. William Winstanley

83. JOHN ADAMS. Oil on canvas; about 1798. Size: 48×36 in. Owners: (a) Charles Henry Hart; (b) Henry Adams (HA); (c) the Adams National Historic Site. Derivatives: Nos. 85, 86.   FIG. 47

84. JOHN ADAMS. Oil on canvas; about 1798. Size: 26½×21½ in. Owners: (a) Alexander Smith Cochrane; (b) the American Scenic and Historic Preservation Society, Philipse Manor, Yonkers, New York.   FIG. 48

85. JOHN ADAMS. Mezzotint by George Graham, probably after No. 83; 1798. Size: 16¼×11½ in. Inscribed: "Publish'd by Dr. John Berkeanhead–Engrav'd by Geo. Graham / John Adams / President of the United States of America. / Hail! Noble Chief! Protector of the cause of purest Freedom Founded on the Laws." Stauffer No. 1160. Example at the Metropolitan Museum of Art, New York City.   FIG. 50

86. JOHN ADAMS. Woodcut by an unknown artist, after No. 83; 1845. Size: 2¾ in. Inscribed: "Fig. 82–John Adams. From an Anonymous American Portrait." Robert Sears, *The Pictorial History of the American Revolution,* New York, 1847, p. 188.   FIG. 49

XIII. Edward Savage (1761–1817)

87. JOHN ADAMS. *The Congress Voting Independence;* oil on canvas; about 1796–1801. Size: 19¾×26½ in. Owners: (a) Charles Henry Hart; (b) The Historical Society of Pennsylvania. Derivative: No. 88.   FIG. 51

88. JOHN ADAMS. Engraving of No. 87; sometimes attributed to Robert Edge Pine; about 1800–1817. Size: 18⁹⁄₁₆×25¹¹⁄₁₆ in. Owners of the copper plate: (a) Edward Savage Jr.; (b) Samuel T. Snow; (c) the Massachusetts Historical Society.   FIG. 52

89. JOHN ADAMS. Oil painting; about 1800. Unlocated; known only through No. 90.   P. 113

90. JOHN ADAMS. Engraving by Savage or by or in conjunction with David Edwin (1776–1841), after No. 89; 1800. Size: 11⅜×9 in. Appears in two conditions: (1) inscribed: "John Adams, President of the United States of America. Philad. Published by E. Savage Oc. 10, 1800"; and (2) as illustrated, "Painted by E. Savage in 1800. John Adams, Second President of the United States of America." These are probably Stauffer's No. 695 (under D. Edwin) and No. 2744 (under E. Savage). Example at The New-York Historical Society. Derivatives: Nos. 91–95.   FIG. 53

91. JOHN ADAMS. Oil painting by William M. S. Doyle (1769–1828), after No. 90; about 1800. Unlocated; in Clarence W. Bowen, *History of the Centennial Celebration of the Inauguration of George Washington,* New York, 1892, facing p. 18.   FIG. 54

92. JOHN ADAMS. Engraving by David Edwin; oval bust portraits of the first four Presidents arranged against an entablature supporting an open book. Size: 6⁵⁄₁₆×4 in. Inscribed: "D. Edwin &–G. Murray / Washington /Adams–Jefferson / Madison." A second state with two ovals added at side and inscription modified to include "Monroe–Adams." A third state adds Jackson, with a new inscription. Stauffer No. 855, Hart No. 598.

93. JOHN ADAMS. Engraving by John Bower, with companion portrait of Washington; Adams, after No. 90. Size: over-all, 5¾×7½ in.; diameter, 1⅞ in. Inscribed: "G. Washington. J. Adams. / J. Bower, Sc. Phila." Stauffer No. 235; Hart No. 504. Example at the Library of Congress.   FIG. 56

94. JOHN ADAMS. Engraving by Nathaniel Dearborn (1786–1852), after No. 90. Size: 11⁵⁄₁₆×9³⁄₁₆ in. Inscribed: "Published by N. Dearborn, Boston / John Adams / Second President of the United States of America." Stauffer No. 471. Example at the Metropolitan Museum of Art, New York City.   FIG. 55

95. JOHN ADAMS. Engraved reproduction of No. 90, by the Pelham Club; 1901. Size: Portrait surface, 11³⁄₁₆×9¼ in. Example at the Library of Congress.

XIV. Charles Balthazar Julien Fevret de Saint-Mémin (1770–1852)

96. JOHN ADAMS. Physiognotrace; Philadelphia, about 1800–1801. Size: 21⅜×15⅛ in. Owners: (a) Baronne de Juigne; (b) William H. Huntington; (c) the Metropolitan Museum of Art, New York City.   FIG. 57

97. JOHN ADAMS. Physiognotrace; Philadelphia, about 1800–1801. Size: 19½×14½ in. Owners: (a) William H. Huntington; (b) John Bigelow; (c) John A. C. Gray; (d) George Gray Zabriskie and the Museum of Fine Arts, Boston.   FIG. 58

Catalogue

XV. Primitives

98. JOHN ADAMS. Oil on glass by Asa Pope; about 1800. Size: 10×8 in. Apparently a copy of a larger picture. Owner: the Quincy Historical Society (John Adams Birthplace).   FIG. 59

99. ABIGAIL ADAMS. Oil on glass by Asa Pope; about 1800. Size: 10×8 in. Pendant to No. 98. Owner: the Quincy Historical Society (John Adams Birthplace).   FIG. 60

100. JOHN ADAMS. Oil on paper by an unknown artist; about 1800. Size: 7¼×5⅛ in. Owner: Thomas Boylston Adams, South Lincoln, Massachusetts.   FIG. 61

XVI. Silhouettes–1809

101. JOHN ADAMS. Silhouette cut by Raphaelle Peale; 1809. Size: 3 in. Framed with No. 102 and others. Owners: (a) John Quincy Adams (JQA); (b) Oliver R. Barrett; (c) David M. Freudenthal, New York City. Duplicate in the Adams Papers.   FIG. 62

102. ABIGAIL ADAMS. Silhouette cut by Raphaelle Peale; 1809. Size: 3 in. Framed with No. 101 and others. Owners: (a) John Quincy Adams (JQA); (b) Oliver R. Barrett; (c) David M. Freudenthal, New York City. Duplicate in the Adams Papers.   FIG. 63

XVII. The Early Stuarts
Gilbert Stuart (1755–1828)

103. JOHN ADAMS. Oil on canvas by Gilbert Stuart (1755–1828); Philadelphia, 1798. Size: 30×24 in. Owners: (a) Gilbert Stuart; (b) Alexander Bryan Johnson; (c) Horatio Seymour; (d) John F. Seymour, Topanga, California.   FIG. 67

104. ABIGAIL ADAMS. Oil on canvas by Gilbert Stuart; 1800. Size: 22×18 in. Unfinished sketch for No. 105. Owners: (a) Catherine Carlton Manson; (b) Charles Francis Adams (CFA2); (c) John Adams, Lincoln, Massachusetts; (d) John Quincy Adams, Lincoln, Massachusetts; (e) the Massachusetts Historical Society.   FIG. 65

105. ABIGAIL ADAMS. Oil on canvas by Gilbert Stuart, from No. 104; 1800–1812. Size: 28½×23⅜ in. Owners: (a) John Quincy Adams (JQA); (b) Charles Francis Adams (CFA); (c) Brooks Adams (BA); (d) Abigail Adams Homans; (e) the National Gallery of Art. Derivatives: Nos. 133, 162.   FIG. 66

106. JOHN ADAMS. Oil on canvas by Gilbert Stuart; Philadelphia and Boston, 1798 and 1815. Size: 28½×23⅜ in. Owners: the same as its pendant, No. 105. Derivatives: Nos. 107–109, 117, 128, 137, 148, 149, 152–155, 163, 165, 171.   FIG. 64

107. JOHN ADAMS. Oil on wood panel by Gilbert Stuart Newton (1794–1835), after No. 106; about 1815. Size: 26×21 in.

Owners: (a) William Smith Shaw; (b) the Boston Athenæum. Derivatives: Nos. 110, 130.   FIG. 69

108. JOHN ADAMS. Oil on canvas by Gilbert Stuart, painted for John Doggett of Boston. Modified replica of No. 106 (probably facing right); 1821. Source for No. 122. Size unknown. Destroyed in the burning of the Library of Congress in 1851.   P. 161

109. JOHN ADAMS. Oil on wood panel by Gilbert Stuart Newton, after No. 106 (or replica of No. 107); about 1815. Size: 24×21½ in. Owner: the Massachusetts Historical Society; on loan to the Adams National Historic Site.   FIG. 89

110. JOHN ADAMS. Oil on wood panel by Bass Otis (1784–1861), after No. 107; 1817. Size: 27¾×21¾ in. Owners: (a) Joseph Delaplaine; (b) Thomas Jefferson Bryan; (c) The New-York Historical Society. Derivatives: Nos. 111–116, 118–121, 125, 126, 134, 138, 151, 156, 157, 159, 160, 161, 164, 167.   FIG. 70

111. JOHN ADAMS. Engraving by William Woodruff, after No. 110 (or one of its derivatives), containing portraits of Washington, Jefferson, and Adams, and the seals of the thirteen states surrounding a facsimile of the Declaration of Independence. Inscribed: "To the People of the United States this Engraving of the Declaration of Independence is most respectfully inscribed by their fellow citizen William Woodruff. Printed by R. Valentine, New York, Published by O. Rogers, No. 67 South 2nd Street, Philadelphia, 1818." *New-York Historical Society Catalogue of American Scenes and Events on Textile,* New York, 1941, p. 5.   P. 155

112. JOHN ADAMS. Engraving by William Woodruff, after No. 110; Washington, Adams, and Jefferson, and the arms of the thirteen original states. Size: 26⅞×18¹³⁄₁₆ in. Inscribed: "Washington / Engraved by Wm. Woodruff / Philadela Published Feby 20, 1819 by William Woodruff / Copyright secured–Printed by C. P. Harmon." Hart No. 595. Also appears without "Printed by C. P. Harmon," Hart No. 595a.

113. JOHN ADAMS. Printed silk textile broadside by Decombereause, after No. 110; about 1820. Size: 28×27½ in. Example at The New-York Historical Society.

114. JOHN ADAMS. Printed silk textile broadside lithographed by H. Brunet et Cie., Lyons, France, after No. 110; about 1820. Size: 28¼×21⅛ in. Inscribed: "To the People of the United States this Engraving of Declaration of Independence is most respectfully inscribed Woodruff." Washington, Jefferson, and Adams, and seals of the thirteen original states surrounding a facsimile of the Declaration of Independence. Example at The New-York Historical Society.   FIG. 71

115. JOHN ADAMS. Printed silk textile broadside, Lyons, France, comparable to No. 114; about 1820. Size: 27½×28 in. Lacks any inscription, and medallions of the thirteen states contain their names and a wreath only, not their seals. A

star in the upper corners and an eagle, displayed, in the lower corners. Example at The New-York Historical Society.

116. JOHN ADAMS. Printed cotton broadside. Design comparable to No. 114, but likenesses of Washington, Jefferson, and Adams are cruder. Size: 33×27¾ in. Inscribed: lower left corner, "The Patriotic Bostonians discharging British Ships in Boston Harbour"; lower right corner, "Genl. Burgoyne's Surrender to Genl. Gates at Saratoga." Examples at The New-York Historical Society and the Museum of Fine Arts, Boston.

117. JOHN ADAMS. Modified replica of No. 106, by Gilbert Stuart; 1825. Size: 25½×21½ in. Owners: (a) Colonel George Gibbs; (b) T. Jefferson Coolidge; (c) Mrs. T. Jefferson Coolidge, Manchester, Massachusetts. Derivatives: Nos. 169, 172.   FIG. 82

118. JOHN ADAMS. Engraving by J. B. Longacre (1794–1869), after No. 110; about 1827. Size: 3⅜×2⅜ in. Inscribed: "Printed by P. Price Jr. Philada / John Adams / Late President of the United States / Engraved by Longacre, from a Painting in Delaplaine's Gallery, from Stuart." A second state omits Price's name and adds, "Published by B. O. Tyler, Washington." Stauffer No. 1916. *Casket,* vol. 1, frontispiece (Jan. 1827).

119. JOHN ADAMS. Engraving by J. B. Longacre, after No. 110; about 1827. Size: 4⁵⁄₁₆×3⁹⁄₁₆ in. Inscribed: "Engraved by J. B. Longacre from a Painting by B. Otis after the Portrait by G. Stuart / John Adams / [autograph of] John Adams." Stauffer No. 1918. J. B. Longacre and James Herring, *The National Portrait Gallery of Distinguished Americans,* New York and Philadelphia, 1834–1839, vol. 4, frontispiece.

120. JOHN ADAMS. Engraving by J. B. Longacre, after No. 110; about 1827. Size: 4¾×2¾ in. Inscribed: "Painted by Stuart–J. Adams.–Engraved by J. B. Longacre–C. S. Williams. New Haven, Ct." Stauffer No. 1917.

121. JOHN ADAMS. Engraving by J. B. Longacre, after No. 110; 1827. Size: 3¾×3¼ in. Inscribed: "John Adams / Drawn & Engraved by J. B. Longacre from a Portrait by Otis after Stuart." Stauffer No. 1919. John Sanderson and Henry D. Gilpin, *Biography of the Signers to the Declaration of Independence,* Philadelphia, 1823–1827, vol. 8, facing p. 201.   FIG. 72

122. JOHN ADAMS. Lithograph by Maurin, after No. 108; 1828. Size: 11¹³⁄₁₆×9⁹⁄₁₆ in. Inscribed: "John Adams / Second President of the United States / From the Original Series painted by Stuart for the Messrs. Doggett of Boston." Example at the Metropolitan Museum of Art, New York City. Derivatives: 123, 124, 131, 132, 135, 140, 142–147, 150, 166.   FIG. 77

123. JOHN ADAMS. Engraving, facing three-quarters left, after No. 122, by Henry R. Robinson. Inscribed: "John Adams / Second President of the United States / Lithographed & Published by H. Robinson 32 Courtland St. N.Y. & Penna.

Avenue, Washington, D.C." Example at the Library of Congress.

124. JOHN ADAMS. Print on cotton cloth from a copper plate; about 1830. Seven Presidents and the frigate *Constitution;* Adams, after No. 122. Adapted from earlier French toile lacking Jackson and the *Constitution.* Examples at The New-York Historical Society and The Brooklyn Museum.

125. JOHN ADAMS. Engraving by William Woodruff, after No. 110; about 1831. Size: over-all, 15⅞₆×16¼ in.; oval, 3¾×3⅛ in. Inscribed: over, "Adams Letter"; below, "Of July 1776 / Published by W. Hill Woodward Main St. Cincinnati. Drawn and Engraved by W. Woodruff Cincinnati." Stauffer No. 3401.

126. JOHN ADAMS. Engraving by Childs & Inman (Cephas G. Childs, 1793–1871, and Henry Inman, 1801–1846), after No. 110; about 1833. Size: 7×5¾ in. Inscribed: "Drawn and Printed by Childs & Inman, Philadelphia / John Adams / Pubd. by Peabody & Co. New York." Example at the Boston Athenæum.

127. JOHN ADAMS. Engraving by John William Casilear (1811–1893), one of group of seven Presidents; 1834. Size: over-all, 10¼×8⅜ in., each portrait 1⅝×1½ in. Inscribed: "Designed by Robert W. Weir–Engraved by J. W. Casilear / The Presidents of the United States / From original and accurate Portraits / Printed & Engraved expressly for the New York Mirror." Example at the Princeton University Library. P. 166

128. JOHN ADAMS. Oil on canvas by Asher B. Durand (1796–1886), after No. 106; 1835. Size: 30×25 in. Owners: (a) Luman Reed; (b) New York Gallery of the Fine Arts; (c) The New-York Historical Society. FIG. 84

129. JOHN ADAMS. Oil on canvas by Asher B. Durand; late in 1835. Replica of No. 128. Size: 28×24 in. Owners: (a) Luman Reed; (b) the Brooklyn Naval Lyceum; (c) the United States Naval Academy Museum, Annapolis. P. 169

130. JOHN ADAMS. Oil on canvas by Jonathan Mason (1795–1884), after No. 107; about 1835. Size: 25⅛×20⅞ in. Owner: the New England Historic Genealogical Society, Boston. FIG. 90

131. JOHN ADAMS. Reproduction, after No. 122, on Tucker porcelain tea cup; about 1835. Size: approx. 3½ in. Helen Comstock, *Concise Encyclopedia of Antiques*, New York, 1958, vol. 2, plate 100; *Antiques*, 51:322 (May 1942).

132. JOHN ADAMS. Woodcut by an unknown artist, after No. 122; about 1835. Size: 3¼×2⅞ in.; facing left, buttons on left side of coat. Alden Bradford, *History of Massachusetts for Two Hundred Years: From 1620 to 1820,* Boston, 1835, facing p. 232.

133. ABIGAIL ADAMS. Engraving by G. F. Storm, after No. 105. Size: 4¼×3⅞ in. Longacre and Herring, *The National Por-*

trait Gallery . . . , New York and Philadelphia, 1834–1839, vol. 4.

134. JOHN ADAMS. Engraving by Abel Bowen (1790–1850), oval bust facing bust of Jefferson. Size: 1 × 1⅜ in. Inscribed: "Bowen & Hoogland, Sculpt / Adams . . . Jefferson / Born Oct. 19, 1735, Born April 2, 1743 / Died July 4, 1826." Fielding No. 160.

135. JOHN ADAMS. Lithograph by Nathaniel Currier (1813–1888), after No. 122; about 1840. Size: 11 × 8¾ in. Inscribed: "John Adams / Second President of the United States / Lith. & Pub. by N. Currier, 33 Spruce St. New York." Example at The New-York Historical Society.   FIG. 78

136. JOHN ADAMS. Lithograph of eleven Presidents surrounding Trumbull's *Declaration of Independence,* by Nathaniel Currier, 1844. Adams derived from No. 122. Example at the Library of Congress.

137. JOHN ADAMS. Oil on canvas by G. P. A. Healy, after No. 106; 1845. Size: 33 × 25 centimeters. Owners: (a) Louis Philippe; and (b) Musée de la Coopération Franco-Américaine, Château de Blérancourt, Aisne, France.   FIG. 85

138. JOHN ADAMS. Lithograph by Albert Newsam (1819–1864), after No. 110; 1846. Size: 6 × 4 in. Inscribed: "On Stone by A. Newsam; P. S. Duval, Lith. Phila." John Wood, *The Suppressed History of the Administration of John Adams* . . . , new edition by John Henry Sherburne, Philadelphia, 1846, frontispiece; and two other variations.   FIG. 73

139. JOHN ADAMS. Lithograph by Albert Newsam, after No. 122 or No. 135, and No. 138; 1846. Size: 13 × 10 in. Inscribed: "Portraits of the Presidents / On stone by A. Newsam–P. S. Duval, Lith. Philada. / Entered according to act of Congress in the year 1846 by C. S. Williams, in the Clerk's office of the District Court of the Eastern District of Penna. / John Adams / 2nd President of the United States / Philadelphia / Published by C. S. Williams, N.E. corner of Market & 7th St." Example at the Library of Congress.   FIG. 74

140. JOHN ADAMS. Lithograph of ten Presidents surrounding Washington, by Nathaniel Currier; 1847. Adams derived from No. 122 or No. 135. Example at the Library of Congress.

141. JOHN ADAMS. Engraving of twelve Presidents and insignia of thirteen states in medallions surrounding facsimile of Declaration of Independence; about 1850. Adams derived from No. 127. Size: over-all, 10⅝ × 8⅛ in.; individual portrait, 1⅚₆ in. Example at the Princeton University Library.

142. JOHN ADAMS. Wood engraving, after No. 122, by Howland Brothers; 1850. Size: 4¾ in. Inscribed: "Howlands Sc." *The American Phrenological Journal and Miscellany,* New York, 12 (1850):41.

143. JOHN ADAMS. Engraving by Vistus Balch (1799–1884),

after No. 122. Size: 3 in. Inscribed: "Engd. by V. Balch from a Painting by G. Stuart / John Adams [autograph]." Fielding No. 89. Example at the Library of Congress.

144. JOHN ADAMS. Lithograph of twelve Presidents surrounding Washington, by Nathaniel Currier; 1850. Adams derived from No. 122 or No. 135. Example at the Library of Congress.

145. JOHN ADAMS. Engraving by Carl Mayer, derived from No. 122. Size: 4×4 in. Inscribed: "John Adams; Stahlstick von Carl Mayer / Stuttgart, J. Scheible's Buchhandlung. Druck v. Carl Mayer Nbg." Example at The New-York Historical Society.   FIG. 79

146. JOHN ADAMS. Engraving by a German artist, after No. 122. Size: 2⅜ × 2½ in. Inscribed: "John Adams / Präsident von 1797 bis 1801." Example at the Boston Athenæum.   FIG. 81

147. JOHN ADAMS. Lithograph by H. Gurnier (or Garnier), after No. 122. Size: 4½ in. Inscribed: "J. Adams President des Etats Unis / ne le 19 Sbre 1735, mort le 4 Juillet 1826 / Galerie Universelle–Publie par Blaisot / Place Vendome No. 24 / Lith de Ducarme r des fr St. Gn Auxois No. 24 Paris / No. 267." Example at The New-York Historical Society.   FIG. 80

148. JOHN ADAMS. Oil on canvas by G. P. A. Healy or Edgar Parker, after No. 106. Size: 29×24 in. Owner: The White House Collection.   FIG. 87

149. JOHN ADAMS. Engraving by Thomas R. Holland and William H. Stinson, after No. 106; 1856. Size: 4½×4 in. Inscribed: "Print by Holland & Stinson / From a portrait by Gilbert Stuart / Boston / Published by Little, Brown and Company." *The Works of John Adams,* . . . ed. Charles Francis Adams, Boston, 1850–1856, vol. 1, frontispiece.   FIG. 83

150. JOHN ADAMS. Engraving by Robert Babson, after No. 122; about 1856. Size: 4¾ × 3¾ in. Inscribed: "Published by Samuel Walker in Boston, New York, Philadelphia & Baltimore." Example at the Boston Athenæum.   P. 166

151. JOHN ADAMS. Engraving by William Wellstood (1819–1900), after No. 110; 1857. Size: 5⅞×4⅞ in. Inscribed: "John Adams / From an Original Portrait by Gilbert Stuart / Johnson, Fry & Co. Publishers, New York." Example at the Boston Athenæum.

152. JOHN ADAMS. Miniature in oil by J. M. R. L. Massard, after No. 106. Size: 4¾×4 in. Owner: the Metropolitan Museum of Art, New York City.   P. 176

153. JOHN ADAMS. Miniature in oil, in brass circular frame, derived from No. 106. Artist unknown. Size: 4 in. diameter. Owner: the Adams National Historic Site.

154. JOHN ADAMS. Oil on canvas by an unknown artist, after No. 106 or some engraving from it. Size: 30×25 in. Owners:

(a) Frances Coonley Farwell; (b) the Chicago Historical Society.

155. JOHN ADAMS. Oil on canvas by G. P. A. Healy, after No. 106. Size: 30×25 in. Signed: "Healy after Stuart / Quincy Oct. 1860." Owner: The Corcoran Gallery of Art, Washington. Derivative: No. 168.　　　　　　　　　　　　　　P. 171

156. JOHN ADAMS. Engraving by Thomas B. Welch (1814–1874), after No. 110. Size: 5½×4⅜ in. Inscribed: "Engraved by T. B. Welch from a portrait by G. Stuart / [autograph of] John Adams." Example at The New-York Historical Society.

157. JOHN ADAMS. Portrait by Alonzo Chappel (1828–1887). Unlocated. The source of No. 158 and probably taken from No. 110 or one of its derivatives.　　　　　　　　　P. 158

158. JOHN ADAMS. Engraving by an unknown artist after No. 157; 1861. Size: 7¼×6 in. Inscribed: "From a Painting in possession of Johnson, Fry & Co. Publishers, N.Y. 1862." Evert A. Duyckinck, *National Portrait Gallery of Eminent Americans,* New York, 1861, 1:107.　　　　　　　FIG. 75

159. JOHN ADAMS. Line engraving by H. B. Hall (1808–1884) after No. 110. Group of six oval portraits: Adams, Patrick Henry, Franklin, Jefferson, Webster, Clay, and Sumner. Size: over-all, 9⅜×5⅞ in.; individual ovals, 1⅞×1½ in. Inscribed: "Engd. by H. B. Hall N.Y." Jesse T. Peck, *The History of the Great Republic,* New York, 1868, p. 259.

160. JOHN ADAMS. Engraving by Joseph Prosper Ourdan (1828–1881), after No. 110; 1867. Size: 2×1⅝ in. Inscribed: "Bureau of Engraving & Printing." James D. Richardson, *Compilation of Messages and Papers of the Presidents,* Washington, 1896, 1:226.　　　　　　　　　　FIG. 76

161. JOHN ADAMS. Engraving after No. 110. Size: 3⅝×3 in., oval. Inscribed: "Boizet del–Barlow Sculp / John Adams." Example at the New York Public Library.

162. ABIGAIL ADAMS. Oil on canvas by Jane Stuart (1812–1888), after No. 105; pendant to No. 163; about 1872. Size: 30×25 in. Owner: the Adams National Historic Site.

163. JOHN ADAMS. Oil on canvas by Jane Stuart, after No. 106; about 1874. Size: 30×25 in. Owner: the Adams National Historic Site.　　　　　　　　　　　　　　FIG. 88

164. JOHN ADAMS. Etching by H. B. Hall, after No. 110; 1876. Size: 3½ in. Inscribed: "Etchd by H. B. Hall N.Y. 1876. From a Painting by G. Stuart. Published by H. B. Hall & Sons, 13 Barclay St. N.Y." Virginia F. Townsend, *Our Presidents,* New York, 1889, p. 24.

165. JOHN ADAMS. Engraving by H. Wright Smith, after No. 106. Size: 7⁷⁄₁₆×5¹³⁄₁₆ in. Inscribed: "G. Stuart Pinxt / H. W. Smith N.Y. / Entered according to Act of Congress in the year 1876 by S. Walker & Co. in the office of the Library of Congress in Washington." Example at The New-York Historical Society.　　　　　　　　　　　　　　P. 167

257

166. JOHN ADAMS. Engraving by John C. Buttre (1821–1893), after No. 122; 1877. Size: 5×4 in. Lillian C. Buttre, *American Portrait Gallery*, New York, 1877, vol. 1, plate 43.

167. JOHN ADAMS. Etching by H. B. Hall, after No. 110; 1880. Size: 3½×3 in. Inscribed: "Etch'd by H. B. Hall N.Y. 1880." Example at the New York Public Library.

168. JOHN ADAMS. Oil on canvas by Eliphalet F. Andrews (1835–1915), after No. 155; 1881. Size: 30×25 in. In the Senate wing of The Capitol, Washington. *Compilation of Works of Art and Other Objects in the United States Capitol*, Washington, 1965, p. 3.　FIG. 86

169. JOHN ADAMS. White-line wood engraving by G. Kruell, after No. 117. Size: 7½×5⅜ in. *Harper's Magazine*, 68:553 (March 1884).　P. 167

170. JOHN ADAMS. Woodcut by Otto H. Parker, after No. 163. Size: 3⅞×2⅞ in., oval. Inscribed: "Otto H. Parker '94." *Scribner's Magazine*, 17:51 (Jan. 1895).　P. 176

171. JOHN ADAMS. Oil on canvas by Edgar Parker (1840–1892), after No. 106. Size: 32¼×26 in. Owner: the Bostonian Society, Old State House.　P. 176

172. JOHN ADAMS. Oil on canvas by an unknown artist. Copy of No. 117. Size: 30×21 in. Owner: Embassy of the United States, London.　P. 167

XVIII. Samuel F. B. Morse (1791–1872)

173. JOHN ADAMS. Oil on canvas; Quincy, 1816. Size: 30×25 in. Owners: (a) Joseph Delaplaine; (b) Alexander M. White; (c) Harriet H. White; (d) The Brooklyn Museum.　FIG. 68

XIX. J. B. Binon

174. JOHN ADAMS. Marble bust; Boston, 1818. Size: 34 in. high. Owner: the City of Boston (Faneuil Hall). Derivative: No. 175.　FIG. 91

175. JOHN ADAMS. Plaster bust, after No. 174; 1819. One, presented to Jefferson by Benjamin A. Gould in 1825, now unlocated. Examples are owned by: (a) the Adams National Historic Site; (b) the Boston Athenæum; (c) Adams House, Harvard University; (d) L. H. Butterfield, Cambridge; (e) Andrew Oliver, New York City.　FIG. 92

XX. The Last Stuarts

176. JOHN ADAMS. Oil on canvas by Gilbert Stuart; Quincy, 1823. Size: 30×25 in. Owners: (a) John Quincy Adams (JQA); (b) Charles Francis Adams (CFA); (c) John Quincy Adams

(JQA2); (d) Charles Francis Adams (CFA3); (e) Charles Francis Adams, Dover, Massachusetts. Derivatives: Nos. 177, 180, 183–187.   FIG. 93

177. JOHN ADAMS. Oil on canvas, replica by Gilbert Stuart of No. 176; 1826. Size: 30×25 in. Owners: (a) John Quincy Adams (JQA); (b) Mary Louisa Adams Johnson; (c) Mary Louisa Adams Clement; (d) the Smithsonian Institution. Derivatives: Nos. 178–179, 181–182.   FIG. 94

178. JOHN ADAMS. Oil on canvas by Charles Bird King (1785–1862), copy of No. 177; Washington, 1827. Size: 30×25 in. Owner: the Redwood Library and Athenaeum, Newport, Rhode Island.   FIG. 95

179. JOHN ADAMS. Engraving by Thomas Gimbrede (1781–1832), after No. 177; 1831. Size: 7⅛×6 in. Inscribed: "Engraved by T. Gimbrede from an original painting by G. Stuart / John Adams / Second President of the United States / (at the age of Ninety)." Stauffer No. 1031. Example at the New York Public Library.   FIG. 100

180. JOHN ADAMS. Oil on canvas by Samuel S. Osgood (1808–1885), copy of No. 176; Boston, 1839. Made for Andrew Jackson Downing, Newburgh, New York; unlocated.

181. JOHN ADAMS. Oil on canvas by Henry Inman (1801–1846), copy of No. 177. Size: 28¾×23½ in. Owner: Tulane University, New Orleans.   FIG. 99

182. JOHN ADAMS. Oil on canvas by John Cranch (1807–1891), copy of No. 177. Unlocated; formerly belonged to Washington University, St. Louis.   FIG. 98

183. JOHN ADAMS. Oil on canvas by G. P. A. Healy, copy of No. 176; 1860. Size: 30¼×25¼ in. Inscribed: "Healy after Stuart, Boston, Oct. 1860." Owners: (a) Mrs. Lysander Hill; (b) the Chicago Historical Society.   FIG. 96

184. JOHN ADAMS. Oil on canvas, copy of No. 176, by Jane Stuart. Size: 30×25 in. Owner: the Adams National Historic Site.   FIG. 97

185. JOHN ADAMS. Engraving by Samuel S. Kilburn, after No. 176. Size: 8×6½ in. Justin Winsor, *The Memorial History of Boston,* Boston, 1880–1881, 3:192.

186. JOHN ADAMS. Wood engraving by T. Johnson, after No. 176. Size: 6⅞₆×4¹³⁄₁₆ in. *Century Magazine,* 34:322 (July 1887).

187. JOHN ADAMS. Engraving by an unknown artist, after No. 176. Size: 5½ in. Inscribed: "John Adams at the age of 89." Example at The New-York Historical Society.

XXI. John Henri Isaac Browere (1790–1834)

188. JOHN ADAMS. Plaster life mask (head only); Quincy, 1825. Owners: (a) Browere's descendants; (b) Stephen C. Clark; (c) the New York State Historical Association, Cooperstown.   FIG. 101

189. JOHN ADAMS. Plaster bust, from No. 188; 1825. Owner: the New York State Historical Association, Cooperstown. Provenance the same as No. 188.   FIG. 102

190. JOHN ADAMS. Bronze bust made in 1938 from No. 189. Owner: the New York State Historical Association, Cooperstown.   FIG. 103

XXII. Paralipomena

191. JOHN ADAMS(?). Miniature in oil, said to be of John Adams, by John Singleton Copley. Unlocated. Known only from photograph in possession of the Frick Art Reference Library, New York City.   FIG. 104

192. JOHN ADAMS. Miniature by an unknown artist, Unlocated. Known from letter from Abigail Adams to John Adams, 24 July 1780.   P. 209

193. JOHN ADAMS. Alabaster or marble medallion by Giuseppe Ceracchi (about 1740–1801); November 1794. Unlocated.   P. 212

194. JOHN ADAMS. Terra-cotta bust by Giuseppe Ceracchi; 1794. Unlocated.   P. 213

195. JOHN ADAMS. Waxwork by Reuben Moulthrop (1763–1814), and Street; figure as large as life; New York, 1797. Unlocated.   P. 214

196. JOHN ADAMS. Transparent painting by an unknown artist from original painting; New York, 1797. Unlocated.   P. 214

197. JOHN ADAMS. Wooden figurehead to frigate *John Adams,* launched at Charlestown, Massachusetts, 3 June 1799; carved by William Rush (1756–1833). Unlocated.   P. 215

198. JOHN ADAMS. Wooden figurehead to frigate *Boston,* launched May 1799; carved by Daniel N. Train. Unlocated.   P. 216

199. JOHN ADAMS. Wooden figurehead to warship *Adams,* launched at Walabout, Long Island, 1799; carved by Daniel N. Train. Ship burned 5 September 1814.   P. 216

200. JOHN ADAMS. Portrait by a Roman Catholic priest; allegedly engraved in great quantity. Unidentified. Known only from letter from John Adams to Joseph Delaplaine, 8 June 1813.   P. 211

201. JOHN ADAMS. Copperplate engraving printed in red on fine white linen kerchief: bust portrait of Washington surrrounded by four labeled medallions: Adams, Franklin, Benjamin Lincoln, and Nathanael Greene; about 1777–1778. Size: 24×27 in. Source of Adams unknown. Edwin Lefevre, "Washington Historical Kerchiefs," *Antiques,* 36:14 (July 1939).   P. 216

202. JOHN ADAMS. Copperplate engraving printed on white linen handkerchief: eight oval portraits surrounding Washington on horseback; about 1783. Adams' likeness the same as in No. 201. Inscribed: "Genl. Washington directing Peace to restore to Justice the Sword which had gained Independence

to America.–Talwin and Foster, Bromley Hall, Middx."
Owner: Edwin Lefevre Jr. FIG. 105

203. JOHN ADAMS. Engraving printed in red on white cotton handkerchief: seven medallions including one containing Adams
accolated with Laurens; England, about 1783. Size: 37×
30½ in. Inscribed: "America Presenting at the Altar of
Liberty Medallions of her Illustrious Sons." Hart No. 872,
listing Adams as derived from Trumbull. Example at The
New-York Historical Society.

204. JOHN ADAMS. Medallic portrait, Indian Peace Medal, by Moritz Furst (1782–?); after 1819. Inscribed: obverse, "John
Adams President of the U.S. A.D. 1797"; reverse, "Peace
and Friendship." Sizes: 76 mm, 62 mm, and 51 mm. Examples at the American Numismatic Society, and the Massachusetts Historical Society. FIG. 106

205. JOHN ADAMS. Medallic portrait by G. H. Leonard, after No.
111; after 1848. Size: 1⅜ in. diameter. Obverse, bust of
Adams facing right, inside wreath, inscribed: "John Adams
Second President of the United States. G.H.L. N.Y." Reverse,
view of Old House, Quincy, inscribed: "Residence of John
Adams. G.H.L. N.Y." Example at the Massachusetts Historical Society. P. 220

206. JOHN ADAMS. Etched by Jules Jacquemart, after No. 111;
1880. Size: 2 in. circumference. Joseph F. Loubat, *The
Medallic History of the United States of America,* New York,
1878–1886, vol. 2, plate XXI. P. 220

207. JOHN ADAMS. Medallic portrait, after No. 111. Artist and
date unknown. Inscribed: obverse, "2nd President, U.S.A. /
1797–1801 / John Adams"; reverse, "Son of Liberty / Minister to England / Vice President two terms / Created U.S.
Navy on Account / of European War Cloud / First President to occupy / White House / Colossus of Independence."
Example in the collection of Mr. George Lye, Singapore,
Malaysia.

208. ABIGAIL ADAMS. Silhouette cut by an unknown artist; after
1809. Size: 5×5 in. Inscribed: "Mrs. Adams." Owner: The
White House Collection. FIG. 112

209. JOHN ADAMS. Oil on canvas by Charles Bird King (1785–
1862); said to be after Stuart. Size: 30×25 in. Owner: the
Redwood Library and Athenaeum, Newport, Rhode Island. FIG. 107

210. JOHN ADAMS. Lightly tinted drawing by Gerard after No.
209. Inscribed: "J. Adams, teint coloré, couleur (Gerard)
. . ."; remainder illegible. Size: 6 in. Owner: the Franklin D. Roosevelt National Historic Site, Hyde Park, New York. FIG. 108

211. JOHN ADAMS. Engraving by François Louis Couché (1782–
1849), after No. 209 or a common source; about 1820–
1825. Size: 3½×3 in. Inscribed: "Couché fils sc. / Adams
Père." Example at The New-York Historical Society. FIG. 109

212. ABIGAIL ADAMS. Oil on canvas by Lydia Smith Russell; about

1804. Size: 38×27 in. Owners: (a) Miss Mary Thacher; (b) The Society for the Preservation of New England Antiquities, Boston.　　　　　　　　　　　　　　FIG. 111

213. JOHN ADAMS. Oil portrait, possibly miniature. Known only from photograph in Library of Congress. No identification except legend on reverse of photograph that painting was by "G. Stuart."　　　　　　　　　　　　　　FIG. 113

214. ABIGAIL ADAMS. Steel engraving by John Sartain (1808–1897), after a painting (now unlocated) by Christian Schussele (1824?–1879); 1854. Rufus Wilmot Griswold, *The Republican Court,* New York, 1854, facing p. 169.　　　FIG. 110

215. JOHN ADAMS. Marble bust by Horatio Greenough (1805–1852); 1828. Size: 22½ in. Above memorial tablet in the Stone Temple (First Church of Quincy), Quincy, Massachusetts. [Daniel M. Wilson,] *The "Chappel of Ease" and Church of Statesmen* . . . [Quincy, Mass.], 1890, facing p. 103.　　　　　　　　　　　　　　P. 231

216. JOHN ADAMS. Marble bust by Horatio Greenough; 1828. Size: 11¾ in. Owners: (a) Mrs. Horatio Greenough; (b) the Museum of Fine Arts, Boston, on loan to the Adams National Historic Site.　　　　　　　　　　　　　　FIG. 114

217. JOHN ADAMS. Marble bust by Daniel Chester French (1850–1931); 1889. In the gallery of the Senate Chamber, The Capitol, Washington. *Compilation of Works of Art and Other Objects in the United States Capitol,* Washington, 1965, p. 172.　　　　　　　　　　　　　　FIG. 115

218. JOHN ADAMS. Line engraving by Daniel Chester French for the two-cent stamp of the 1938 Presidential series. Size: ⅞ × ¾ in.　　　　　　　　　　　　　　FIG. 116

Index

NOTE ON THE INDEX

The principles on which the *Adams Papers* indexes are compiled have been stated in a "Note on the Index" appearing at the beginning of each published Index. A recapitulation of these need not be given here, although it is important to say that the indexes are designed in some measure to supplement the annotation by supplying standard forms of proper names, by filling out—as far as possible—incomplete names, and by furnishing at least minimal identifying data for persons who cannot be fully named. Surnames for which forenames cannot be given with certainty always follow those given more completely; they may in some instances represent persons already entered. Wives' names normally follow their husbands' names, with *see*-references under their maiden names.

The content of this volume being specialized, some devices used in other *Adams Papers* indexes have not been employed here, but these need not be specified. On the other hand, it should be pointed out that particular pains have been taken in this Index to tie together the several elements and parts of the work. For each likeness, not only are all discussions and mentions in the text cited, but, if it is illustrated, both its place in the List of Illustrations and the page on which it is illustrated are given; and for every likeness, whether or not illustrated, both its Catalogue number and the page number of its listing in the Catalogue are cited. It is hoped that this scheme will obviate the difficulties that users so often encounter in books of this kind when they try to find their way back and forth among the pictures themselves, the primary discussions and passing mentions of them in the text, and the formal entries in the Catalogue.

The Index to the *Portraits of John and Abigail Adams* was both planned and executed by Mrs. Carl A. Pitha. The fact that it is the third she has compiled for the Adams Papers enterprise will attest the editors' confidence in her ability to do exacting work in the most exemplary way.

Index

AA. *See* Adams, Mrs. John (Abigail Smith, 1744–1818)

AA2. *See* Smith, Mrs. William Stephens (Abigail Adams, 1765–1813)

ABA. *See* Adams, Mrs. Charles Francis (Abigail Brown Brooks, 1808–1889)

Active (ship), 25

Adams (warship), Train's figurehead for (Cat. No. 199), 216, 260

Adams, Abigail. *See* Smith, Mrs. William Stephens (1765–1813)

Adams, Abigail Louisa Smith. *See* Johnson, Mrs. Alexander Bryan

Adams, Brooks (1848–1927, son of CFA, designated as BA in *The Adams Papers*): owner, Stuart portraits of AA and JA (Cat. Nos. 105, 106), 135, 251; mentioned, 95

Adams, Charles (1770–1800, son of JA, designated as CA in *The Adams Papers*), 47, 141

Adams, Charles Francis (1807–1886, son of JQA, designated as CFA in *The Adams Papers*): and Adams family portraits, xi–xiii; and Blyth's portraits of JA and AA (Cat. Nos. 1, 2), 12–13, 240, 241; and 1783 Copley portrait of JA, 35, 38, 243; and Stuart's portraits of AA and JA Cat. Nos. 105, 106), 135, 251; and engraving of Stuart's 1798–1815 portrait of JA (Cat. No. 149), 167, 256; and Stuart's 1823 portrait of JA (Cat. No. 176), 188–89, 191, 201, 258; King's portrait of, 192, 221; Browere's life mask of, 203; Browere's bronze bust of, 208; mentioned, 82, 187

Adams, Mrs. Charles Francis (Abigail Brown Brooks, 1808–1889, CFA's wife, designated as ABA in *The Adams Papers*), xi, 187

Adams, Charles Francis, 2d (1835–1915, son of CFA, designated as CFA2 in *The Adams Papers*): and Blyth's portraits of JA and AA (Cat. Nos. 1, 2), 11, 12; and Winstanley's portraits of JA, 104, 106; and Stuart's

sketch of AA (Cat. No. 104), 137, 251; on French's bust of JA, 234

Adams, Charles Francis (1866–1954, son of JQA2, designated as CFA3 in *The Adams Papers*), 137, 259

Adams, Charles Francis (of Dover, Mass.), 191, 259

Adams, Elizabeth Coombs (1808–1903, daughter of TBA, designated as ECA in *The Adams Papers*): and Blyth's portraits of JA and AA (Cat. Nos. 1, 2), 11, 12, 240; and Sharples' tempera of JA (Cat. No. 65), 90; mentioned, 9

Adams, Fanny. *See* Adams, Georgeanna Frances (1830–1839)

Adams, George Washington (1801–1829, son of JQA, designated as GWA in *The Adams Papers*): silhouette profile of, 129, 131; and Stuart's replica of 1823 portrait of JA (Cat. No. 177), 192, 195; mentioned, 161

Adams, Georgeanna Frances (1830–1839, daughter of JA2, called Fanny), 221

Adams, Henry (1838–1918, son of CFA, designated as HA in *The Adams Papers*): number of portraits and photographs of, xi; and W. J. Williams' portrait of JA (Cat. No. 72), 95, 248; and Winstanley's portrait of JA (Cat. No. 83), 104, 106, 249

Adams, Mrs. Henry (Marian Hooper, 1842–1885, wife of HA, designated as MHA in *The Adams Papers*), xi

Adams, Henry (1875–1951, son of CFA2, designated as HA2 in *The Adams Papers*), 12, 92, 240

Adams, Deacon John (1692–1761, father of JA), 5

ADAMS, JOHN (1735–1826, designated as JA in *The Adams Papers*): extent and style of portraits, x, 2–4; views on art, xii–xiv, xv–xvi; comment on France, xiii, 23, 25; and West's portrait, xiv, 41–42; and

265

Index

Bailyn, Bernard, on Blyth's portraits of JA and AA (Cat. Nos. 1, 2), 9

Baker, G., proprietor of Panorama museum, New York City, 215

Balch, Vistus, engraving after Maurin (Cat. No. 143), 255–56

Baltimore, Md., 58, 81, 95

Bancroft, George, 12

Barbour, Philip, 208

Barlow, ———, engraving of JA after Otis (Cat. No. 161), 257

Barrett, Oliver R., and Raphaelle Peale's silhouettes of JA and AA (Cat. Nos. 101, 102), 131, 251

Bass, Seth, comment on Newton's copy of Stuart's portrait, 151

Beale, Mrs. B. A., 167

Beaumont, Charles, 162

Bedford House, Katonah, N.Y., 66

Belper, 1st Lord. See Strutt, Edward

Belper, 2d Lord. See Strutt, Henry

Bentley, Rev. William, 8

Berkeanhead, Dr. John, publisher of Graham's mezzotint (Cat. No. 85), 249

Berry, Mr. (friend of Copley), 33

Bigelow, John, and Saint-Mémin's physiognotrace (Cat. No. 97), 120, 250

Bingham, George Caleb, portrait of JQA by, 82

Binon, J. B.: 1818 bust of JA (Cat. No. 174), 181–82, 184–85, 258; illustrated, xxv, 183; JA's comment on bust, xv, xvi, 185; plaster reproductions of bust (Cat. No. 175), 184–85, 187–88, 258, illustrated, xxv, 186; mentioned, 3, 130, 220, 234, 235

Bliss, William H., copy of Sharples' profile (Cat. No. 69), 86, 247

Block, Marion (curator, Huntington Art Gallery), 141

Blyth, Benjamin: pastel portraits of JA and AA (Cat. Nos. 1, 2), xiii, 3, 5, 8–12, 22, 53, 68, 227, 240, illustrated, xix, 6–7; pastel copies (Cat. Nos. 7, 10), 12, 241; engravings (Cat. Nos. 3–6, 8–9), 12–13, 241

Boizet, ———, engraving of JA after Otis (Cat. No. 161), 257

Bolton, J. B., and Kimberley's engraving (Cat. No. 56), 246

Boston: public subscription for Binon's bust of JA in, xv, 179–81; Trumbull's *Declaration* exhibited in, 58. *See also* Boston Athenæum; Bostonian Society

Collection; Boston Museum; Faneuil Hall; Museum of Fine Arts; Society for the Preservation of New England Antiquities; State House

Boston (frigate), figurehead of JA for (Cat. No. 198), 216, 260

Boston Athenæum: and Brown's portrait of JA (Cat. No. 41), 52, 244; engravings of Stuart's portraits (Cat. Nos. 126, 146, 150, 151), 137, 254, 256; Newton's copy of Stuart's portrait (Cat. No. 107), 151, 252; Binon's plaster bust at (Cat. No. 175), 184, 185, 187, 258; Greenough's bust exhibited at (Cat. No. 215), 231; example of H. R. Hall engraving at (Cat. No. 31), 243

Boston Gazette, publication of "Novanglus" essays in, 14

Boston Magazine, 22, 242

Boston Museum (Tremont Street): Winstanley's portrait of JA at (Cat. No. 83), 104; painting by Savage at (Cat. No. 87), 109; Doyle's portrait of JA at (Cat. No. 91), 116

Boston Transcript, 82

Bostonian Society Collection, Old State House, Boston: copy of Copley's portrait in (Cat. No. 34), 38, 244; copy of Stuart's portrait in (Cat. No. 171), 176, 258

Bowen, Abel, engraving of oval bust of JA (Cat. No. 134), 255

Bowen, Clarence Winthrop: on Blyth's portraits, 11; reproduction of C. W. Peale's portrait of JA, 72; and Winstanley's portrait of JA, 104; reproduction of Stuart's portraits of JA and AA, 137; reproduction of Morse's portrait of JA, 149

Bower, John, vignette engraving of JA and Washington (Cat. No. 93), 117–18, 250, illustrated, xxiii, 117

Bowers, Henry: and Sharples' portrait and copy by unknown artist of JA (Cat. Nos. 64, 69), 82, 84, 86, 90, 91, 247

Boylston, Ward Nicholas, owner, Copley's portrait of JA (Cat. No. 18), 33, 35, 38, 242

Brady Studio, daguerreotypes of JQA, x

Bristol Fine Arts Academy. See Royal West of England Academy

British Museum, 38

Brook, Joseph, inventor of "polyplasiosmos," 49

268

Index

Index

King, Charles Bird: copy of Stuart's 1823 portrait of JA (Cat. No. 178), 192, 195, 259, illustrated, xxvi, 194; portrait of JA (Cat. No. 209), 221, 224, 261, illustrated, xxvii, 222

King, John Crookshank, bust of JQA, 184

King, Rufus, 146

Knoedler & Co., owners, replica of Copley's portrait of JA (Cat. No. 24), 243

Knox, Katharine McCook, comments on Sharples' portraits, 82, 84, 86

Knox, Gen. Henry, 230

Kruell, G., engraving after 2d Stuart replica (Cat. No. 169), 167, 258

Lafayette, Marie Joseph Paul Yves Roch Gilbert du Motier, Marquis de: Browere's bust of, 202; mentioned, 49, 64, 187

Lambdin, James Reid, portrait of JQA, 82

Laurens, Henry: at peace negotiations, 39; in West's *American Commissioners* (Cat. No. 35), 42, 43; in engraving on handkerchief (Cat. No. 203), 261

LCA. *See* Adams, Mrs. John Quincy (Louisa Catherine Johnson, 1775–1852)

Le Bas, Jacques Philippe, 14

Lefevre, Edwin, Jr., owner, engraving on handkerchief (Cat. No. 202), 261

Leney, William S.: engraving of JA (Cat. No. 29), 243; mentioned, 145

Leonard, Daniel, "Massachusettensis" articles, 14

Leonard, G. H., medallic likeness of JA (Cat. No. 205), 220–21, 261

Leslie, Charles Robert, 147, 192

Lewis, John Frederick, owner, Williams' portrait of JA (Cat. No. 71), 95, 247

Library of Congress: owner, Stuart's copies of Presidential portraits (including Cat. No. 108), 161, 251; photograph, anonymous portrait of JA (Cat. No. 213), 229–30, 262; example, Kimberly's engraving (Cat. No. 56), 246; example, Bower's engraving (Cat. No. 93), 250; example, engraved reproduction of Savage's engraving (Cat. No. 95), 250; example, Robinson's engraving (Cat. No. 123), 254; examples, Currier's lithographs (Cat. Nos. 136, 140,

144), 255, 256; example, Newsam's lithograph (Cat. No. 139), 255; example, Balch's engraving (Cat. No. 143), 256

Lincoln, Abraham, Shober's 1865 lithograph of, 108

Lincoln, Gen. Benjamin, in textile engraving (Cat. No. 201), 217, 260

Lippincott's Magazine, 81

Literary Magazine and American Register, Tanner's engraving in (Cat. No. 80), 98, 249

Little, Mr. and Mrs. Bertram, Essex, Mass., owners, anonymous portrait of JA (Cat. No. 27), 243

Livingston, Brockholst, 80

Livingston, Chancellor Robert R., 80

Loeb, Capt. Richard A., owner, Hicks' copy of Trumbull's *Declaration* (Cat. No. 54), 246

London, England: JA in, xiv, 23, 41, 42, 45, 46, 48; AA in, 25; Copley's house in, 27; West's paintings exhibited in, 41; U.S. Embassy, owner of copy of Stuart's replica (Cat. No. 172), 167, 258

Longacre, James B.: Storm's engraving of Stuart's portrait of AA (Cat. No. 133) published by, 140; engravings "after Otis" of JA (Cat. Nos. 118, 119, 120, 121), 151, 154, 155, 253, illustrated, xxiv, 157

Loud, May Hallowell, pastel copies of Blyth's portraits of JA and AA (Cat. Nos. 7, 10), 12, 241

Louis XVIII, King of France, 120

Louis Philippe, King of France: collection of portraits of Americans, 27; and Healy's copy of Stuart's portrait of JA (Cat. No. 137), 171, 195, 255

Low, Seth (mayor of New York City), 161

Lucretia (ship), 48

Lye, George, owner, example of medallic portrait of JA (Cat. No. 207), 261

Lyndhurst, Lord. *See* Copley, John Singleton, the younger

McLellan, Henry B., 187

Madison, James: in Gimbrede's engraving of Stuart's portrait of (Cat. No. 26), 31, 33, illustrated, xx, 34, 243; Stuart's copy of his portrait of, 161; Ceracchi's bust of, 212; in Edwin's engraving of Presidential busts (Cat. No. 92), 250; mentioned, 146, 202

Manson, Catherine Carlton, owner,

275

Index

New York University, Hall of Fame for Great Americans, example, Paramino's bust of JA (Cat. No. 43), 52, 245

Niles' Weekly Register, 62, 179

Noble, [George?]: engraving of Copley's portrait of JA (Cat. No. 20), 29–30, 242, illustrated, xx, 29; engraving of B. Franklin, 30

Norman, John, engraving of JA (Cat. No. 16), 22, 242, illustrated, xix, 21

"Novanglus." *See* JA

Old House (JA's home at Quincy; now the Adams National Historic Site): Adams family materials at, vii, xi–xii; Brown's portrait of AA2 at, 47; Williams' portrait of JA at (Cat. No. 72), 92, 95, 98, 248; examples of Graham's engravings at, 108; Savage's portrait of Washington at, 118; Stuart's portraits of JA and AA at (Cat. Nos. 105, 106), 135; Jane Stuart's copy of Stuart's portrait of JA at (Cat. No. 163), 176, 257; Newton's 2d copy on loan to (Cat. No. 109), 176, 252; reproduction of Binon's bust at (Cat. No. 175), 185, 258; Jane Stuart's 2d copy of Stuart's portrait of JA (Cat. No. 184), 195, 259; on medal (Cat. No. 205), 220–21, 261; Greenough's bust on loan to (Cat. No. 216), 234, 262; anonymous miniature at (Cat. No. 153), 256; Jane Stuart's copy of Stuart's portrait of AA at (Cat. No. 162), 257. *See also* Stone Library

Oliver, Andrew; owner, anonymous sanguine drawing (Cat. No. 75), 101, 248; owner, Binon plaster bust (Cat. No. 175), 185, 258

"Original," defined, 4

Orr, John William, engravings of JA and AA (Cat. Nos. 6, 9), 241

Osgood, Samuel S., oil copy of Stuart's 1823 portrait of JA (unlocated; Cat. No. 180), 259

Oswald, Richard, 39, 42, 43

Otis, Bass: portrait of JA after Newton (Cat. No. 110), 2, 141, 151, 154–55, 252, illustrated, xxiv, 153; lithographs and engravings after, 155, 158, 253

Otis, Harrison Gray, and public subscription for bust of JA, 179–80

Otis, Capt., 185

Ourdan, Joseph Prosper, engraving of

vignette of JA (Cat. No. 160), 160, 257, illustrated, xxiv, 160

Panorama (gallery or museum, New York City), 215

Panorama (sale catalogue), 53

Pantograph. *See* Physiognotrace

Paramino, John Francis, bronze bust of JA (Cat. No. 43), 52, 245

Paris, France: American peace treaties at, 23, 39, 42; JA in, 19, 39, 42, 46. *See also* France

Park, Lawrence, *Gilbert Stuart,* 141, 154

Parke-Bernet Galleries, 131

Parker, Edgar: copy of Stuart's portrait ascribed to (Cat. No. 148), 171, 176, 256, illustrated, xxv, 174; copy of Stuart's portrait (Cat. No. 171), 176, 258

Parker, Otto H., engraving of Jane Stuart's copy of Stuart's portrait (Cat. No. 170), 176, 258

Parkman, George Francis, owner, Brown's portrait of JA (Cat. No. 41), 52, 244

Paschal, Mrs. Dorothy Iselin, owner, anonymous copy of West's painting (Cat. No. 36), 244

Peabody & Co., N.Y., publisher of Childs & Inman's engraving (Cat. No. 126), 254

Peabody Museum (Salem), owner, Binon's bust reproduction, 185

Peale, Charles Willson: JA's meeting with, xii–xiii, 70; and West, 39, 41, 45; portrait of JA (Cat. No. 58), 70, 72, 234, 246, illustrated, xxi, 71; mentioned, 73, 130

Peale, James, portrait of JA (unlocated; Cat. No. 60), 73, 246, illustrated, xxi, 74

Peale, Raphaelle, silhouette profiles of JA and AA (Cat. Nos. 101, 102), 129–31, 229, 251, illustrated, xxiii, 130

Peale, Rembrandt, portrait of Jefferson, 171

Peale's Museum, Philadelphia, 70, 81, 130, 246

Pelham, Henry, 210

Pelham Club, reproduction of Savage's engraving (Cat. No. 95), 250

Pelton, Oliver, engraving of Blyth's portrait of AA (Cat. No. 8), 12–13, 241, illustrated, xix, 11

Pendleton, John B., publisher of "American Kings" series, 164

278

Index

❮ The *Portraits of John and Abigail Adams* was composed on the Linotype by the Plimpton Press. Rudolph Ruzicka's *Fairfield Medium,* with several variant characters designed expressly for *The Adams Papers,* is used throughout. The text is set in the eleven-point size, and the lines are spaced one and one-half points. The printing is by the Meriden Gravure Company, and the binding by the Plimpton Press is in a cover fabric made by the Holliston Mills, Inc. The paper, made by the S. D. Warren Company, is a grade named *University Text.* It was developed by Harvard University Press for first use in The Belknap Press edition of *The Adams Papers.* The edition was designed by P. J. Conkwright and Burton L. Stratton. This volume was designed by Burton J. Jones and Burton L. Stratton.